No More Neckties

A Memoir in Essays

LOREN A. OLSON, MD

OAK LANE PRESS

Oak Lane Press
2815 100th Street #274
Urbandale, Iowa 50322

ORDERING INFORMATION

Quantity sales: Special discounts are available on quantity purchases by corporations, associations, and others. For details, please contact the "Special Sales Department" at the above address.

Orders by US trade bookstores and wholesalers: Please contact BCH: (800) 431-1579 or visit www.bookch.com for details.

Printed in the United States of America

Cataloging-in-Publication data

Names: Olson, Loren A., author.
Title: No more neckties : a memoir in essays / Loren A. Olson, MD.
Description: Urbandale, IA: Oak Lane Press, 2022.
Identifiers: LCCN: 2021924942 | ISBN: 978-1-7379956-2-3
Subjects: LCSH Olson, Loren A. | Psychiatrists--United States--Biography. | Gay men--United States--Biography. | Essays. | BISAC BIOGRAPHY & AUTOBIOGRAPHY / Personal Memoirs
Classification: LCC HQ75.8.O589 2022 | DDC 306.76--dc23

First Edition

26 25 24 23 22 10 9 8 7 6 5 4 3 2 1

No More Neckties

Praise for *No More Neckties*

"Olson's essays will make you laugh and squirm with discomfort—in the best way. They inspire you and help you see yourself and those around you with compassion and care. Grab a cup of coffee and a slice of banana bread for what feels more like a conversation with an old friend than a book with a beginning and an end."

—*Carly Thomsen, PhD, author of*
Visibility Interrupted: Rural Queer Life
and the Politics of Unbecoming

"An amazing collection of essays, providing insight as to what LGBTQ+ life was like growing up in the '50s and '60s in middle America when we had no road map to help us understand this very private journey."

—*Matt Skallerud, President, Pink Media*

"*No More Neckties* had me at the first line of the preface and then drew me in. Like Olson, I was the good boy, and as a man on the cusp of sixty, I am sick of it too. This book is raw, personal, intimate, emotional, relatable, and real."

—*Scott A. Oakman, MD, PhD,*
Program Director, Hennepin-Regions
Psychiatry Training Program

"Olson brilliantly captures society's historical view of being gay and how churches' cold dogmas filled us with guilt and shame. We felt unwanted and unloved. Like Olson, I have found a freedom in embracing my sexual identity, and this book is a great joy and solace for me."

—*Fr. "Lee" (Ireland)*

"Loren paints vivid scenes of his experiences, from the hayloft to counseling rooms to relationships to aging as a gay man. . . . A wonderful memoir of overcoming pain and achieving happiness. I wholeheartedly recommend *No More Neckties* for anyone coming out later in life."

—*Mark Hatten, President, Prime Timers Worldwide*

"*No More Neckties: A Memoir in Essays* by Loren Olson is a collection of captivating and authentic vignettes that offer a window into the gritty complexity of what it means to be human. A genuine delight to read."

—*William Huggett, MD, psychiatrist and psychoanalyst*

"Olson articulately captures the complexities of sexual orientation, intimacy, trust, hurt, and communication. His stories show how acceptance, compassion, forgiveness, and connection have the power to transcend and transform. You will be empowered by his refreshing openness, honesty, and authenticity."

—*Craig White, PhD, Honorary Professor,*
Institute of Health & Wellbeing, University of Glasgow (Scotland)

"Powerful and candid, *No More Neckties* will appeal to readers of all ages and backgrounds. Younger readers will see how much our world has changed while older readers will recognize their own journeys. Everyone will be reminded how much we need each other."

—*Ginger Campbell, MD, author of*
Are You Sure? The Unconscious Origins of Certainty

"*No More Neckties* is a fitting representation of the refreshing authenticity, intimacy, and candor that readers will discover within its pages. Dr. Olson is a gifted writer and storyteller who captures readers' attention and deepens their interest as his life story unfolds. His analysis transcends his personal experience, which makes reading these pages a deeply personal experience for readers. Highly recommended!"

—*Basil Vareldzis, MD, MPH (Canada and Switzerland)*

"With the sensitivity of a gay man over forty, Olson's stories guide the reader on a path to self-discovery."

—*William Smith, founder of Gay Life After 40.com*

For Lefty

Contents

Preface

Growing up, I was always the good boy, and I'm sick of it. Not only was I a good boy, but I also felt self-righteous about how good I was. Yet I knew that another part of me wasn't so good and wanted to be one of the bad boys. I was lonely because I felt I needed to hide those thoughts I believed to be bad.

After I wrote my first book, one of my patients came into my office and said, "Dr. Olson! I read your book. You told me a lot more than I needed to know. Why did you do that?" It was her last therapy session after my having seen her for twenty-five years. The final thing she said to me when she left my office that day was, "I've always thought I was a lesbian." Only after learning some of my secrets did she finally feel the courage to tell me her deepest, unspoken conflict.

As you read through this book you, too, may think, "You told us a lot more than we needed to know," but I have written this book to come clean. I want you to know me as I am even though some of you might prefer not to. I went through much of my life feeling like an impostor. I tried to be someone I was not because I thought I had to fit in. But nothing makes one feel lonelier than to feel like you can't show up as yourself.

I couldn't have published this book earlier in my life. The potential consequences would have been too great. But I am old now. Old age gives us the freedom to be who we are. But we can never entirely sever our concern that others will disapprove of us. As scary as writing this book feels, if I am known at all in this world, I want to be known as myself. I know there will be consequences because some people are not going to want to let me be that person. I hope that you will accept me knowing who I am, but I no longer need that approval from you as I once did. As I wrote in the final chapter, "Old age allows us to say, 'Fuck off!'"

The events I have written about are intensely personal, and yet variations of these stories are nearly universal whether you're gay, straight, bisexual, or something else. These are topics we're not supposed to talk about. But not sharing them cuts us off from others and leads us to feel isolated and disconnected. So often I hear from others, "I feel like I'm the only one who's ever felt this way." But I know that the only reason they feel so alone is because they've been too afraid to talk about the hard stuff. And we all have hard stuff.

Someone once told me that if you want to write a memoir, start with the most difficult chapter first because if you can't write that one, you can't write the book. I did that. I wrote that first chapter about ten years ago. For all those years, I wondered, "Will I ever have enough courage to hit Send?"

Anne Lamott, author of the book *Bird by Bird: Some Instructions on Writing and Life*, said, "If people wanted you to write warmly about them, they should've behaved better." Telling my story inevitably involves telling parts of other people's stories, and those stories aren't mine to tell. Sometimes I was hurt by the ways they behaved, but many times I hurt them. Loving people means setting them free to behave the way they choose. And my hope is that those I have hurt when I behaved badly will forgive me and continue to love me.

Why would I write about death and suicide, sex and infidelity, betrayal and forgiveness? I've written about them because we think about these topics constantly, but don't talk about them enough. Knowing that others have felt the same way or done the same things helps relieve us of our shame and guilt.

Facts don't change minds; our stories do. When I was a resident in psychiatry, we were told never to have anything personal in our offices. Even wearing a wedding ring disclosed more information than our supervisors wanted us to. We were to be a blank screen onto which our patients projected their desires and conflicts. I presented to the world an image of someone with all the answers while hiding the fact that I hadn't found solutions in my own life. I hate hypocrisy, and I hadn't dealt with my own conflicts. I've always loved hearing other people's stories while being afraid to tell my own.

I agree that too much disclosure, too soon, can damage a therapeutic relationship. But sometimes—as when I'm working with an older man who has same-sex desires—if I tell him, "I'm gay. I've been married to a woman, and I have children," I can immediately drive the therapy to a deeper level. On the other hand, disclosing that too soon could send another man into a panic, as if I were saying, "This is what I did. This is what you should do too." My choices are not necessarily the right choices for you.

Through the years, I have found that many of you want to talk about those hidden elements of who you are with someone you know will accept you. My hope is that as you read my story, you may come to accept that some of the bad things you believed about yourself really weren't so bad after all.

I have used a conversational tone in this book because I want you to imagine that we're sitting together in a coffee shop, sharing our stories. The essays are arranged by topic rather than chronological order. Although we may disagree about certain points of discussion, deep conversations lead to connections, and all of us want connection. Those connections also allow us to work through the subjects where we disagree. Walk away from me if you feel you must; I won't walk away from you.

Brené Brown, a researcher in intimacy, says that to connect in our relationships, we must be seen, and seen deeply. I hope that this book allows you to see me in that way. But I also hope it lets you see yourself—and to see yourself deeply. My wish is for you to find someone with whom you can share your stories and have these hard conversations, and I hope that talking about the hard things will make them easier.

Although the term *gay* is preferred to *homosexual,* I have sometimes used *homosexual* because of its historical context. I have also used the term *queer,* which some will consider offensive or pejorative. Young people in particular use this term when the words *lesbian, gay,* and *bisexual* are thought to be too limiting or laden with cultural overtones they feel don't apply to them.

This book is a work of creative nonfiction. Our memories are never factually accurate. We alter them as we reconstruct them, and they are further altered each time we tell them. I have reconstructed my memories to be accurate to the true spirit of what happened rather than to the details. I have recreated dialogue as carefully as I can recall it.

I want to thank those who have trusted me with the most intimate details of their lives through emails and correspondence. I have included some of their stories in this book with their permission. In some cases, two stories have been combined. To protect them, details have been modified by changing names, ages, physical characteristics, locations, and personal details. Some people will be easily identified whether I use their names or not.

I also want to thank everyone who helped me with this book, even those who should've behaved better. You all have enriched my life.

Illusions of My Father

All memories are but reconstructions. We believe our memories are like video recordings of our earlier lives. But they are like ambiguous inkblot images onto which we project our unconscious thoughts, motives, and desires. Here, then, are the illusions of my father.

On a sauna-like day in late August 1946, I skipped to meet our family, friends, and neighbors as they alighted from their cars. They looked filled with dread as they arrived at our small, white clapboard farmhouse in northeast Nebraska. I was three years and a few months old. My mother had carefully parted my curly blond hair, and I wore my Sunday-best bib overalls.

I was too young to understand that the party I awaited was for mourners coming to pay their last respects to my thirty-three-year-old father. He lay

Loren, at age 3, with his mother, Martha Katherine Koester, and father, Alva "Alvie" Harold Olson, about 1946 on their farm in Cedar County, Nebraska. (Courtesy of Loren A. Olson.)

Merlin "Lefty," age seven, Marilyn, age five, Janice "Jan," age three, and Loren, age one, in 1944. (Courtesy of Loren A. Olson.)

wearing his Sunday-best suit in a blue velveteen-covered coffin in the corner of our tiny dining room, as was the custom in those days.

I expected them to ask, "What's your name, young man?" to which I had always answered, "My name is Loren Alva H. Olson." I always emphasized the *H*. I had seized the *H* from my father, who signed his name *Alva H. Olson*. I wanted to be just like him.

But on that day, no one wanted to play our familiar game. We had played it over and over in the past, invariably leading to laughter and smiles of approval. I always needed that approval too much.

I wondered, "Where are the kids? Why is everyone so gloomy at a party?"

They arrived for the reception in their Sunday-best clothes, too hot for that stifling, humid day. They lingered as they approached the house to greet my thirty-one-year-old mother. Uncharacteristically, she stood in the doorway like a cut flower that was too wilted to be saved but still too pretty to throw away. Her eyes focused on nothing more than an unknowable future.

My father played the saxophone in the Olson Family Band. The band was composed of my Uncle Ralph, who'd purchased a violin through the Sears-Roebuck catalog and learned to fiddle by studying the book that came with it, and my aunt Vivian, who played the piano "by ear,"

The Koesters were a close-knit family and always celebrated holidays and major life events together. This photo of the cousins was from Christmas 1946. *From left:* Gary Schroeder, Loren, and Delaine "Dee" Isom Trim. (Courtesy of Norman Koester.)

meaning she had little if any formal training. My Uncle Glen was too young to join the family band.

In the early 1930s, the Olson Family Band played for house dances. These dances were held in farm homes with furniture cleared to the side to make a dance floor. It was at one of these dances in the 1930s where my father met my mother, who had come to the dance with her sisters. Grandma Olson never approved of their relationship since my mother was German. The Olson lineage was a lot of things, but certainly not German.

My Aunt Sophie took charge of the funeral reception. My mother's mother was undoubtedly there, but my memory of her is like faded and peeling wallpaper: always there but barely noticed. Aunt Sophie had replaced Grandma as the matriarch of the family. Aunt Sophie always wore practical black lace-up orthopedic shoes. She greeted the arrivals

Members of the Olson Family Band about 1922 before they became a band. *From left:* Loren's father, Alva; Aunt Vivian Olson Lindley; and Uncle Ralph Olson. (Courtesy of Loren A. Olson.)

and directed them to put their hot dishes and Jell-O salads on the enameled table in the small kitchen. They had prepared their favorite recipes (almost always named something "delight"), which they heard on *The Neighbor Lady* radio broadcast from WNAX in Yankton, South Dakota.

Aunt Sophie instructed them to leave their bouquets of handpicked flowers (mostly gladiolas) beside my father's coffin. For many years after, my mother complained of the stench of gladiolas, even though hybridizers had long ago sacrificed fragrance for varieties of color. My mother always hated gladiolas after that day.

My mother extended her hand to greet everyone as if it were reserved for children or adults behind closed doors. She wore her best dress. It was her only suitable dress. The balance of her wardrobe consisted solely of "wash dresses" that farmers' wives wore every day—dresses they had scrubbed in homemade lye soap, which removed all the color as well as any stains.

The house may have been purchased from the Sears-Roebuck catalog, as some were in those days. It had four small rooms downstairs: a kitchen, dining room, living room, and the parents' bedroom. Upstairs were two bedrooms, one for boys and one for girls, no matter how many of each were in a family.

Martha Katherine Koester, age twenty, and Alva Harold Olson, age twenty-two, were married on January 23, 1935, during the Great Depression. They married in the home on the Koester "home place" in Allen, Nebraska. The $150 in wedding gifts was used to purchase furniture, including a piano. (Courtesy of Marilyn Olson Robinder and Norman Koester.)

A few days before he died, Daddy was making hay in our meadow alone. He had introduced a new horse into his team that pulled the hay wagon. Hitching a new horse to an older, well-trained horse was a common practice to help break a new horse into working as a team. A high-spirited horse that is not well trained continually challenges the older horse and the driver's skills. He will wait for just the right moment to attempt to break away. The older, well-trained horse acts to stabilize the team, anchoring them in place.

Since my father worked alone, no one could help reconstruct what transpired. Something spooked the horses. The strength and excitement of the young horse overpowered the more compliant one. They ran about a mile back to the security of their barn, pulling the hay wagon. When they reached the barn, the doorway, narrower than the wagon, abruptly blocked the horses from entering the barn.

My father, who was trapped in the harnesses beneath the hay wagon, died a few days later of a ruptured spleen. Ten years later, surgeons developed a procedure to remove a spleen, a procedure that could have saved his life. I never knew my father; I hope he knew me.

In small towns, people judge a man's reputation by the size of his funeral. My mother regularly boasted of the one thousand people that attended my father's funeral.

Some have suggested that my young father was no match for the spirited horses that killed him. When I was young and pitying myself for not having a father, I became angry and blamed him for abandoning me through his carelessness. But my Uncle Glen—who knew my father best and loved him as much as I do—set me straight. Uncle Glen insisted that my father was an excellent horseman. He and my dad acquired wild mustangs through a government agency and brought them to our farm in Nebraska. They would break the feral horses to ride, then sell them to other farm families as well-trained horses.

Fathers teach boys the code of masculinity even without knowing they're doing it. How does a boy without a father learn to become a man? Several years later, my sister Jan and I had a conversation about how we studied fathers in our friends' families to try to understand what a father's role was. I didn't know how my father looked or the sound of his voice. What made him laugh, and what was the sound of his laughter? I didn't know the feel of his touch.

My small town in Nebraska held an annual father-son banquet. I envied the boys who could go with their fathers, but I did not want to go with a proxy. When I was about nine years old, a neighbor man who had no children asked my mother if he could take me, although I'm not sure why. I don't think he wanted to go any more than I wanted to go with him. We were surrogate father and son. It only called attention to the fact that he was childless and I was fatherless.

He was older than my father would have been. He was short and squat with a potbelly, unlike my father, who had been slim and athletic. My proxy father seemed ill-suited to be the insurance salesman he was; he seemed even less suited to being a father. My lungs seized up as I got in his car from the stench of cigarette smoke. My father had never smoked. Although I hungered for the touch of my father, I resisted having this man touch me with his cigarette-stained fingers. We spoke very little, unable to find anything we could share.

Being with him as a boy without a father felt like being a plus one at a party. I imagine it felt the same for him. You weren't invited; you came only because a friend invited you. You didn't make the A list of invited guests. You might have fun. You could even meet some interesting people. But the feeling of being slightly out of place never left me. The evening seemed much longer than it actually was. I couldn't wait to get home, where I felt like I belonged.

My Uncle Glen idolized my father, but he was only nineteen years old when my father died. He and my mother tried to manage the farm for a time, but grief undermined their success. Emotionally they had nothing left over for me.

Grandpa Olson was locked inside his body with Parkinson's disease. I actively searched for men to be surrogate fathers, but none measured up to the canonized image of my father. I had uncles we saw often, but they were all much older than my mother. Her brothers had young adult sons of their own. My cousins treated me well, but they were ten to fifteen years older. They called me Henry, but my name was Loren Alva H. Olson. I felt more like a puppy than their peer.

Several years later, when I was about thirteen, my friends and I showered and dressed after football practice. My best friend, Fred, caught his penis in the zipper of his Levi's. Fred hid his privates with his hands and walked home to wait a couple of hours for his father. Who would help me extract my penis from my zipper if I got it caught? There are some things a boy doesn't want to ask his mother to do. I wanted a father whom I could call and say, "Dad, I need some help with my penis." Once, for a high school play, I needed a man's suit. My mother said she still had an old suit of my father's in a trunk in the attic. As she dug through the chest, she found his suit under her mother's wedding veil and old pictures of relatives I didn't remember. She removed his suit from the trunk and pulled it to her chest. As she inhaled deeply, she began to cry softly. She said, "I can still smell your dad on his suit." I wanted to be able to smell my father too.

From time to time, I would ask my mother about my father. She dismissed my questions by saying only what an incredible man he was. She characterized him as flawless. She portrayed him as an idol that I knew I could never be. No matter how good I might be, I would always come up short.

Loren's mother, Martha Koester, graduated from Allen High School in Nebraska in 1932. (Courtesy of Loren A. Olson.)

Loren's father, Alva Harold Olson, like so many farm boys of the era, only received an eighth-grade education. He died in a farm accident on August 1, 1946, at age thirty-four. The local newspaper estimated over one thousand people attended his funeral. (Courtesy of Loren A. Olson.)

I met my wife, Lynn, in Omaha, Nebraska, during my last year of medical school. She had worked with my mother, and she had left something in the office when she went off to her first teaching job in Bellevue, Nebraska, just outside of Omaha. My mother's motives to get us together were obvious—and effective.

I was thunderstruck when I met Lynn. She won my heart immediately, but I doubted I had a chance at winning hers. We became engaged during my last year in medical school and her first year of teaching, and we got married after graduation. When we made our vows in front of family and friends, we expected to be married "till death do us part." We didn't make our vows with our fingers crossed.

Lynn came from Laurel, Nebraska, less than thirty miles from Wakefield, where I grew up. Our backgrounds were similar. We had the same values. We were both Lutherans. In another culture, our parents would have arranged our marriage; perhaps my mother did.

Lynn and Loren on their honeymoon in the Teton Range, Wyoming, June 1968. They married a few days after he graduated from medical school at the University of Nebraska. (Courtesy of Loren A. Olson.)

When I was in my thirties, Uncle Glen's son, Gayland, came to stay with Lynn and me. I asked Gayland to tell me about my father. Our conversation lasted well into the night. "Tell me some dirt," I said. "I need some balance, something to attach my dad to the ground." I thought my cousin might have heard something in his family that would pluck a few feathers from the angel's wings my mother had given him. I needed to remove the shroud that prevented access to his humanity.

Gayland replied, "I've got nothin'. My dad worshiped him. Dad might have said he was a bit arrogant." I felt as if he had manufactured something to satisfy me.

In 1975, when I was thirty-two years old and my mother was sixty, she married Martin Mortenson. She'd been a widow for nearly thirty years. I'm sure she never married earlier because no man could live up to my exalted father. I asked her once why she never dated anyone, and she responded, "I had a boyfriend once." She was referring to my father.

As I lay in bed on my mother's wedding night, I suddenly sat straight up and said to Lynn, "Oh, my God! Do you think Mom and Marvin are doing it?" Twenty years too late, I first thought about my parents as sexual beings.

I loved Grandpa Marvin, as we called him after welcoming him into the family. Although he was said to have been quite stern with his own children when they were young, with me and my siblings, he was always warm and gentle. I loved him as much as I could love any man who wasn't my actual father. Grandpa Marvin had many characteristics that I imagined my father would have had. He was a warm and gentle man who had been a successful cattle farmer. He was a sports fan and particularly liked baseball, as my father had. He had a great sense of humor with an infectious laugh. A proud Swede, he was as Lutheran as my Grandpa Koester. He didn't question his faith. I remembered from my childhood that his name topped the list of contributors to Salem Lutheran Church that was printed in the back of the yearbook.

Grandpa Marvin was a somewhat simple man who read the newspaper but didn't question authority. At times, he said things that would make a bigot blush, but he would have been ashamed if he thought he had ever said anything hurtful. I loved the fact that he cried, and he wasn't humiliated like I was when tears came to my eyes. He couldn't fill the hole left by my father's death, but he plugged it rather well.

I loved Grandpa Marvin most one Christmas. After coming out as gay, I had started dating Doug, and I brought him with me to Nebraska to meet my family for the first time. We had arranged to stay in a hotel because I assumed my mother and stepfather would be uncomfortable if Doug and I slept together in their home. The temperature was twenty degrees below zero when we got up to leave.

Grandma Martha and Grandpa Marvin Mortenson in the mid-1990s. They were married twenty-four years before Loren's mother died. Each of them had four children of similar ages. All eight children had attended school and church together in Wakefield, Nebraska. (Courtesy of Loren A. Olson.)

As we opened the front door to go, Grandpa Marvin said, "It's foolish for you to go out on a night like this. We have room, stay here." It not only assured me they liked Doug but that they also accepted that I am gay. Only years later did I learn that Grandpa Marvin had struggled with my relationship with Doug even more than my mother.

Throughout my early life, I blamed my father's death for my feeling like a flawed man. I had buried my same-sex desires until I was in my forties. My conflicts with my sexuality and a normative life were much like the power of my father's horses. My desires and my dreams were competing forces that I seemed unable to control. Now at seventy-eight years old, I feel the forces are in balance.

It is up to me to master my desires. I can balance the competing forces of my desires and dreams. I am Loren A. Olson, with an emphasis on the *A* for my father, Alva.

Fitting in Is Not Belonging

The sign that welcomed visitors to Wakefield, Nebraska, said Pop. 1030. The town's size didn't vary in all the years I lived there. It was a close-knit community linked by culture, economy, religion, and blood. The people not only knew each other, they knew each other's histories. Most families had many interconnecting links. In the generation before me, four Anderson brothers had married four sisters. Most of the family names were Swedish, although a few Germans had settled there too. Five Lutheran churches were scattered over a ten-mile radius from Wakefield. Church services were held in both English and Swedish until the early twentieth century. Most people looked alike, thought alike, and believed alike.

Wakefield was pastoral, but not in the sense of its being a charming and serene small town in rural America. It was pastoral because the Lutheran pastors were leaders in the community who made clear the distinctions between right and wrong. To an outsider, Wakefield appeared normal. The people who lived in Wakefield thought it was better than normal. They believed it was definitely better than Emerson and Allen, the two closest towns.

When I was nine years old, a neighbor had made a deal with me. If he bought a power mower, I could use it to mow lawns around Wakefield to make some money for the family. The one condition of the deal was I would mow his lawn regularly too. We needed the money.

I always struggled to start the mower. One day, I called my widowed mother at her work and sobbed, "I can't get the lawnmower started again."

She responded, “Of course you can. You’re a man, aren’t you?”

How does one answer that question? I thought, “Men fix machines; I can’t fix mine; I must not be a man.” I felt as if she’d ripped off one testicle.

Men’s and women’s roles were dogmatic, and if people strayed too far from those roles, they paid the penalty for it. My mother knew the values of her generation and wanted to teach them to me. Had I been a girl, she might very well have said to me, “Of course you can cook. You’re a woman, aren’t you?” It was the way she understood the world.

My mother was a kind woman and protective of my feelings. Now, as an adult, I can see she had intended to encourage my nascent manhood. All I could think was, “If my dad were here, he would have taught me. How can I learn to be a man without a dad? I will never measure up.”

The number of people in Wakefield never changed during the entire fifteen years that I lived there. The people who lived in my hometown didn’t change much either. Although a few new people came to town from time to time, they usually didn’t stay long. It would have been hard for them to feel welcome when the people who lived there had been there for generations and could recite everyone’s history down to the most intimate details.

My wife, Lynn, and I lived in Maine for ten years, and our children were both born there. People whose families have lived for generations in Maine think of people like us who move there as “from away.” As one story goes, a man who had moved to Maine and raised his children there asked an old Mainer, “I know that I will always be considered ‘from away.’ But since my children were born here, are they Mainers?”

The old Mainer responded, “If a cat has its kittens in an oven, you don’t call them muffins.” Although you may find a new life in a new place, the place you came from never entirely lets go of you.

In Wakefield, if someone asked for directions to a farm home, the directions weren’t given in distance. Instead, that person more likely would be told something like, “Go down the cemetery road past the old Dahlgren place. Then take the next left. You’ll pass the Anderson place and then the Fisher's. The next lane on the right will be the one you want. Can't miss it." And no one ever did.

The people of Wakefield were taciturn. They meted out discipline through quiet shame. The citizens kept their houses painted and their lawns mowed at the same height as their neighbors' lawns. One Sunday morning, my friend Fred and I were called out by Pastor Carlson in the middle of his sermon. The congregation turned to us with disapproving looks when he said, "Loren and Fred, will you be quiet!" My mother punished me by saying, "Loren, I am so disappointed in you." That was enough.

Wakefield didn't have any bad boys. Sure, some would squeal their tires, throw eggs at Aunt Edna's house, or drink a little beer after a football game. But your parents always knew what you'd done by the time you got home. We lived by a universally subscribed moral code enforced by the fact that there were no secrets. Having everyone know your business wasn't seen as a bad thing. My mother always left her keys in the car. When I asked her about it, she responded, "You just never know when someone might need to borrow your car."

A farmer knew that if he lost his arm in a corn picker that the neighbors would harvest his crops. Those who helped out thought, "There but for the grace of God go I." When I was in Lutheran catechism class, I learned that GRACE stood for "God's riches at Christ's expense." I used to wonder—at least when I had more faith in God—"If God's grace kept you from losing your arm, why didn't that same God's mercy keep him from losing his arm? On what basis does God dispense grace? If God has so much grace to hand out, why had she skipped my family?"

Behavior was monitored through gossip. For the gossipers, accusations trumped truth. I once dressed up as a girl for Halloween. I knew almost immediately after leaving the house that I had done something wrong. No one bullied or taunted me, but I could sense the whispering of the town gossips as I walked by in the parade.

I tried to play Little League baseball because it was expected, not because I wanted to. But the coach said, "Loren, you throw like a girl."

He implied that he didn't want someone like that on his team. I never went back.

We are hard-wired to seek belonging, but acceptance in Wakefield was illusory. You were accepted, providing you played the role. Schoolteachers drove to the next town if they wanted to have a beer. People kept their indiscretions to themselves.

When I was eleven or twelve, I bought a baton and an instruction book through the Sears-Roebuck catalog with the money I saved from mowing lawns. We lived on the edge of town where there was little traffic. I put a forty-five-rpm record player in the window to broadcast Sousa's marches and practiced between the garage and the house. I ran into the garage if I heard a car coming. I was the best baton twirler in my eighth-grade class of twenty-six students. I was good at something I felt ashamed of being good at.

I thought no gay people lived in Wakefield. A couple of "confirmed bachelors" lived there, and two inseparable women were long-term "roommates." Years later, when I asked my mother if they were gay, she responded, "We assumed they were, but there was no reason to talk about it."

No one spoke of any possibility that these couples were in loving, committed relationships. We didn't even have the language for it. Others may have whispered and giggled about them, but if they were discreet about their sexuality and participated in the community as "normal" people, the community of Wakefield ignored it.

As I grew older, people seemed less willing to overlook my unconventional interests. Social disapproval grew stronger. I went out for football. Everyone did. I played well enough to make varsity as a sophomore. My older brother, Lefty, taught me the plays. I was big and powerful enough to play tackle and linebacker. But I never could get to a place in my head where I wanted to hurt someone.

When I was about thirteen, a handsome senior boy was the lifeguard at Wakefield's swimming pool. I wanted to be like him in every way. I even fancied dating the popular homecoming queen he dated. Now I recognize he was the one I was smitten with. A mutual desire for a

Loren's football photo from his senior year at Wakefield High School, 1960–61. (Courtesy of Loren A. Olson.)

woman triangulated my desire for him. It wasn't the only time I disguised my attractions.

I have man boobs, and I've always felt self-conscious about them. When I went swimming as a teenager, I either stood shoulder-deep in the water or lay facedown on my towel. When that wasn't possible, I always had a T-shirt handy. On my chest was physical evidence that I wasn't quite a man; it was as obvious as if I had a giant tattoo saying SISSY on my chest.

After football practice, my teammates and I showered together, and I faced the wall to hide my shame. I hated exposing my naked body to anyone. One night, while we showered, Coach Pappy yelled at me, "Olson, with tits like that, you should wear a bra! Ha, ha." The other guys snickered nervously; they knew they could be the next victim of Coach Pappy's verbal assaults. He hadn't singled me out for his bullying. All of us had vulnerabilities. He sought them out, and then he struck.

He may have meant to toughen us up. As young men, we heard often enough, "This will make a man out of you." Maybe he wanted to piss us off, hoping we'd transfer that anger onto our opponents. But the only person on the football field I wanted to hurt was Coach Pappy. Had I told him that, his response would likely have been, "Don't be such a fucking sissy." Real men were supposed to be able to take it and give it back.

Boobs are feminine. Women were thought to be weak, and I needed to be strong. I hated my boobs because I presumed boobs excommunicated me from the fraternity of manhood. I was ashamed of this physical evidence because I wasn't the man I wanted to be. Coach

Pappy humiliated me by shaming me in front of my friends. The worst kind of pain comes from being exposed for something you already believe is true.

My sense of being a misfit in small-town America picked up momentum during my last years in high school. I felt cramped by the small size of our school. Opportunities were limited. You were either headed toward farming or college. Boys who lived in town couldn't take shop classes. Only girls could take home economics and cooking.

Mrs. Hughes taught English, but for three years we did little beyond diagramming sentences. All twenty-five of my classmates took her classes. I'd mastered diagramming by my sophomore year, while some in my class never did. Either way, all of us were bored. In my final semester of English, Mrs. Moller taught our class, and for the first time, I was exposed to literature. I grasped at the chance to discover more about the world away from the prairie.

Mrs. Hughes also directed our senior play. In the part I played, I needed to put on an overcoat. The first time I did it, she said, "Loren, you put on the coat like a girl." I couldn't throw a ball or put on a coat like a man. I constantly surveilled my actions to correct any errors, but I wasn't always successful.

As the country grew more conservative during the Red Scare and the McCarthy era, our teachers reminded boys who excelled academically that we had a patriotic duty to study math and science. Girls were told to choose nursing or teaching until they married into financial security or to have "something to fall back on" if left alone. With the Soviet launch of the Sputnik satellite in 1957, those cautions were accelerated. When someone asked me what I wanted to do when I grew up, I always answered, "I don't know for sure, but it will be something in math and science." That's what good boys answered.

I felt continuously pressured to play a role. I would have been more honest if I had said, "I'll do anything that will get me the hell out of Wakefield." It wasn't that Wakefield was such an awful place. My brother, Lefty, served as mayor for many years, and he thought there was no place on earth like Wakefield. But Lefty's attitudes fit in; mine didn't. This town was right for others, but it just wasn't the place for me.

I hungered for the diversity of an urban environment, even though I'd had little exposure to one. I wanted to make my own choices in a place that had a wide variety of options. I had not yet thought of this desire in terms of conflicts about sexual orientation. I wanted to find my own identity apart from the constraints of the world I'd known.

During my senior year, I saw an ad from United Airlines for flight attendants that said, "'Marriage is fine! But shouldn't you see the world first?" I sent for brochures from every major airline to see if any were hiring men. But the 1960s was the era of stewardesses: beautiful, elegant, single women who were hired out of high school and forced to retire either at about thirty years old or if they became pregnant. International airlines hired men as stewards, but they required that applicants be bilingual. My one year of poorly taught Spanish hadn't made me fluent. Airlines didn't actively begin recruiting men until a Supreme Court decision against Pan American Airways in 1971 forced them to. From that point on, *flight attendant* replaced the word *stewardess* in support of gender neutrality.

It might be reasonable for you to ask, "How could you not know you were gay?" For many years, I asked myself that same question. I admit I missed a few significant clues along the way. My earliest self-explanation was that my father died when I was three years old. I had no father to teach me how to be a man. Many years later, I realized that I couldn't continue to blame my father for feeling like I didn't fit in. I didn't begin to feel like a man until I accepted that I was a gay man.

When I try to explain how I didn't know I was gay, I say it was like a child's belief in Santa Claus. A young child never doubts that a fat old man flies through the air with eight reindeer plus one with a light on the end of his nose. Then Santa drops down a chimney and leaves gifts under the Christmas tree. As the child matures, things don't quite add up. But the child is reluctant to let go of this myth. He or she has a lot of good reasons not to investigate the discrepancies. Finally, the secret is exposed. The child must accept the fact that he or she can no longer cling to a deceitful legend.

Some people in the twenty-first century would like to return to the cultural values of the 1950s. Not me. Those who are nostalgic for that idealized past are dissatisfied with the present. But they are also disillusioned about what small-town America was like for some of us. We understood complete truth was not possible. Those of us who tried to fit in but couldn't believed there was no place for us.

In Truman Capote's book, *The Grass Harp*, Judge Cool spoke to his misfit friends while they sat in their treehouse looking down at the small town they hated. "It may be that there is no place for any of us. Except we know there is, somewhere, and if we found it, but lived there only a moment, we could count ourselves blessed."

Through those years in Wakefield, I asked myself, "Do you have a place for me?" I never felt it did. The people of Wakefield would be surprised that I felt that way. Their myopic attitudes did not allow small-town Americans to see how pressures to conform suppressed our differences and excluded us. I needed a sanctuary—a place where I could misbehave and still be accepted, feel free to reveal the hidden truths about myself, and choose another life made of my own decisions.

I tried to fit in, but fitting in isn't belonging. And nothing is lonelier than pretending to be someone you're not. My escape began in 1961 when I left Wakefield to attend the University of Nebraska.

Lefty

Life for my brother, Lefty, was a continuous battle against gravity. Until he was sixteen, his primary battles with gravity were on the baseball field. Lefty was passionate about many things, but nothing exceeded his enthusiasm for baseball. He practiced it, played it, read about it, and listened to it on the radio. He often fell asleep at night cuddling his radio like a teddy bear. He listened to the scratchy broadcasts of whatever game he could bring in on his portable radio. But most of all, he loved the Brooklyn Dodgers.

Lefty played first base for the Junior Legion team. One night, someone in the crowd called out to him, "Nice play, Lefty." After that, he never wanted to be called anything but Lefty. Many people didn't know his given name was Merlin.

In July 1952, someone other than our mother startled my sister and me awake far too early for a summer morning. We were scrambled out of the house to spend a few hastily arranged and unexpected days in the country. Everything about it felt wrong. They told us Lefty had been hurt in a car accident returning home from a Junior Legion baseball game.

As the car he was riding in came over a hill, it plowed through a bridge that sat at a forty-five-degree angle with the road. Road construction had caused traffic to be diverted to this detour, which was used almost exclusively by local farmers. At that moment, Lefty's fight against gravity escalated. Lefty's body was torpedoed from the backseat in the car before it slammed to an abrupt stop when the vehicle landed in the bottom of the creek. The driver and one other passenger escaped injury. Charlie, my brother's friend, was killed upon impact.

Dr. Coe, Wakefield's beloved and only physician, told my mother immediately he did not expect Lefty to survive. I have two sisters, Marilyn and Jan, both older than me but younger than Lefty. My mother kept the prognosis to herself. Dr. Coe explained to my mother that Lefty was "a high quadriplegic." Lefty's injuries mucked up the connection from his brain to his arms and legs. He lost sensation, bowel and bladder control, and the ability to regulate his body temperature. He had spasms and exaggerated reflexes. He had difficulty breathing, coughing, and clearing his throat. The functions he lost exceeded those he retained. A neurosurgeon from Sioux City, Iowa, came to Wakefield to place bolts in his skull. The bolts were attached to cables that held weights to keep him motionless. The wires were hardly necessary since he couldn't move much anyway.

Too young to visit Lefty in the hospital, my sister Jan and I could see him only if we stood on a pipe railing beneath his window. Lefty, at age sixteen, had been the man of the house since my father's death six years earlier. Over the next few months, I watched with my sister Jan, two years older than me, as our athletic brother transformed into a nearly helpless wounded warrior. Occasionally, my best friend Fred's mother, who was a nurse at the hospital, sneaked us in for a quick visit. Marilyn, my sister who was four years older, had more access to visits. My mother worked full time, and between work and visits to Lefty, we didn't see much of her. My sister Marilyn, who was just thirteen years old, had her adolescence stolen from her as she assumed responsibility for managing the household. All our lives were upended again.

When I started fifth grade in the fall of 1952, on my way to school, I walked past Wakefield's fourteen-bed hospital, where Lefty faded away on a bed in the corner room. I walked by Wakefield's hospital each night in my dreams too. I had a recurring nightmare in which I walked past the hospital on the way to school. But in front of the hospital was a brick display case with a glass front. Inside the box lay the spotlighted body of Charlie. In my dream, I was terrified because the only way to get to school was to walk past the entombed body.

After six months of being confined to his bed by his body's dead weight—now reduced by 50 percent—Lefty developed huge bedsores.

He had outlived Dr. Coe's prediction of his life expectancy. My memory is vague, but I believe the man for whom my mother worked, who'd moved to Wakefield from New York City, arranged for Lefty to be transferred. He was flown in an air ambulance to the rehabilitation center at New York University Hospital under the care of Dr. Howard Rusk, one of the pioneers in the field of rehabilitation of the physically disabled. The people in Wakefield collected money to pay for the trip.

Dr. Rusk knew that to encourage progress, he needed to attend to more than just his patients' physical needs. He must also address their psychological and social needs to an equal degree. He taught Lefty not to let his disability define him: Dr. Rusk viewed all his patients not by their diagnoses but as humans with varying challenges to overcome or manage. Lefty went on a stretcher to see his beloved Brooklyn Dodgers play. He peed in a shower cap filled with absorbent cellulose. If he shit himself, he shit himself. Those were natural functions, something to deal with without shame or embarrassment. I think that's why he so readily later accepted my being gay. It was a complication to be dealt with without shame.

Lefty was in New York City for several months and had a number of surgical procedures. My mother left Wakefield to be with him. She worked as a secretary, lived at the YWCA, and visited Lefty every day in the hospital. My sister Marilyn, just thirteen, managed the family under my mother's direction from afar. Marilyn did it splendidly, but she sacrificed her own teen years in the process. Today, child welfare would have yanked us out of the home and placed us in foster care, a thought that horrifies me.

When Lefty returned to Wakefield, he was still on a stretcher. I remember the first time I pulled back the sheets to expose his body. I saw the disfiguring scars from his many surgeries and skin graftings. The scars on his neck and places where the skin had been removed and repositioned shocked me. Instead of the smooth and rounded buttocks of a young man, his butt resembled a topographical map. Surgeons had moved a flesh tube (shaped like a Slinky) from one place on his body to another to heal the bedsores.

Family photo at their home in Wakefield, Nebraska, in 1954 after Lefty's stay at Bellevue Hospital, affiliated with New York University in New York City. (Courtesy of Loren A. Olson.)

Lefty approached his disability without saying he could not do things; instead, he tried to discover ways for them to be done. He fed himself with a fork held in a clawlike hand about as functional as a pirate's hook. Whenever he asked me for help, he rolled slightly to one side. I slid out from under him the cellulose-filled, pee-soaked shower cap and replaced it with a fresh one. When I cared for Lefty's personal hygiene needs, he often had a powerfully erect young man's penis. As I was a preadolescent boy, it was the first time I'd ever seen anything like that.

Paralyzed men get normal erections fully capable of penetration, but they are only a reflex mediated through the spinal cord. The severed spinal cord cannot carry a sexual message to the brain. Paralyzed men can masturbate and sometimes ejaculate. But orgasms are in the brain and ejaculation is in the sex organs. For Lefty, these weren't connected.

Numbness is a feeling quite like silence in a symphony. It intensifies feeling by its absence. Imagine, as a paralyzed person, intimately rubbing the leg of your partner only to realize that you had actually been caressing your own leg—wasted intimacy.

One Christmas, Lefty received an entire box of Mounds candy bars from a local businessman. I would ask him, "Do you want a Mounds?" I knew his response would be, "No, but you can have one if you want one." Sometimes I took two. I ate them until they were all gone. It wasn't that

Family Christmas photo in 1954 at their home in Wakefield, after Lefty's return in a wheelchair from Saint Mary's Hospital and the Mayo Clinic in Rochester, Minnesota. (Courtesy of Loren A. Olson.)

difficult to steal from him; gravity protected me since he lay on a sawed-off gurney in the next room.

I once asked my mother if she'd ever heard Lefty complain about his limitations. She told me the only thing she'd ever heard him say was that sometimes he would dream of standing on first base. A fielded ball was thrown to him. As he tried to catch it, his first baseman's mitt kept falling off his right hand. Gravity won. Dreams can be more punishing than reality.

After being at home on a stretcher for several months, Lefty was referred to the Mayo Clinic. He was in Saint Mary's hospital in Rochester, Minnesota, for a few months. When he came home, he was in a wheelchair. He had no usable trunk muscles and could remain upright only by forming a triangle with his butt and two elbows acting as sentries. One day, I rushed him in his wheelchair through the yard in front of our house. I hit a hole in the lawn, projecting him out of his wheelchair like an unrestrained crash-test dummy. I was horrified at what I had done, but Lefty said nothing. Perhaps he thought, "If you shit yourself, you just shit yourself." By then I was strong enough to lift him back into the chair.

Another time, as he crossed the alleyway, a car rushed out and hit him, throwing him out of the chair and breaking his hip. Although he couldn't feel pain, he appeared pale and had goosebumps with some sweating, but only on his brow. When asked what he was feeling, he said, “Nothing.” But we learned to recognize the physical signs of his body’s response to pain.

When Lefty was twenty-three and I had just turned sixteen and gotten my driver’s license, I occasionally took Lefty on a boys’ night out to Sioux City, Iowa. He always asked me to take him to an adult bookstore at the end of the evening. He browsed the adult magazines of nude women. He pointed out his selections. I held them for him until we reached the clerk, who required an adult to purchase them. Upon our return home, I hid the magazines in the now-empty Mounds candy bar box.

When the two of us were home alone together, he would ask, “Loren, will you bring me the box?”

Then I left him alone to his fantasies. When he called me to return the box to the shelf, I looked through the magazines. I saw that he had caressed the naked women’s photos by drawing lingerie on them with a Magic Marker. We never talked about it. It was our man-to-man secret, an intimacy shared but unspoken. It was my payback to him for stealing all his candy bars.

The essential characteristic of a man of honor is that he takes risks, faces others, and stares them down. When someone offered their hand for Lefty to shake, he stretched his hand to meet theirs. He showed no embarrassment or shame about his shrunken and contracted hand. He grasped their hand with his emotion if not with his physical strength as if to say, “I am a man among men.”

Although Lefty struggled with gravity, he soared. My sisters encouraged him to start classes at Wayne State College, ten miles away from Wakefield. My mother took him to Wayne State in the morning before going to work and picked him up after classes. The students at Wayne State helped him get from class to class. He graduated magna cum laude with a degree in accounting in 1968, the same year I graduated from medical school. He opened his own accounting business in Wakefield.

In 1978 Lefty was elected mayor of Wakefield and served consecutive terms until 1998. In 1981, he married Sylvia Magnuson. As mayor and first lady of Wakefield, they traveled together throughout the

United States as Wakefield's ambassadors. They visited twenty-two other communities named Wakefield, including Wakefield, England.

Lefty continued to be an avid sports fan and became the sports reporter and photographer for local and regional newspapers. He took pictures holding his camera with both hands and clicked the shutter by a cable that connected the shutter to his teeth. He was elected an honorary member of the semipro baseball hall of fame and Outstanding Disabled Person of the Midlands in 1981. Lefty was instrumental in having Wakefield named the Baseball Capital of Nebraska.

Lefty and Sylvia, along with my mother and Grandpa Marvin, never missed a Cornhusker home game. At one of those games, my mother had a stroke and Grandpa held her up through the national anthem. When he got to the hospital, he said to the doctor, "I guess I should have gotten help right away."

The doctor replied, "Don't worry about it. Most Nebraska fans would have waited until the end of the game to get help."

Although he received a lot of help from my mother, Sylvia, and Grandpa Marvin, Lefty, though damaged physically, was the strongest man I've ever known. He embodied this message: when gravity pulls you down, discover new ways to do what needs to be done.

Lefty was my mentor and my hero. Sadly, gravity eventually took his life. He contracted the

Lefty married Sylvia Magnuson in the backyard of Lefty's and his mother's home, June 19, 1981. (Courtesy of Loren A. Olson.)

flu at sixty-two years old, and because his coughs were ineffective, he couldn't clear his lungs. He died in his sleep. He lives in my heart.

When Lefty received the Wakefield Community Club's Citizen of the Year award, he quoted these words from an anonymous poet:

> I got nothing that I asked for, but everything I hoped for.
> Almost despite myself, my unspoken prayers were answered.
> I am, among all men, most richly blessed.

Lefty was more than a big brother to me. He was my champion, and he always had my back. He had plenty of reasons not to. Lefty never said to me, "Don't be such a baby," even when I was.

Although we had very different passions, he always made me feel safe. I experienced soft-shaming criticism for my emotionality and nontraditional interests whispered between others. But never from Lefty. He was the shield that protected me from being shamed. I lived in the protective shadow of his masculinity until I could discover it for myself.

Lefty realized that he had challenges and I had challenges. Although our challenges were different, they were our own challenges. I watched Lefty outstretch his deformed hand unapologetically and hold his head high even when he'd been unable to control his bowels in a public place. The automobile accident broke my brother's body but did not destroy his soul. From him I learned to have the strength to believe that I could face my challenges and not feel ashamed.

Suicide and Other Family Secrets

"Aunt Martha, could you tell us about Grandpa's suicide?" a cousin asked my mother at a family reunion several years ago.

My mother's two sisters and all my cousins were stunned as my mother's face grew red and she shot back, "We don't talk about that!"

An agonizing silence fell upon the room. My mother then slammed the door shut so hard that everyone knew it would be impossible to reopen it. It took several moments for the family gathering to recover and move on to another piece of our shared history.

My mother sat on a panel with her two younger sisters, the only three surviving siblings of the eight children born to my German immigrant grandparents. The hosts of the reunion had asked my mother and my aunts if they would answer cousins' questions about our family history. Everyone knew that before long, we would lose the history they had lived.

I didn't learn Grandpa had shot himself until twenty years after it happened, even though we were living with him when he took his life. I learned of it by chance in conversation. I was in medical school and had an interest in psychiatry. I was walking with Lefty, who was in his electric wheelchair, past the home of a woman from Wakefield whom I knew had been hospitalized many times for depression when I was quite young.

I asked Lefty, "Whatever happened to Mrs. A——?"

"She killed herself," he answered, almost as if he were trying to suppress a belch.

"Oh, I'm so sorry." Then I added somewhat self-righteously, "I just don't understand how anyone could ever do that." I was very new to psychiatry.

Loren's grandfather, Friedrich Gerhard Koester, married Anna Matilda Wessel on February 12, 1902. Both had immigrated with their families to the United States from Elsfleth, Germany, in 1890. (Courtesy of Loren A. Olson.)

"I guess it's sort of like Grandpa." He was trying to help me understand.

I screamed, "What? Twenty years later, and I'm just finding out about this!"

"I guess we thought you knew."

By the time of that family reunion thirty years later, I had discovered more about Grandpa's suicide. I had asked Jan, Marilyn, and Lefty some questions, but I had never discussed it with my mother. Before Grandpa's suicide, my grandma, my mother's mother, had simply withered away and died without explanation, as people did in those days. After the farm accident that killed my father, my mother was too grief-stricken to make any decisions for herself, so her sister, my Aunt Sophie, took charge again and decided that since my mother and Grandpa were both alone, we should move in with Grandpa.

Grandpa Koester immigrated with his family to the United States from Germany when he was fourteen years old, and he became a naturalized citizen in 1899 at twenty-three. In 1902, he married my grandmother, who had also immigrated with her family from Germany. My grandfather came from a family in Germany that made rope for sailing ships, a dying industry, but when they learned of cheap land available in the newly opened western United States, they became

Grandpa and Grandma Koester and their eight children in 1924.
Top row, from left: Herbert Diedrich, Oscar John, Paul Gerhard, and Sophie Louise.
Middle row: Martha Katherine and George Arthur ("Judd").
Front row: Marjorie Patience Mathilda ("Pete"), Grandpa Koester, Helen Elizabeth, and Grandma Koester. (Courtesy of Loren A. Olson.)

hardscrabble farmers near Hooper, Nebraska, where a number of other German families had settled. Grandpa decided that Hooper was too German, maintaining many Old World traditions, so when he started his own family, he moved seventy miles away to Allen, Nebraska. The fact that Great-Grandpa Koester drank too much beer may have been the bigger reason.

Grandpa and Grandma Koester and their young family spoke only German at home until World War I. After the war began, other students at school harassed the older siblings about their nationality and broken English. My mother was raised on a farm in rural Allen, Nebraska, the fifth of eight children born to her German immigrant parents. German was the only language spoken in my grandparents' home until the oldest siblings went to school. Memories of World War I lingered, and they were bullied for their German heritage. Speaking a different language always confers an outsider status, but particularly when it is the language of the enemy.

From that time forward, Grandpa Koester did not allow German to be spoken in the home. My mother recalled him saying, "Ve are nicht Germans. Ve are Americans!" They had come to America to be Americans, and Americans spoke English. He spoke with a heavy accent; my grandmother never mastered the new language. The only exception to speaking English in the home was when they spoke German to keep secrets from their children.

When my older uncles took over "the home place" (as everyone referred to family farms), my Grandpa moved about fifteen miles to Wakefield. Grandpa was as Lutheran as he was German; even Martin Luther would have envied his faith. The spire of Salem Lutheran Church was the highest point in Wakefield, visible across the prairie from miles away. Wakefield had only a handful of Roman Catholic families. One Jew arrived later, but he later became a Lutheran.

Church attendance was expected. During Lent, the school administration released the entire school to attend lunch served by the women of Salem Lutheran Church. Each morning in school, the Pledge of Allegiance was followed by the Lord's Prayer. The community was so homogenous that no one challenged the assumption that they were equally important or considered that it might offend others.

On May 7, 1945, all forces under German control surrendered. I was two years old at the time. Because my father was a farmer, he had not been drafted, and many years later my mother told me, "The war was good to us. Grain prices were high, so we could pay off our mortgage on the farm." In war, some lose, some win. My mother wasn't a selfish woman, but her world didn't extend much beyond the ten miles to Hartington, Nebraska, where she sold her eggs and cream every Saturday night to get money for the groceries the family needed.

In 1949, Grandpa Koester decided to return to visit Germany for the first time since he emigrated. Germany was still in the early stages of reconstruction, though the devastating effects of the war surrounded

The Swedish Evangelical Lutheran Salem Church, also known as Salem Church, was established in 1883. This late Gothic Revival–style church was built in 1905–06 and is now in the National Register of Historic Places. (Public domain.)

them already. The trip was too soon. Grandpa Koester became terribly depressed during the visit, and his depression had sucked energy out of our household for quite some time.

He arrived back home in Nebraska on a Friday and shot himself Sunday night; an unintended consequence and noncombatant casualty of World War II. I learned from my sister Marilyn, who'd heard it from our mother, that Grandpa had not believed in the Holocaust. He could not accept that the Christians of his beloved homeland could have perpetrated such a heinous crime. During Grandpa's trip to Germany, he learned the truth about the Nazis, and he came home unable to bear the shame.

I sometimes wonder if Grandpa had known that the Germans also imprisoned thousands of gay men. Some were castrated because they could not or would not have sex with the state's female prostitutes. Did he know about the medical experiments performed on them and that the majority of them died following those procedures? Could he have learned how the ones who did survive were too frightened to talk about their experiences?

The Lutheran legacy was handed down from my grandfather to my mother and subsequently to me. It was a critical part of my identity for many years. We said the Apostles' Creed every Sunday. In later years, I found myself moving my lips silently as we came to "born of the Virgin Mary" and "rose again from the dead." I wanted to believe it, but I struggled.

After my mother died, I searched in her dresser for clothes for her burial. I found a drawer filled with books she had hidden. Her pastor gave her these books—books that condemned me for being gay—written for parents trying to understand their child's homosexuality from a Lutheran viewpoint. An incredible sadness compounded my grief for her passing. My mother always accepted me; she just wanted to understand me. Her greatest fear about my being gay was that she would not see me in heaven. She had never hinted to me that my behavior had put her Christian faith to such a test. She was trapped, caught between her love for me and her passion for her inherited faith. How I wished that we could have talked about that too.

Now I find it is easier to understand why my mother didn't want to talk about Grandpa's suicide. He shot himself two years after my father was dragged to his death by a team of runaway horses. She had found my father trapped in the harnesses beneath the horses. Then she found Grandpa on the floor in our basement with a bullet wound to his head. Her blood-spattered memories muted her voice. My cousin's question about Grandpa's suicide had triggered a flood of emotions that through the years she had tried to suppress.

Who's the Boss of You?

Growing up in small-town Nebraska, I knew what everyone expected from me. Kindred values hung over Wakefield like a tornado-producing dark cloud that could drop a twister on you at any moment. As the saying goes, "No prisons are more confining than those we know not we are in."

I followed all the social rules, and damn, I was good at doing that! Yet I never felt good about myself. Other mothers would say to my mother, "I wish my boy would be more like Loren." That never felt good. And note: they said more like Loren, not just like Loren. I wanted to be more like those other boys who were a little bit naughty. I wanted to flaunt the rules and have adults look amused and say, "Boys will be boys."

No one demanded I be a good boy. I never really believed that my family would stop loving me if I misbehaved. Still, I felt I couldn't risk the disapproval of people I loved. The driving force behind my good behavior was shame. Guilt is a feeling you've done something bad; shame is a feeling you are bad. A lot of gay men and women say they felt different, but the feeling is heavier than being a misshapen tomato. I felt different in all the wrong ways. I felt if I could get everyone to ratify my goodness, it would take the shame away.

When I think back on the validation I received, I get a bit nauseated. I'd often hear, "What a sweet boy. Such a nice young man." It feels like I just ate all my Halloween candy in one sitting. I knew they were lying if they added, "I wish my son could be more like Loren." All they really wanted was a child who was more compliant with their wishes. I am distressed when I remember how self-righteous I felt about being such a good boy.

On the rare occasion I did something wrong, I always got caught. When I was about ten years old, I stole a pack of cigarettes from the Rexall drug store to smoke with some friends. When I got home, my mother asked, "When did you start smoking?" Gossip travels fast in small-town Nebraska. Where everyone knows everyone, it's hard to keep secrets. I felt like a surveillance camera was on me all the time. I had no place to escape to where I could safely be naughty.

Most people want approval, but some of us need it more than others. We seek the approval of our parents most of all, but we also demand the collective endorsement of our lovers, our kin, and all of society. We even want approval from people we don't like or respect.

I excelled at being good because approval was my heroin. I'd take a hit, but it didn't last long. Then I'd have to shoot up another. And another. I sought validation from my family, my kinship, my community, and my religion. I adopted their values, and those values directed my choices. It was a delusion to think I would feel good about myself if I followed their rules, but the delusion was pervasive and seductive. I let them direct my choices even though they didn't recognize they were doing it. I didn't recognize it either. The truth is, though, that I didn't know who I was apart from the roles I played. I see now that I feared knowing who I was outside of those good-boy roles. I was an actor waiting for the director to coach my performance. I couldn't find a place to feel safe to be myself.

I believed that something out there—a person, social stature, or ideology—would give me some validation that I was worth something. But in the process, I lost my sense of self. Adopting others' values as my own was confusing. Those values sometimes conflicted with each other. I was a paint-by-numbers person. Someone else had drawn the lines and chosen all the colors.

I once said to my younger daughter, Krista, "What I like best about you and what I like least about you is the same thing." What I like best is that she is her own person. But that means she will always do what she wants, not what I want her to do.

Some people want to be just like their parents. Others decide to be anything but like them. In either case, their parents are still the template for how they live their lives, but either approach doesn't feel right. The first time I remember setting myself free was when I told my mother I wanted to be a psychiatrist.

She asked, "Why do you want to stop being a doctor?"

I assured her, "I'll still be a doctor, but I want to do something that will give my life meaning." I knew that being the small-town family doctor—particularly if I returned to my hometown in Nebraska—would give her life meaning but would have been a disaster for me.

It was not until 1987 at age forty-four that I broke free of the bondage when I ripped off the chains and came out as gay. The world didn't fall apart as I had anticipated. As I matured, I discovered that someone wasn't going to grant me permission to live my life; I had to find my own place and seize it. I wasn't going to find myself by looking "out there somewhere." It was within me. Approval provided highs that were transient and superficial. Obtaining approval from others gave their lives meaning while sacrificing my own life.

After my book *Finally Out: Letting Go of Living Straight* first came out in 2011, to promote it I traveled throughout the United States and Canada to speak to any group that would listen. At these talks, I often ask, "How many prefer chocolate ice cream?" Then I ask, "How many prefer vanilla?" I follow that by asking, "Who's right? How might it affect your decision if someone said, 'Only faggots eat vanilla' or 'You'll go to hell if you eat chocolate?'"

If we demand that chocolate is the right answer, we deny the humanity of those who prefer vanilla. If we say we like vanilla because we were told it was better, we deny our own humanity. The more we wish another person to satisfy us, the more dissatisfying a relationship becomes. Any relationship can expand no more than the highest level of maturity of each partner.

Excessive reliance on other people for approval leads to an estrangement from our souls. It arises from two false assumptions: one, that we are powerless, and two, that the power we attribute to the other person is unlimited. When someone puts you in your place, it isn't your place. It is their place for you. Sometimes, in service to our emotions, a distorted logic leads us to do crazy things. We recognize it as illogical only after we begin to recognize the patterns in our lives. We resist this insight because it makes it hard to blame our parents, our society, or someone else.

I wanted the freedom to choose either chocolate or vanilla. Being loved is being accepted for your own choices. To love someone is to give them the freedom to like whatever they choose. Grab the sense of purpose in your own life; set those you love free to find meaning in theirs.

Yoga for the Penis

As we stripped down to our underwear to get into bed, Randy said, "Hey, Loren, I got somethin' to show you." Circumstances had thrown Randy and me together that summer when he was fourteen and I was eleven years old. Randy and I spent a lot of time together during that summer, and occasionally he would sleep over.

Late in the afternoons, one of us would call our parents to ask if we could stay for supper at the other's house. (The last meal of the day was never called "dinner" in Wakefield, Nebraska.) We'd play together until it started to grow dark, and then we'd make the second phone call to see if we could sleep over. We were hardly ever refused. Our families were church friends at Salem Lutheran Church but otherwise didn't socialize. Good Lutherans assume it's always safe to be with other Lutherans.

Many of us as preadolescent boys played "I'll show you mine if you show me yours." It was more like collecting butterflies than anything sexual. The girls in fifth grade watched a movie about menstruation, but I think it must have been shown to prevent embarrassing accidents rather than to provide any introduction to sex. No one seemed to think boys needed to know about the unexpected onset of wet dreams.

Boys in farming communities escaped to the privacy of haylofts for childhood sexual explorations. As clothes came off, we piled them on the scratchy hay bales. We thrilled at the wonder of our grubworm-sized penises becoming erect. I am sure that our parents knew precisely what we were doing in those haylofts. As they recalled their own childhoods, they probably thought, "Boys will be boys."

Sonograms reveal boys in utero can have erections, and infant boys experience erections with diaper changes. They may even experience orgasms. These are normal reflexes, not sex as adults understand sex. Starting as early as age three, children begin to explore their bodies and the bodies of other children, but infants and young children do not differentiate one type of pleasure from another. Their exploration comes from curiosity, physical pleasure, or behavior they have observed.

A child experiences sexual response long before he or she has any understanding of adult sexual behavior. Boys begin to masturbate before they can conjure explicit fantasies of sexual activity. Young children may masturbate together, play "doctor," hug and kiss, or lie on top of each other. Adults may interpret this as sex; children do not. Because children's play is commonly separated by gender, sexual exploration with a same-gender friend is not a reflection of sexual orientation. It is a matter of convenience. Sexual orientation is neither caused by nor an effect of childhood sex play.

When I had this experience with Randy, my knowledge of human reproduction was in its infancy. For a while after that day, my only words for orgasm were "that good feeling." It takes a while to learn the language of sex. About all I understood was that it took both a man and a woman to make a baby. I knew that only because I had extrapolated from farm boys who told me a bull had to be introduced to the cow herd to have calves. I didn't know that sex could be for pleasure and an expression of love, not only for the purpose of creating offspring.

When I reached adolescence and grew those first pubic hairs, I had a surge of sexual interest. My erections were out of control. Erections occurred when I was called on in class, when I read or slept, while I was talking with Grandma, or when I waited for my football physical. By the time my testosterone really kicked in as an adolescent, my developing brain associated nakedness with something sexual, but the sexual act was about as real as reading a travel brochure for some place you might want to visit.

When my voice began to change, I still had some of my baby fat. My older sister, Marilyn, who worked at the Rexall drug store, brought me home my first spray-on deodorant. She also told me I needed to learn to shave with a safety razor because, according to her, girls didn't like boys who sprouted facial stubble, and an electric razor would never shave close enough. I inspected myself daily in the shower for the first sign of a pubic hair. Nothing. I ached to become a man.

Randy and I were about the same height, even though he was three years older. He was lean, powerful, and muscular. Unlike most of the other high school boys, he never had to get himself in shape for football. He was always in shape. There was no weight training in the late 1950s in Wakefield. If you had muscles, you earned them through hard work. Farmers always needed help stacking hay bales in the barn, and Randy was often asked to help because he could throw them like the best of the men. The only time I remember seeing his breathing accelerate was that night in bed.

I had not seen Randy naked before we climbed into bed together. Except for when I assisted Lefty with his care, I had never been that close to a man-sized penis before, and as I remember it, Randy's was definitely man-sized. He had a thick bush of pubic hair. I had seen only little-boy penises.

As Randy pulled down his underwear, his penis was already hard. Randy was well pleased with himself and appreciated my fascination. He said, "Watch this! It feels really good." He began to stroke his penis, and within moments, he ejaculated. I felt as if I were some wimpy kid watching a burly young man swing the mallet and ring the bell on the carnival midway at the Dixon County Fair. All I could think was, "I want to do that!" I immediately pledged allegiance to the code of manhood.

If Randy hadn't taught me about masturbation, I can confidently state I would have discovered it on my own. I had an erection and masturbated when I put on my first jockstrap. A new pair of underwear triggered the same response. These erections were unrelated to explicit sexual fantasies. Telling me to control my feelings of lust would not have changed this. Erections were not a result of conscious thoughts of sexual desire. But having those first man-sized erections was as exciting as seeing the ocean for the first time.

I didn't associate what Randy and I had just done with sex. Telling someone who has never had sex what it's like to have sex is like trying to explain what eating a Snickers bar is like to someone who has never tasted candy. You can't accurately envision what you've never experienced. I had no reference point to think of what I'd just observed as sexual behavior.

With Randy, I began my initiation into the rituals of manhood. Nothing separates men from women or boys more than the capacity to ejaculate. At eleven years old, what point of reference could I have? I had not yet experienced anything like that. The only association I had was once before when I was about nine. I had had "a good feeling down there" when shimmying up a metal post on a swing set.

When I was in the eighth grade, I stayed overnight with a male friend who was a year older. We practiced kissing "so we'd know how when we started dating girls." At that age, we often slept over at friends' homes. We frequently ended up finding each other with an erect penis and jerking each other off.

Exploration became more direct with teenage sleepovers. Side-by-side masturbation became routine. I discovered that size differences in erect penises were less than the sizes observed in our communal locker-room showers. I always had some fear of getting hard in the shower with so many naked bodies nearby. A few times, lingering in the shower with one friend, the fear was replaced by desire as we jerked off in the shower together. After I came out as gay, he did not want to have anything to do with me.

Everything became more sexual. We watched and compared penises in the showers after football practice. But the secretive examination of other boys' penises was more about competition. Whose is bigger? Who has more pubic hair? But somehow, we understood not to get caught looking too long.

American culture is full of contradictions. Americans love sex, and yet we shame it. We resist acknowledging sexuality in the young. We say "Not in public. Not in front of the children." Yet children are surrounded by sex. The foundation of our culture suggests it is imprudent to speak openly about sexuality, which is at odds with respectability, dignity, and self-worth.

Masturbation is one of those topics polite society doesn't talk about. Like breathing, blinking, and pooping, we assume everybody does it. Attitudes toward masturbation are extremely varied and linked to the perceptions within a given culture of its nature and consequences. The roots of American culture go back to seventeenth-century Puritanism. In that era, stoicism, self-reliance, and denial of sensual pleasure were extolled. Sensual pleasures—at best—were a waste of time. At worst, they were considered depraved and sinful.

No one taught me that sex was wrong or sinful. I was taught, however, that love was good, lust was bad, and they should never be confused. Our Lutheran pastor didn't talk about masturbation. I guess he felt if he didn't mention it, we would never know about it. Perhaps teaching us that gluttony was sinful was a surrogate for the uncomfortable topic of masturbation. Although I was never taught masturbation was sinful, anything so pleasurable must be bad. I must have had some guilt, or I wouldn't have made all those promises to stop. Children absorb these beliefs even if they are not being specifically taught about them. We internalize these attitudes about masturbation during adolescence, where they often remain unchanged throughout the course of our lives.

Leaders of religious faiths can decide what constitutes sin. I don't have a problem with their right to do that. I do have a problem, however, when they justify their positions on grounds that are totally contrary to science. Although religions teach sexual purity and abstinence, in those states where conservative religion is ingrained in the culture, people have the highest consumption of pornography. Someone is not telling the truth. Rules are outdated mistakes that need to be either replaced or broken.

In response to something I'd posted on Facebook, someone responded, "Why, in the twenty-first century, are we still talking about guilt for masturbating?" But masturbation remains taboo in many cultures, and this is not without consequences for mental and sexual health. Some studies suggest that even today, university students feel guilty about masturbating, but their guilt rarely reduces their frequency of it.

In medical school we had zero training about sex. Research on masturbation is complicated because it remains one of the most sensitive sexual topics to discuss. Physicians and therapists often find it difficult to talk about masturbation. It often makes both the interviewers and interviewees uncomfortable. Few studies go beyond asking, "Do you masturbate? If yes, how often? To what extent do you experience guilt?"

Whatever the source of negative attitudes about masturbation, they set the stage for feelings of shame and guilt. Children and adolescents are told to exert self-control before they are developmentally capable of doing so. Then they are blamed for their failure. But even adults aren't successful with self-control.

I have a gay cousin who said to me, "You're married. You can have sex any time you want it." Anyone who believes that marriage puts sex-on-demand at your disposal has never been married or is still listening to eighteenth-century moral authorities about male dominance. Masturbation does not decrease with age. It is not always a compensation for a missing sex partner. Its frequency is almost unrelated to the relationship status and years spent in a relationship.

Masturbation, from a scientific perspective, is normal, acceptable, and beneficial. Masturbation will not cause you to become sick or your intelligence to diminish. It doesn't steal your energy. You won't go blind or grow hair on your palms. It doesn't affect fertility. Scientists generally agree the positive aspects of masturbation include becoming familiar with one's body, forming healthy sexual fantasies, and achieving sexual satisfaction without risk. Masturbation relieves stress and promotes good sleep. Some evidence suggests that masturbation may even reduce the risk of prostate cancer. The only negative effect of masturbation is a pervasive sense of guilt that results from its taboo. Masturbation is a safe, independent way to experience sexual pleasure whether or not other alternatives to sexual satisfaction are available. Masturbation is transcendental, like yoga for the penis.

One of the most common questions I'm asked is, "How much is too much?" Most often, the question originates from someone who has promised to stop but finds it difficult, if not impossible, to do so. What's normal? In the past, more than one orgasm a day was considered problematic. Current writers suggest that no specific number separates masturbating just enough from too much. The key question is, "How much do your sexual habits interfere with other important aspects of your life?" A good test is to stop for a few days and see what happens.

We begin to form our identity in childhood, but formation of a sexual identity accelerates in adolescence. Some gay men say they knew they were gay before they started school but didn't develop a stable sexuality identity until much later. I suspect they were beginning to experience erotic desire through attraction to men, but they still had little idea how that desire would later manifest. Gay men talk more openly about masturbation than straight men. For mature straight men to admit they masturbate suggests they've failed in their sexual prowess, as if to say, "If I were better at being a man, I wouldn't have to masturbate."

Randy and I were only beginning to consolidate our physical and sexual maturation with ideas about our futures. I came to my sexual identity later in life than many men. As I began to formulate ideas of who I was, I had sealed away same-sex attraction as a part of my embryonic identity.

I assume that most of my friends with whom I carried on my childhood sexual explorations understand sex better now than we did back then. Our sexual activities were a sexual placeholder until we could begin to have healthy sex with a suitable partner.

Some may raise the question about whether I was sexually abused by Randy, and some fourteen-year-old boys in similar situations have been charged with being sexual predators. I would argue that I was not abused. I was under the age of consent in any jurisdiction, and although Randy was sexually mature, he was not mature enough to understand how some young boys might be harmed. I wasn't threatened or coerced. I wanted to be there as much as he did. In my mind, what we did was an extension of childhood sexual exploration. Even looking back on it now, I don't feel he was exerting any power over me. Randy didn't demand anything of me. When does sexual exploration become sexual trauma? Age alone is not enough to define it.

Clearly, prohibitions against masturbation aren't stopping it, and they do result in a great deal of mental anguish about it. Setting a goal of perfect self-control is unrealistic, and there is also a great deal of hypocrisy in what people say we should do and what is done. If your goal is to be totally abstinent from any sexual self-pleasure, you'll fail. It will lead to guilt, shame, and a sense of failure. Restraint and moderation are more realistic goals and may even lead to better health.

As a psychiatrist, I often discuss masturbation with my patients, and women often seem more comfortable with it than men. To ease men into the discussion, I often start by saying something like this: "I assume that you masturbate; most men do." The statement is designed to say that while talking about masturbation may not be common, the behavior is natural and normal. Some will consider it imprudent or unprofessional for me to speak about my own history of masturbation, and I wouldn't do it with a patient. But why don't we talk about it? I assume that you masturbate; most people do. You've probably assumed this about me too.

When Cardinals Appear, Angels Are Near

On one of those days pictured in travel brochures, my husband, Doug, and I were sitting outside on our deck. A bright red cardinal landed in a shrub nearby. I said to him, "I always feel like my mother is nearby when I see a cardinal." He smiled. My mother loved Doug as much as she loved me, and he returned that love to her.

On the deck floor near us was a crudely shaped concrete lawn ornament in a cardinal shape. The red paint chipped away as if the cardinal were molting. It wouldn't get a second look at a flea market, but it was one of the few things of hers I wanted after my mother passed over twenty years before.

When I remarked to Doug about the cardinals and my mother, I had no idea many people feel the same intense spiritual connection with departed loved ones when they see a cardinal. Cardinals seem to be a part of our collective unconscious.

My first memory of feeling connected to cardinals was during the spring of my freshman year in college. I worked as the night orderly at the student health infirmary at the University of Nebraska. After my final rounds of checking patients early in the morning, I walked to my dormitory room or my first class.

When spring taunted us with only promises of warmer weather, I heard the male cardinals' songs like a Gregorian chant in the Vatican coming from high in the trees. I chanted a whistled response. It was as if I sat at my childhood kitchen table with my mother, catching up on our lives.

A few months after my mother died in the spring of 1999, I visited the flight cage in the Saint Louis Zoo, commissioned by the Smithsonian

Grandma Martha; Whitney, age nineteen; Krista, age sixteen; and Loren at a Koester family reunion in Casper, Wyoming, in 1990. (Courtesy of Loren A. Olson.)

Institution for the 1904 World's Fair. It now serves as an aviary displaying cold-hardy birds year-round. As I entered the flight cage, I heard a cardinal singing. I thought, "Mom, you're here! I know you're with me."

I whistled back as I had done when walking back to my dorm at the university. It responded to me. As I proceeded through the exhibit, I repeatedly whistled. Then I noticed speakers high in the corners of the aviary. The cardinal's song had been recorded and was piped into the display.

Embarrassed, I looked around to see if anyone had seen me whistling. I thought, "Mom, you've played quite a trick on me." My mother loved to laugh, and I knew it was she who had played this trick on me. Even though the songs were artificial, her presence was real.

I don't believe in ghosts or spirits or even an afterlife. I'm a scientist, and I'm not one to buy into the paranormal. Still, when I see a cardinal, something happens to me that makes me question my skepticism about the unexplainable. I want to believe in angels and that my mother's spirit is singing from the treetops or eating the tiny fruit on our crab apple tree near my deck.

Many people feel that a cardinal's appearance is a sign from heaven. Cardinals are often considered gifts of hope and energy from God for people of faith, like my mother. Cardinals make me believe only a skinny space separates something "in here" from something greater "out there." People of many different faiths—and some with no faith at all—feel a cardinal's presence in their garden is the spirit of a loved one who has passed, someone who wants you to know they are watching over you during periods of celebration or despair.

People attribute to cardinals just about every characteristic value humans aspire to: romance, devotion, hope, strength, leadership, pride, determination, and protection of loved ones. My mother would have wanted all of these for me.

Humans could take some lessons from cardinals. They form pairs devoted to each other and their offspring. The female primarily incubates their eggs, but after hatching, the male begins a manic pattern of food gathering and feeding, with nestlings fed up to eight times per hour. Parent cardinals live a well-balanced family life, giving both of them the chance to nurture their youngsters.

Cardinals are typically the first bird to visit feeders in the morning and the last to visit in the evenings. During courtship, males feed their female partners in a way that resembles kissing. They become territorial and will attack any intruders if they feel visitors threaten their brood. Like humans, they may battle their image in a mirror or anything that reflects it.

How you might interpret a cardinal's appearance will depend on your religion, circumstances, and cultural beliefs. You may not find a deep spiritual connection when you see a cardinal as I do. Hearing their song may tempt you to whistle at some long-departed ancestor. When I hear a cardinal brightly singing "bird-EE, bird-EE, bird-EE" from the treetop, I smile and feel at peace as if I've just received a hug from my mother.

Empathy and Dissent

Upon arrival at the University of Nebraska in the fall of 1961, I found most of the other students were from small towns in Nebraska. They looked, thought, and believed like the people I'd left behind in Wakefield. In 1961, girls wore skirts and pantyhose to class, and boys wore long pants and socks. We weren't referred to yet as men and women.

Boys' and girls' dorms, as they were known then, were separate. Housemothers locked the doors to girls' dorms at nine in the evening on weekdays and eleven at night on weekends, but men had no restrictions. University policy prohibited alcohol anywhere on campus, even at the University of Nebraska Cornhusker's football games. If the university caught you with alcohol in your room, that could lead to dismissal from college. We could and did smoke everywhere on campus, including in class. College etiquette discouraged girls who smoked from doing so while standing because it wasn't considered ladylike.

I began to smoke during my first semester of college. Marlboro Reds were the obvious choice because I wanted to be the Marlboro Man. If you're over age thirty, the mention of the Marlboro Man conjures images of manliness: toughness, swagger, ruggedness, virility—a don't-take-no-shit kind of guy. The Marlboro Man knew the ropes and commanded respect. He was a man's man. The ads flirted with me through variations of this message: "I own this ranch, ride my horse from end to end every day. Feels good to be the boss." Then, after I was seduced, he'd add, "Like to smoke too." I couldn't have been more enchanted if he'd said, "Like to suck dick too."

Even the Marlboro box was masculine. It was a bold, red-and-white box, with an angular design that suggested power, strength, and confidence. The red also suggested courage, lust, and love. The box protected cigarettes from damage as men confronted a dirty and challenging world. You may even be singing the flip-top box jingle about now.

What's not to like? The tattoo on the Marlboro Man's hand hinted at an acceptable degree of naughtiness. Boys will be boys, but boys become men. Marlboros weren't sissy or effeminate. The Marlboro Man was everything I wanted to be and everything I feared I wasn't. Marlboros were a prosthetic device for my crippled manhood. I so wanted to be a bit naughty.

My first act of defiance was to leave the red-and-white box on my dresser when I went home for Thanksgiving. I grant you, it was a small step. But my mother hated smoking. Mom said, "If you must smoke, please don't do it around me." It was like the town's reaction to the two lesbians who lived in Wakefield: "If we don't see them kissing or holding hands, and they try to fit in, we can pretend everything is normal." I imagined striding across the prairie, a cigarette hanging from my lower lip. The Marlboro Man spoke to all my growing desires and well-established insecurities.

Americans elected John F. Kennedy to the White House the year I entered the university. Even some Republicans got caught up in "Ask not what your country can do for you." Americans were upbeat. We'd survived a nuclear confrontation with Russia during the Cuban Missile Crisis. The public was optimistic about the economy. Middle-class people were satisfied with their incomes. With an approval rating of 70 percent, President Kennedy received much of the credit.

Trouble was brewing. The earliest civil rights protests sprang up in the 1950s. Peaceful lunch-counter sit-ins started in the early 1960s, and nonviolent protesting began to pay off. After six months of sit-ins, Black people integrated lunch counters. Television brought the often-brutal responses to these protests into people's homes.

The Freedom Riders, the civil rights activists riding interstate buses to the segregated South, began the year I started college. Resisters threw a bomb into one bus, and the Ku Klux Klan attacked a second bus. Klan members had arranged with the police to allow them fifteen minutes alone with the bus. In 1963, the 16th Street Baptist Church in Birmingham was bombed, with four young Black girls killed. FBI director J. Edgar Hoover equated civil rights demonstrations with communist subversion.

In June 1963, Kennedy proposed comprehensive civil rights legislation, saying the United States "will not be fully free until all of its citizens are free." In November of that year, Kennedy was assassinated. Lyndon B. Johnson, his successor, used the nation's anger over Kennedy's assassination to push through civil rights legislation.

Meanwhile, I lived in a bubble. On the university campus, the few Black men were usually athletes. The most significant social issue was whether a Black man could pledge any of the all-white fraternities. And yet, my only protest was placing a pack of Marlboro Reds on my dresser in my mother's home.

In 1970, when I was a flight surgeon in the US Navy, my wife joined a bridge foursome with three other flight surgeons' wives. They were all from the Deep South. Nannies had raised them, and they had nannies for their young families. My wife had grown up in a family and a town like mine, where we had no exposure to Black people. My wife commented to her bridge group, "When Loren and I moved to Florida for Loren to go to flight surgeon school, we drove through the South for the first time. We were surprised to see African Americans living in rural areas. There aren't many Black people in Nebraska, and they live only in the cities."

One of the belles turned to her and said, "Well, who does your work then?"

My wife stuttered her response, "W-w-well, *we* do!" The others looked at each other with disdainful expressions, their heads down, eyes half closed and darting from one to another.

We empathize when we can understand the world from another person's perspective rather than our own. We feel what they feel, although less intensely. We do not need to have endured the same situation. Empathy means we care enough about the other person that we want to join with them in their pain. We share their emotion if not the experience. The three women in the bridge group weren't empathizing with my wife; they were pitying her. Pity is patronizing; empathy is supportive. When we walk down life's darkest corridors, as we surely will, we all want someone there to hold our hands and say, "I don't know how, but we'll get through this. Together." Empathy means, "We're in this together." Pity means, "You're on your own."

The Marlboro Man never said, "I feel your pain. Like to smoke too." The Marlboro Man never showed signs of weakness and vulnerability. Empathy didn't sell those cigarettes. I no longer feel the need for a pack of Marlboros to make me feel like a man. None of those things ever worked anyway. I can always find other ways to be naughty if I choose to be.

The real heroes were those Freedom Riders. They had empathy, but they combined it with action. I'm good at empathy. I have not been as good at putting empathy together with action. Empathy is what makes us human. It allows us to put ourselves in another's shoes even when we have not experienced their struggles. We may not feel their feelings with the same intensity, but we can ride the bus with them.

I Didn't Expect Sex to Be This Difficult

I tried to fall in love with Joyce. I really did. She wasn't the first woman or the last I thought might alleviate the loneliness I felt.

It was 1966, and I was in my second year of medical school at the University of Nebraska. Without a doubt, it was the most difficult year of my entire life. I've experienced a lot of losses in my life, but with each of them, there were also moments of reprieve. The pain was relentless during my sophomore year in med school. I am horrible at the game of Trivial Pursuit and remembering birthdays, telephone numbers, and names of books and their authors. My mind is not designed to capture facts.

The course work in that second year seemed like one huge game of Trivial Pursuit. I underlined, highlighted, and drew stars and arrows in my microbiology and pharmacology texts, but none of it mattered. Exams flew at us like rabid bats. I studied every moment I could. When I wasn't studying, I felt guilty that I wasn't studying. The pressure was unrelenting. I craved some nurturing. But instead, I earned my room and board by caring for and nurturing a rich old invalid who'd been overnurtured his entire life.

Joyce was a recently graduated nurse, like most of the women I dated. I met her on a blind date. She was as eager as I was to find someone to share her life. She also came from a small town in Nebraska, and we shared similar values. She was a Lutheran. She was an attractive woman with a personality starched as stiff as her white nurse's cap. Her hair was held in a hair-sprayed bubble cut. She was never out of control. When she laughed, which wasn't often, even her laugh was controlled.

She was efficient. Her major attractive feature was that she was available and willing to date me. It should have been an ominous warning about our relationship that I never took any pictures of the two of us together.

I was a twenty-three-year-old virgin. I doubt Joyce was. I was needy but emotionally unavailable. I had no energy to invest in a relationship. I think I wanted someone to salve my wounds rather than someone to love. I didn't want a relationship where I would be cared for like a patient in intensive care even though I felt like someone on life support. I wanted to be married, but I didn't want to marry Joyce. Some men my age bragged about their sexual exploits, but most didn't talk about sex. The FDA had approved birth control pills only a few years before. I knew that one female classmate was on the pill, supposedly to manage her menstrual periods. I assumed I was older than most men when I had sex for the first time. Perhaps that should have been a clue. On the other hand, in the 1960s, we'd all heard "Save yourself for marriage." Some did.

My mother's voice rang inside my head again as it did when I was an adolescent: "Don't go getting Joyce pregnant because you'll have to get married, and you'll be miserable the rest of your life." In this case, she would have been correct. The pill eventually revolutionized women's healthcare and allowed sex for pleasure as well as procreation. Joyce's doctor didn't buy into the sex-for-pleasure idea. He would not prescribe the pill for her. But his disapproval was not going to stop me. Condoms were the only option.

It was a different era. No one said the word *pregnancy*. Instead, it was either "in a family way" or only "PG." Schoolteachers had to resign at the first sign of a baby bump. My sister who worked in the Rexall drug store wrapped Kotex boxes in plain paper in the back of the pharmacy before putting them out on display. Pharmacists concealed condoms in locked drawers behind the pharmacy counter in the back of the drug store. Only later did "tickler" condoms and pleasure-enhancing lubricants begin to appear in vending machines in the bathrooms at truck stops.

I'm a bit ashamed to admit dating Joyce was more a matter of convenience than of passion. She never seemed like the right match for me, yet we had discussions about marriage. Joyce was readier than

I was. While she wasn't the right one for me as a wife, at least she was right for my initiation into sex. Our physical relationship was becoming progressively more intimate. I remember thinking, "I am going to have sex. I am going to have two-person sex," instead of the solo sex to which I'd been accustomed.

Perhaps because I'd waited so long, I wanted to have sex for the first time but make it look like it wasn't my first. I wanted to make that first time extraordinary. But I had never had any sex education, even in medical school. I had collected bits and pieces of misleading information, mostly overheard in the locker room at the gym. Men are expected to innately have some understanding of sex, but few do. The only references I had were the sexual fantasies I'd used to masturbate. In 1966, porn videos weren't readily accessible to use as study guides.

Masturbation is not a good measure of what to expect. When you masturbate, there is no negotiation. You oversee all variables. I was nervous about two-person sex. I had longstanding doubts about whether I was man enough to be a good sexual partner. But with masturbation, you have nothing to prove except to yourself. No one is there to applaud your performance. With a partner, questions about being good enough loomed large. The longer I delayed it, the larger those questions became.

I knew I would have to speak with a pharmacist to prepare myself for my great sexual awakening. A neighborhood drug store with a soda fountain sat on a corner in the Dundee neighborhood of Omaha. I walked into the small drug store and meandered to the pharmacy at the rear of the store. Along the way, I stopped to look through the magazines, even ones like *Field and Stream* and *Sports Illustrated*, which held no interest. I examined the tchotchkes as though I were shopping for a gift. My hesitancy must have blared out to everyone in the pharmacy why I was there.

The older, gray-haired pharmacist, in a starched white jacket as stiff as the muscles in his face, looked so professional that he could have been in an ad for arthritic pain relievers. I approached him nervously and said quietly so as not to be overheard, "I need some condoms."

"I'm sorry. Could you speak up?" he said abruptly. I thought, "I can, but I don't want to."

I repeated a bit louder, "I need some condoms." I knew he had heard me the first time.

He spoke as if he were talking to one of his hearing-impaired, geriatric customers. "What size do you want?"

I thought, "They come in different sizes?" Confused about how to answer, I thought back to locker-room comparisons. I replied, "Average." I wanted to add, "Maybe a little more."

"Rubber or lambskin?" He wasn't wasting any words.

I didn't know they make condoms out of lambskin. We'd always just called them "rubbers." I had never heard them called anything else. I knew I could nail this question, so I confidently said "Rubber."

"Lubricated?"

Once again, not knowing how to answer, I responded, "Yes."

"Reservoir tip?"

"Yes." If his goal was to make me uncomfortable, he had succeeded. "Do the tips come in sizes too? I think I will need a large one," I thought.

Joyce shared a one-bedroom efficiency apartment with Beverly, another nurse. We all lived in a complex near the medical school that was filled with nurses and medical students. The night of the anticipated event, with Beverly safely asleep in the adjacent bedroom, Joyce and I lay together on their beaten-up couch and began to get intimate. She lay across my right arm, which fell asleep. It was as useless to me as my appendix. I had to use my left hand to move my right arm to where I wanted it to be.

I unfastened my belt, unzipped my jeans, and wriggled out of them. I kicked them off at the foot of the sofa. I repeated this with my white briefs. I removed Joyce's clothes from the waist down. Then I realized I needed to retrieve the condom, which was in my Levi's pocket, which lay in the pile of clothes just off the end of the narrow couch. I stretched my toes to recover them.

I needed the condom. My right arm was useless. I fumbled with my left hand to get the foil package out of my jeans pocket. I now had the condom in my left hand, which was nearly as worthless as my right one. I resorted to tearing the package using my teeth. I'd never put a condom on a banana before, much less my penis, but this was no dress rehearsal. It was the main event.

I couldn't tell which side was up to roll the condom onto my penis. My clumsiness embarrassed me as I struggled with an untrained left hand to roll the slippery condom onto my erect penis. The lube on the condom and the precum on my penis made the condom very slippery, and it kept popping off before I could get it unrolled. Perhaps I should have bought one without the lubricant! Or maybe I should have asked for a larger one! Even though what little romance had been there at the start had dissipated, I realized that if I labored much longer, I would cum before I got the damn thing on.

I finally had the condom on my penis, which was so hard, I hardly recognized it as mine. With Joyce's help, I thought, "There, it's in. I think I've got it in! Maybe it isn't. I'm not sure." The condom made it difficult to know for sure.

Did all of this come easily to other men? Men fix machines; they should know how to condomize a penis. I should have jerked off before my date with Joyce. Maybe then I wouldn't have been so sensitive.

As I began to move my hips in an oft-imagined way, Joyce's roommate, Beverly, walked sleepily out of the bedroom, through the tiny living room where Joyce and I lay on the couch. She walked to the kitchenette, cracked open a Coke, took a swig, and lit a cigarette. She took a few more drags before she walked back into the bedroom. She did not acknowledge our presence. Despite the intrusion, sex was over very quickly.

The following morning, I stared at myself in the mirror as if I had just returned from climbing Mount Everest. I examined my chest hairs to see if they had grown. A smile curled across my face. I had finally crossed to the other side. But inside my head, I could hear the haunting voice of singer Peggy Lee, as she sang about a life without meaning.

I broke off the relationship with Joyce shortly after that. She was very angry with me, apparently believing that having sex was a proposal. I think I broke off the relationship for exactly the same reason. After a few weeks, I began to wonder, "Perhaps this is all there is." Maybe marriage is nothing more than as if you're on the same bowling team.

I called Joyce once again to ask if she would consider going out with me. She was justifiably still angry.

"Why? So you can dump me again?"

"No, I think I made a mistake. I'm sorry."

"Yes, you did."

I promised even though warning sirens were going off in my head. I was desperate to have someone in my life.

We went out again, and both of us had a miserable evening. She knew it and I knew it: this wasn't going to work. Whatever feelings she might have had for me were gone. The feelings I had for her were never enough to begin with.

Was Joyce my default sexual pleasure? The baseline to which I would keep returning? But I always felt like I was her default doctor-husband prospect too. I used her. I make no excuses. I had committed relationship malpractice. Perhaps she was using me, too; I don't know.

In 1988, a few months after I came out as gay and Doug and I had started living together, I received several phone messages at home on my answering machine from a woman whose name I didn't recognize. I disregarded the messages, thinking it was one of my psychiatric patients. My telephone number was listed, but I had a rule: don't call me at home unless it's an emergency. She persisted in her attempts to reach me.

One evening she called while I was home, and I answered. A young woman asked, "Are you Dr. Olson?"

"I am."

"Did you graduate from the University of Nebraska Medical School?"

"Yes."

"In 1968?"

"Yes."

"Did you know Beverly?"

"Yes."

"I think you're my father!"

I quickly reviewed my list of women with whom I could have fathered a child before I married my wife, and it was very short: Joyce.

I was gobsmacked. I couldn't think clearly and I had difficulty saying anything. My hesitancy must have made me sound very guilty. As we talked, her disappointment grew increasingly evident, and anger permeated her voice.

Could Joyce have been her mother? I knew that Beverly had gotten pregnant and relinquished her baby, as most single women in those years did. I knew it because I was on my obstetrics rotation when Beverly delivered. I could not ethically disclose that. Had Beverly used my name as the father? It was clear that the caller had been searching for me as her presumed father for quite some time. Having found me, she was not ready to let me go.

I knew she thought I was lying. She abruptly hung up without saying goodbye. I never heard from her again. After she hung up on me, I began to think more rationally, and I wished I could have had a different conversation with her. Would it have mattered? I'm sure that she saw me as just another man who was unwilling to take responsibility for his indiscretions. She'd already charged me and found me guilty.

I knew I'd never fucked Beverly. I had barely fucked Joyce.

Tarnished Mettle

It frightens me to think of what I might have become had I been raised in my grandfather's Germany. The promise that joining *die Herrenrasse*, would have been almost irresistible. I was searching for something to plug the holes in my sense of self: my feelings of weakness, my fragmented ideas of manliness, my shame at having been born poor and raised fatherless.

The Nazi Party targeted German youth with its propaganda. Young people were told that to die for Hitler was to die a hero, to value honor before death. And I was a good boy who followed the rules and didn't question authority. I would have been easy prey for their propaganda.

The best US soldiers are patriotic, religious, and come from small-town America. I had the essential tools to be a good soldier. A soldier is loyal to his country, his unit, his seniors, and his fellow soldiers. He—in my head, it was always a "he"—is willing to fight and die for them. Could someone really love me enough to die for me? Could I become honorable enough to die for someone? Good soldiers accept that it is okay to be afraid, but they understand that in the face of their fears, they proceed with calmness and resolve. They take orders and say "Yes, sir" without question.

My father's death granted him heroic status. He was a farmer, an athlete, a leader, and a man of God. No one ever spoke ill of my father. My Uncle Glen, his younger brother, still cried when he spoke of my father, even eighty years after my father died. My sisters, Marilyn and Jan, visited him and Aunt Janet when Uncle Glen was ninety-five years old. We knew it

In 2016, Loren and his sisters, Marilyn and Jan, visited their Uncle Glen and Aunt Janet Olson, who were in their nineties. On this visit, Uncle Glen drove them around Cedar County to visit all the "home places." (Courtesy of Loren A. Olson.)

might be our last chance to ask them questions like, "Did Daddy have a sense of humor? What was the sound of his laugh?" We were all in our seventies, but we never knew our father.

Being the son of a father-hero has disadvantages. As the son of a hero, I had to be worthy of his hero status in every way. Hearing people say, "You'll have to be a man now," put a great deal of pressure on a suggestible boy who felt that even just being an ordinary man was out of reach.

After my brother, Lefty, was paralyzed, he became a hero, too. He was said to have been a gifted athlete, but how talented was he? Everyone knew he was more gifted than me. After he was injured, he did, in fact, do some heroic things. But is there inflation of the gifts of fallen heroes? The stories about Lefty always ended, "Lefty has two sisters and a little brother." I lived in the shadow of a man confined to a wheelchair who couldn't even cut up his own pork chop. But did God get it wrong? I could have been the one whose body had been broken. Maybe I should have been the one.

Especially when you're young, everyone tells you how perfect your heroes were at everything. If my father did anything wrong, it was buried with him. My brother's faults were as immobilized as his hands and legs. Survivors don't need to be only as good as those they've lost. They need to be better than the heroes they represent.

My mother's tragic losses carved out for her a hero-mother status too. As a thirty-one-year-old widow raising four kids alone, she was deservedly a sympathetic figure. It wasn't easy to rebel against a saint. How do you rebel against the holy hero-mother or a hero-widow?

I was never cut out to be a superhero, so I chose to be the best little boy anyone had ever seen.

Uncle George Koester, whom everyone called, "Uncle Judd" was the kind of warrior I wanted to be. He was the complete man: patriotic, honorable, and principled. My mother always harbored a bit of resentment toward Uncle Judd, who had been encouraged to go to college. She wasn't encouraged to go to college because she was a woman. I remember her saying, "Grandpa gave Uncle Judd a typewriter when he graduated from high school. When I graduated a year later, my gift was to share Judd's typewriter. But he'd taken it to college with him." In German families, men were the heads of households; no exceptions were made for women who, like my mother, might be widowed and left alone to raise four children.

The army sent Uncle Judd to Harvard to study radar, a new technology at the time. The army then assigned him to the Manhattan Project in Los Alamos, New Mexico. Its mission was to design an atomic bomb that would hit its target without the shock waves destroying the B-29 aircraft that delivered it. To do that, the aircraft had to make a 155-degree turn to reverse direction within two minutes.

Uncle Judd was assigned to supervise a team that fused the A-bomb in flight just prior to its launch. The teams drew lots to determine the order of the crews that would drop the atomic bombs. Uncle Judd's team drew number three. On August 6, 1945, an American B-29 bomber dropped the world's first deployed atomic bomb over Hiroshima. It created a crater where a city had once been. On August 9, a second B-29 dropped an A-bomb on Nagasaki. Had a third bomb been dropped, Uncle Judd's team would have armed that bomb.

I wonder if Uncle Judd experienced a moral conflict between duty and sedition, over death versus deliverance for noncombatants. Uncle

Judd never talked about his role in the Manhattan Project. But a quiet Koester family legend surrounds him as the consummate warrior.

I envied the mentality of a warrior I saw in others but couldn't find within myself. I wanted to fight my way out of my fucked-up self-esteem. I wanted to stop feeling like dog shit under the shoes of those I looked up to. I wanted to be what others wanted me to be, not what I imagined myself to be. I, like many others, was drawn to the military for those reasons.

My wish to be a warrior wasn't about wanting to kill—which is, after all, one of the roles of being a warrior—but rather to compensate for my own feelings of weakness and vulnerability. I think about how the mettle of those warriors has been tarnished by those who need to feel powerful. In the safety of their citadels, the powerful have exploited the innocence and idealism of young patriots by sending them to war.

I first began to worry that I might die when I was a ten-year-old boy during the Cold War. I learned that an atomic bomb could be dropped on the Strategic Air Command base in Omaha, less than one hundred miles away. We would have been the next Hiroshima or Nagasaki. After that, I worried I might die when I turned thirteen only because it was an unlucky number. I turned eighteen in 1961, and I had to register for the military draft. Some of my friends and cousins were drafted. I had a deferment for college and then medical school, but afterward, I'd be headed to Vietnam. I registered proudly while secretly asking myself, "So this is how it ends?"

In the fall of 1966, when I entered my third year of medical school at the University of Nebraska, my class was convened in the large amphitheater where most of our classes were held. The speakers were all military recruiters. "Gentlemen." (They didn't address the eight women in my class, the most women who had ever been at that time in a med school class at Nebraska.) "We're here to speak with you about the opportunities in the military."

We listened as military recruiters said, "We are engaged in a significant conflict in Vietnam against the Viet Cong. The military is in serious need of your help." The military was running out of doctors for

Vietnam. We all understood that our risk of being drafted was high. The recruiters were telling me that I would become a warrior.

The recruiter went on: "There are ninety-six members of your class. Eight are women and not subject to the draft. Twelve of you have previously served in the military, so you will not be drafted. We're gonna need about seventy-five members from your class. Most of you will be drafted." I had already done the math.

This was my chance to accomplish heroic things, to achieve eternal honor in the minds and hearts of others. Not only was the military running out of doctors, but it was also running out of marines. Full platoons of marines were being killed. I knew I might be sent to a field hospital in Vietnam where mass casualties would flood in and I would triage the wounded and be forced to make a decision between "You are likely to die" and "I may be able to save you." The job demanded treating wounded men whose mangled needs went far beyond my limited skills. My fears of being incompetent exceeded my fears of dying.

Believing the navy was my safest option, I left that meeting and drove straight to the US Navy recruiting office. I enlisted in the navy on deferred status. I spoke with another student who recommended I sign up for flight surgeon school in the navy. He told me that I would put in an extra six months for the school, but I could learn to fly and travel with flight crews. I applied and was accepted. I didn't know when I signed up that the navy supplied the physicians for the marines. During the Vietnam War, one-third of my flight surgeon class would be assigned to combat forces in the marines.

By the time I graduated from medical school in June 1968, veterans were throwing away their medals while I prepared to take my medical board examinations. I hadn't paid much attention to the resistance. Around July 1, 1969, I was one of about seventy young physicians who arrived at Naval Air Station (NAS) Pensacola to enter the flight surgeon training program. We had all volunteered to be there and contrasted sharply with those young physicians who had been drafted, begrudgingly, into the military.

On my first day in uniform, I stood outside the Naval Aerospace Medical Institute, leaning against a pillar and waiting to go inside. I hoped I had put everything on my uniform in the right places. Then I thought, "Oh my God, I hope I don't have to salute anyone." Just as I finished that thought, a young ensign walked out of his way to address me, as they all were required to do. He stopped directly in front of me, offered a snappy salute, and said, "Good morning, sir!"

"Good morning," I replied, saluting casually as if I had done it a thousand times, but hoping I had saluted with the correct hand.

The drill sergeants tried to teach us how to march, but marching was far more important to the drill sergeants than it had ever been for any of us. They were accustomed to loudly dressing down the flight candidates when they got it wrong, but they only shook their heads and smiled at the mistakes of those of us who outranked them but still didn't know our right from our left.

I both appreciated the importance of the training and dreaded the requirements that were demanding and at times somewhat frightening. I had to jump off a tower and swim underwater across the pool. I spent time in a chamber where I experienced the impact of hypoxia, low levels of oxygen, on our fine-motor skills. Although I'd rarely handled a gun, I earned an Expert Pistol Shot ribbon shooting a .45 caliber pistol. I was nervous about having to swim a mile in our flight suits: I feared I couldn't finish unless I swam the entire mile doing the backstroke. Others who were in better shape and more accomplished swimmers passed me repeatedly and finished a long time before I did. I spent four hours floating around in Pensacola Bay in a yellow rubber one-person raft out of sight of the other men who bobbed around in theirs.

Our final exam was the "dipsy dunker," a simulated cockpit seat that slid down a large metal support beam into the water and flipped upside down. Safety divers rescued anyone who might become entangled. Once strapped into the chair, I began a slow slide into the water, and I gasped my last breath as my head descended beneath the surface. Then when completely upside down, I released myself to return to the surface. My lungs felt like they might fly around the room like overinflated balloons once the pressure was released.

On my trip to the woods for overnight survival training, in the bus on the way to the woods I ate the Hershey bar that was part of our survival rations. We were given a portion of rice, which we pooled to make soup out of a boiled raccoon. I couldn't eat the fatty broth made of something that smelled like road-kill soup. I wished I still had that Hershey bar. I decided I would reward myself with a Peanut Buster Parfait at the Dairy Queen when we returned home. I tried to avoid capture during the escape-and-evade portion of the experience, a kind of navy paint ball. Strategy has never been my strength, so I was "dead" exceedingly early in the game.

It was obvious that experiencing all these trials were designed not only to drill into us the technical skills to survive but also to teach us the critically important attitude of survival, the idea that we could survive a dangerous situation if it ever became necessary. We took the training seriously because flying can be dangerous. We knew that aircraft sometimes went down, and we wanted to be prepared should the math ever prove to be against us. Even though I am a big and muscular man, my attitude had never matched my stature, but the training enhanced my self-confidence. I relished the cohesiveness and camaraderie among those of us going through the training.

Flight training began about six weeks prior to the end of our six months of training, and I anticipated it with excitement. I loved to fly, and I could be a pilot instead of a flight attendant. For several decades, the navy, marines, and coast guard had used the T-34 as the introductory aircraft in the flight training program. It is a low-winged, single-engine, propeller-driven aircraft, and we were told it is a forgiving machine that is virtually impossible to stall. Shortly before we were to begin flight training, it was announced to our class that because of the high training demands on the navy for new pilots, all the T-34s were committed to their training program.

Instead, our training was to begin with the T-28B, a more powerful three-bladed, propeller-driven aircraft with a cockpit design like early jets and with structural modifications that permitted higher performance. This aircraft was used in the second tier of aviator training. I sat in the forward part of the cockpit with the training pilot directly behind me, and we communicated over a two-way radio. It was like learning to ride a motorcycle on a Harley-Davidson with a Porsche engine.

The power of the T-28B allowed it to be used in acrobatic maneuvers, and I loved having a training copilot to coach me through them. The T-28B was so powerful that when practicing stall maneuvers, if rudder and power were not applied correctly, the robust rotary engine could flip the aircraft upside down. I practiced stall maneuvers in my final week of flying, right before deciding whether I would fly solo. I flipped my aircraft upside down. Twice. I was completely disoriented, I had absolutely no idea what to do, and my rational decision making stalled like my aircraft. I thought, "If I were up here solo, how would I get out of this?" I was about to soil myself when I heard the trainer's voice coming from my radio, "I've got it. I've got it." I was not man enough for the T-28B.

After completing our six months of training, a list of next assignments was posted. The training officers in the flight surgeon school told us that when we graduated, they would post the available billets. We would choose our billet based on class standing. It felt like a lottery for human sacrifice. Although I felt called to serve the men in combat, I also thought I would die.

When I entered medical school, someone told me to pick out a member of our class I thought was the dumbest and said, "If he's still in school, you're safe." When the student I picked out left school before the end of the second year, my buffer was removed. Once again, I had to find one person I thought I could surpass.

Upon graduation from flight surgeon training, I didn't place high enough in the class to pick the choicest assignments. About a third of the available billets were assigned to the marines. I was sure that I would go to the marines. Some of the alpha males who needed to be a hero more than I did chose the marines even though they didn't have to. As we

Loren A. Olson, MD, receives his wings as a US Navy flight surgeon from his wife, Carolyn "Lynn" Olson, in early 1970 at the US Naval Aerospace Medical Institute in Pensacola, Florida. (Reprinted with permission from the Wakefield Republican, February 5, 1970.)

Lt. Loren Olson Receives Wings of Gold

Navy Lieutenant Loren A. Olson, Medical Corps, son of Mrs. Martha Olson, recently graduated from a 24-week course for aerospace physiologists at the Naval Aerospace Medical Institute at Pensacola, Fla.

He has been designated a Naval Flight Surgeon and awarded special "Wings of Gold" which indicate he is qualified in aerospace physiology.

His wife, the former Carolyn Zimmerman, is a native of Laurel and a 1967 graduate of Wayne State College. Her parents, the Robert Zimmermans, now live in Scuth Sioux City.

Lt. Olson and his wife live at 838 LeBlanc Way, Pensacola.

moved down the list, I grew more anxious as most of the assignments to the marines remained.

When it came time for me to choose, only two billets other than the marines remained. One was for a staff physician at the Naval Aerospace Medical Institute in Pensacola, where I would do nothing but flight physicals on incoming cadets. The other position was for a year in Antarctica. I picked Pensacola. Being the sole physician for a small group of scientists on that colorless iceberg frightened me even more than flying solo in the T-28B or being assigned to the marines. As I looked down the list to make my choice I thought, "A warrior chooses war and the risk of a shortened life."

I chose a life of security. I wanted to be a warrior, but the truth is I was never good at it. The man with the lowest standing in the class got Antarctica.

It was an increasingly difficult time to be in the military. Resistance to the war was growing. When I entered the military, we were required to take commercial flights in uniform. By the end of our service, we were not allowed to fly in uniform because of public hostility to the war and warriors. I remained naïve about the resistance to the war. I believed in our mission. I was angry with those who spit at returning soldiers who had honorably served our country. How could I have been misled by people I had helped elect to offices of leadership? How could anyone not trust our commander in chief? I was still trying to be worthy of being a hero's son.

My mother wrote to me that Steve Wilkerson, a recent graduate from Wakefield High School, had been killed in combat in Vietnam. Steve was a good athlete and a self-trained artist. My mother had commissioned him to paint a picture of the farmstead near Allen, Nebraska, where she grew up. The people of Wakefield were also innocent. They believed that Steve had given his life for a noble cause. He became a local hero.

Dissent grew in the military as well as in the civilian population. Many of the enlisted men had been drafted. They had never felt the same call to serve like those of us who came from rural and small-town America. Nor did they blindly serve their leadership as we did.

When I was reassigned to NAS Brunswick, Maine, our mission was to find Russian submarines in the Atlantic. I loved those men and our mission, and they loved their Doc Olson. I was the one who would decide if they were fit to fly. They welcomed me to go with them on every training mission I had time to fly.

We were first deployed to Sicily for six months. While there, I went on training flights with my squadron to places all over southern Europe. After they arrived in Italy, my wife, infant daughter, and my wife's grandmother toured Italy, Germany, and Switzerland. My second deployment was to Bermuda, where I swam in the ocean, played tennis, and kept a bar for the flight officers. I flew with the crews whenever I could. One of our training flights was to watch the Newport-to-Bermuda yacht races, where we flew about 150 feet off the ocean's surface, pretending they were submarines.

My friends were being shot at in helicopters. After a year in Vietnam, my friends qualified for one week of rest and relaxation (R and R) outside of Vietnam while I had thirty days of leave from the military. As much as I enjoyed exploring Europe, I couldn't stop thinking about my colleagues in Vietnam. They were in Vietnam sorting casualties. "This one may live. This one will probably die." Like Uncle Judd, most of them didn't want to speak about it.

Throughout my early life, I trusted what the military leadership fed me about the Vietnam War. I assumed that those in authority knew what was right. They would only ask me to do the right thing. I didn't understand the protests against the war, and I was confused by the disdain many felt for those who served in the military. Warriors are heroes, aren't they? It took many years and much more life experience to become jaded and cynical about war.

After I left the navy, one of the flight crews from my squadron with whom I'd frequently flown was lost in the Atlantic. Our squadron of about 250 men knew each other well and was bonded together. These were my men. Death became personal since I knew the names of every lost crew member. I could have been on that plane.

I began to question the ethics of war, not only the ethics of the Vietnam War but of all conflicts. I began to see war not as a holy cause but as the consequence of inflated egos of powerful men whose need for more power was insatiable. I felt lied to. I felt all those small-town boys who honorably served their country had been deceived.

The grace of God may have saved my life, but it didn't keep me from feeling the guilt and shame of providing medical care to mostly healthy men on both sides of the Atlantic Ocean while my friends were making choices of life or death in the Pacific. Survivor's guilt can happen after a person experiences a trauma in which they wish they could have done something different to prevent another person from emotional, mental, or physical damage.

I heard two stories after leaving the military that convinced me that wars not only take a terrible cost in terms of loss of life but also create immeasurable and long-lasting problems for those who survive. One man, who'd been involved in heavy combat while in Vietnam, was discharged and returned home. Shortly after arriving back home, he invited his young nephew to go fishing with him. While out fishing, the engine on his boat exploded. He reacted quickly by diving in the water to save himself. He left his nephew on the boat, where he burned to death. His guilt drove him to want to kill himself.

Another man saw himself as the ultimate warrior, a real man. He loved combat so much that he had signed up for three separate tours in Vietnam. He had experienced several disagreements with the leader of his platoon. Once when out on patrol, he shot the platoon leader. An American soldier, in that lawless environment, took the life of another American soldier. War scrambles human values beyond the point of repair.

I have now been out of the military for nearly fifty years, but I still ask myself, "Why? Why was my life spared? Why did my grandfather kill himself after witnessing the destruction of his homeland after he visited Germany for the first time after the end of World War II? Why did those men and women die in Vietnam? Why wasn't I on that plane that went into the ocean?" I feel blessed that I escaped all those things, but my relief is tainted by guilt. My life is no more valuable than the lives of those lost. And I bristle at the thought of those who wrap themselves in the flag and consider themselves great patriots but who did all they could to avoid serving in the military.

How many soldiers feel pressured to live life to revere their heroes who have died? How much they must suffer because they are not superheroes! And yet their lives can never compensate for those losses. No matter how good I was, it was no compensation for my father's death or my brother's injury.

Several years later, I visited the Vietnam Memorial in Washington, DC. My sadness was profound as I looked over the names of the 57,939 women and men who died. I cried as I read a card on the ground that said, "Dad, I miss you so much, even though I never knew you." I cried again when I found the name of Steve Wilkerson and did a rubbing of his name that I've fastened to the back of a painting of the Koester homestead my mother had commissioned Steve to do.

My footsteps were heavy as I walked away from the wall of names. I walked over to the Vietnam Women's Memorial. I saw a statue of one nurse embracing a fallen soldier as another nurse gazed to the sky, watching for the next helicopter that would bring in more wounded. I collapsed in sobs knowing that helicopter could have been bringing someone to me to try to save. Or it could have been bringing me for someone else to save. But I wasn't there. Instead, I swam in the ocean in Bermuda, watched a yacht race, had wine and cheese in the Schwarzwald of Germany, and visited the island of Capri. I don't feel lucky. The guilt of surviving persists.

For the most part, I live my life without regret. I believe I have always made the best decisions I could make with the information I had at the time I made those decisions. If it later turns out that things didn't work out the way I'd hoped, so what? I couldn't have done it differently. But if I have regrets, it is those times when I wish I had done something different because the decision I made hurt someone else.

I'll Have Just One of Those Brownies

As I read through the *Washington Post*'s top ten baking recipes of 2020, I came across a recipe called Gooey Pot Brownies by Tom McCorkle. I love brownies, and I thought, "I've never heard of using a kettle to bake brownies." Then I read, "Made possible by medical-grade marijuana procured from my friend's then-boyfriend." I thought, "Ohhh, those brownies." I should have known. The *Washington Post*'s article began "If it's legal where you live..."

He went on, "In many places, you no longer need a friend with medical connections and pro-level skills to acquire excellent edibles." I read on to learn that bakeries are baking edibles, and television shows and cookbooks like *Bong Appétit* are available. And the domestic goddess Martha Stewart has launched her new line of CBD pâte de fruit. I'm reminded daily how naïve I am and how much the world has changed since my days in the US Navy.

My first attempt at smoking marijuana almost cost me my marriage, my military career, and my profession.

In 1970, I had become bored with my assignment at NAS Pensacola. Day after day it was the same: physical exams on healthy young men who wanted to be pilots. These flight candidates were all handsome and fit, but they began to all look alike (except for the Mormons, who wore one piece underwear). About the worst news I had to deliver to any of them was to tell them their vision was 20/200 instead of the 20/20 required to become a pilot. They were disappointed, but on the scale of bad-news deliveries physicians make, it didn't rank very high. Walking around a circle of forty men bent over spreading their cheeks so I could check for hemorrhoids was not why I suffered through all those trivia exams in medical school.

Flight surgeons kept a file of reviews of various duty stations, and the reviews of Brunswick, Maine, sounded appealing. My wife, Lynn, and I had been married a year and a half by then, and she didn't like living in the South any better than I. At the time, the Florida Panhandle was often referred to as Southern Alabama. I requested to be reassigned to a Navy Patrol Squadron in Brunswick, Maine.

It wasn't great timing. Lynn had just learned that she was pregnant with our first child. If we moved to Maine, I would soon be deployed to NAS Sigonella, Sicily, near Sicily's eastern coast, ten miles from Mount Etna. I would miss the birth of our daughter, and we were to move in January. In our first week in Maine, it snowed twenty-four inches in one day.

Newly attached to the squadron, I met the commanding officer to introduce myself. He informed me that before our departure, I was to give a lecture on drug use and sexually transmitted diseases to the 250 officers and enlisted men in my squadron.

The captain explained that recreational drug use was having a destabilizing influence on some military forces. Most of the younger men had been drafted into the military and resented the disruption in their lives. Drug use proved to be the perfect way to act out their resentments and to numb their anger at being drafted to serve in a war in which they didn't believe. In Vietnam, service members had easy access to cannabis, opium, and heroin. Fighting men—they were mostly men—narcotized themselves against the horrors of war.

I hadn't met anyone other than the commanding officer and executive officer before I was asked to give the predeployment lecture on substance-use disorder. I was nervous. I hadn't done much public speaking at the time, and I knew next to nothing about the subject. I needed to do some research.

As I spoke to the men, the enlisted men in the front rows reminded me of when I had spoken to a high school class. They either slumped over or stretched out, closed their eyes, and smirked. In fact, many of the men weren't much older than that high school class. I could feel the senior career military men in the back of the room sit back in their chairs and shake their heads as if to say, "Yeah, Doc, you tell 'em."

When I turned my comments to alcohol-use disorder, the men in the back shuffled their feet and shifted their weight. Even the commanding officer looked as if I had taken it too far. Their message seemed to be, "Doc, don't be messin' with alcohol." But I pressed on with my comments about alcohol because I believe it is a drug of abuse with health and social consequences as bad as many illegal drugs. Little did I know at the time how embedded drinking is in the military culture.

In February of 1971, my squadron readied to deploy to NAS Sigonella, Sicily. On the day we were to depart, another nor'easter struck the coast of Maine, and it was uncertain if the planes could take off. It is difficult to say goodbye to those you love, knowing you won't see them for several months, only to have it delayed for another day and have to go through it all again. And there are no do-overs for the birth of your first child. Even though Lynn and I both had some doubts about our decision, we never regretted it.

The enlisted men and women in the medical corps spoke cryptically about how much fun they had using marijuana. But you didn't have to be a cryptologist to understand what they discussed. The more they talked about it, the more it intrigued me, and I decided I wanted to try it.

Toward the end of my time in the navy, Lynn decided to drive from Maine back to Nebraska with our infant daughter to visit our families, leaving me alone for two weeks. I spoke in confidence to a young "short-timer" second class corpsman. Corpsmen are the navy's EMTs. I asked him if he would come over while my wife was away and bring some marijuana with him.

The military forbids fraternizing between officers and enlisted men, and for a good reason. Officers care deeply about the men who serve under them, but they must love them as a unit, not as individuals. How much more difficult must it be for an officer to send into harm's way an enlisted man for whom he cares in a deeply personal way? Such emotions compromise objectivity in the same way those feelings might compromise objectivity between psychiatrist and patient. Compassion? Sure. Empathy? Most definitely. Love? Never one above another.

I invited the corpsman to our home on Mere Point Road, and he came over to the house on a snowy and frigid March evening. Darkness came early. I had carefully closed all the drapes and turned off any nonessential lights. I had some music playing through the Fisher speakers as big as end tables I'd brought home from Sicily.

My guest was a good sailor and a hard worker who followed the rules, at least when on duty. He was an attractive man in his mid-twenties, blond, tall, and slender. He wore neat but casual civilian clothes except for his highly polished, inspection-ready black military shoes. I asked him to have a seat on the sofa as I took my usual overstuffed chair. We made small talk about our plans once we left the military.

He brought out the weed and a cigarette rolling paper and showed me how to construct the doobie. He instructed me as if he were explaining to a new corpsman how to apply a wound dressing. I bungled through rolling the joint. Then he took it from me and repaired it.

He said as he demonstrated, "First, you light it. Inhale deeply. Then hold your breath for as long as you can. Then exhale." Only wafts of smoke returned with his exhale.

I took a drag and inhaled it deeply. Since I planned this as a one-time event, I was determined to make the most of it.

"That's harsh!" I said, choking, as I exhaled all of that first drag.

"Try it again. It'll get easier," he said.

At that time, I smoked cigarettes, but I never inhaled them deeply. This smoke was more acrid than cigarette smoke. I inhaled, held it, and exhaled. I waited. Nothing. He continued to take a toke occasionally. Each time he handed it back to me, I inhaled deeply and held it for as long as possible before exhaling. Nothing.

"Are you feeling anything?" I asked him. I wasn't sure what to expect, but I didn't seem to be experiencing the same thing he was.

"Yes, sir." He remained fully aware of our rank differences even though I had billed this as a social visit. "Feelin' pretty mellow."

I was determined to make the best of this one-off experiment. I still wasn't feeling anything—or so I thought. I continued to inhale deeply until I had smoked the whole joint. Suddenly, the doobie morphed into an improvised explosive device. I felt battered and broken. I began to believe that naval intelligence agents surrounded the house and used infrared devices to watch me smoking dope with an enlisted man.

I panicked. I needed to move around. So I asked, "Would you like to see the rest of the house?" It was a small Cape Cod, not much to show. We had two small bedrooms and a three-quarter bath on the first floor, and another two dark bedrooms and a bath on the second floor. It had a separate dining room, which was too small to hold even an average-sized dinner party. The large eat-in kitchen had a floor covered with cheap, olive-green carpeting that could have been a military issue. The tour didn't last long enough, and I was still not thinking clearly.

"Let me show you the basement" (where there was nothing at all to see). I opened the door, stretched out my hand, and invited him to descend first. As he passed in front of me, I experienced an overwhelming urge to touch this young man, to feel his body, to kiss him, to fuck him.

Even without the impact of the THC in marijuana, my thoughts had been twisted. Everything I was doing went against military regulations. My rational judgment was impaired, and I was losing control. I imagined that not only could the NIS (Naval Investigative Service) see through the drapes, but they could also see directly into my mind.

I thought, "My military career ends disgracefully. My marriage is over. My medical license is in jeopardy. I have desires I don't want to have."

I was a married man, a recent father, and a navy officer fraternizing with an enlisted man, smoking dope, and wanting to do something strictly prohibited in the Uniform Code of Military Justice. Talking about being gay was riskier than talking about smoking weed. The most frightening realization was that I knew I could do nothing to help me regain control. The paranoia overpowered my sexual desires until my distorted thinking safely passed.

Looking back, any one of several enlisted men or women could have mentored me through my first experience with marijuana. But I had chosen a young corpsman whom I had always assumed was gay. And I liked him—more than I realized. I now believe that when he came to the house that evening, he had suspected that I was curious about more than just a trial run of smoking weed. But the military code loomed large for both of us. With his more experienced use of marijuana and less-impaired thinking, he had the good judgment not to encourage any sexual advances.

Now I'm gay, divorced, remarried, and retired. I think I'll have one of those brownies.

You Are Delicious to Someone

My man boobs plagued me. Ever since I was a teenager, I've been ashamed of my body. My body never looked like I wanted it to. But most of my self-hate centered on the excess fat tissue in my breasts. Man boobs further undermined my fragile sense of manhood. I think I understand why transgender men always first want to get rid of their breasts.

When I was about fifty, I finally had enough money to consider seeing a plastic surgeon to have a breast reduction. I contacted a plastic surgeon who'd gained his reputation by creating lips out of vaginal tissue. Perhaps that should have been a warning.

When I arrived for my appointment, he said, "Loren, take off all your clothes and stand here in front of me." That was just the beginning of the trauma. I didn't like being naked in front of anyone. As I stood there, he took out a dry-erase marker and began drawing black lines all over my body. "We can nip this, tuck this, suck the fat out of that." And on and on he went.

He found flaws on every part of my body, a lot more than I thought I had. He recommended several procedures, gave me a cash-only price for the overhaul, and suggested I would probably want to schedule a three-week vacation in the Caribbean for my recovery. I had no idea my body was so disgusting. The entire visit was traumatizing.

When I was in my early sixties, I reconsidered having the surgery. I had a patient who was a nurse for a plastic surgeon. I asked her, "Who do you think is the best plastic surgeon in Des Moines?"

In response, she asked, "Oh, are you going to do something about the hooding over your eyes?"

I thought, "Hooding? What hooding? I didn't know I had hooding." I asked, "What's hooding?"

"It's all that loose, baggy skin that hangs down over your eyes so you can't see very well."

She was barely out the door when I called the plastic surgeon. "I want to consult with you about a breast reduction and to have you look at my hooding."

I called my husband and said, "I've scheduled a visit with a plastic surgeon to have a breast reduction. And I'm also going to talk to him about my hooding."

"What's hooding?" he asked.

By the time I got home, Doug had scheduled an appointment with the same plastic surgeon to have his hooding removed too.

That evening we were going out. I was still wound up about the surgeon. As I backed the car out of the garage, I backed it into a tree that had been there for twenty years.

"Watch where you're going!" Doug said, less supportive than I'd hoped.

"I can't see. I've got hooding!"

I had breast reduction and the "hooding-ectomy." I was pleased with the results, and I felt more comfortable in my skin, albeit with less of it. My life didn't change dramatically following the surgery. The only change was in my attitude about my body.

Now I often joke, "Apparently God wanted me to have boobs because they seem to have grown back." And yet my attitude about my body remains improved.

Body dysmorphic disorder is a mental disorder in which people can't stop thinking about some perceived flaw in their appearance. It may be a flaw that doesn't exist or is so minor nobody else notices it. It leads to feelings of embarrassment and shame. Sometimes people with the disorder avoid social situations because they feel their "defect" will be on display. A fairly common example is people who have multiple rhinoplasties to fix their imagined nose defect. And yet after each surgery, they are always dissatisfied with the results.

Psychiatrists make diagnoses of a disorder when a collection of the symptoms reach such a degree that they begin to interfere significantly with one's life. People may have some of the symptoms of a disorder without having those symptoms interfere in their lives. I was distressed by my man boobs, but I didn't spend hours and hours checking them in the mirror every day. But I have seen men at the gym go to the locker room several times during a single workout to check in the mirror for improved muscle definition. That's the difference.

The perception that men are protected from concerns about body image is false. A preoccupation with your body build being too small or not muscular enough occurs more frequently in males. When I was a child, people measured men's attractiveness by their behavior and achievements. Our parents told us, "Never hit a woman," but the implied message was "Never hit a woman, but always hit a man when you need to." We were told to be confident, one of the guys, and tough enough to take a beating. Any preoccupation with the appearance of our bodies was considered a girl thing.

I've always struggled with my weight. The stereotype of fat men and women is that we are lazy, unmotivated, and undisciplined. Being fat leads to discrimination in employment, healthcare, and education. Men are judged by body size, muscle definition, and fat composition. The stereotype of the optimal male body is lean, athletic, and V-shaped, with well-defined muscles. Men crave more muscles and less body fat even at the expense of their health and well-being. We have in our heads an image of the ideal body. We judge others by that idealized image. We also judge ourselves by it.

Like all stereotypes, they are always true for some but never true for all. Some men like skinny, some like fat. Some like hairy, some like smooth, some like younger men, some like older. But the body type promoted in marketing products to us is a man who is heavily muscled and has low body fat.

Is depression a cause or an effect of obesity? The answer is yes because it is both. We isolate ourselves if we are fat, and we eat to lose the pain of loneliness. Then we isolate ourselves even more because the added weight makes us even more depressed. We begin to feel hopeless, and we want some immediate relief. So we eat. It becomes a vicious cycle.

Like most of us who are fat, I've been on lots of different diets. To lose weight means continuous self-denial of foods I love. To deny ourselves those things, we must believe that there is a brighter future ahead. What if we lose hope that a brighter future is possible? Whenever I have tried to lose significant amounts of weight, I needed to become obsessed with it—every thought and conversation centered on my diet.

The last time I had an acceptable BMI (body mass index) and body weight, I was running six miles four to five days per week and biking more than one hundred miles per week. I couldn't maintain that lifestyle. It required too much time and too much sacrifice of a life I loved, like spending time with family and friends. I always felt hungry. I was pissed off because others seemed to maintain their weight without those sacrifices. My dominant mood was self-pity. It made me bitchy and irritable. I didn't like feeling that way about myself. So I wanted to do something, anything, that would give me some relief. Often that momentary relief came in a package of Oreos. And then the guilt returns like a yo-yo with more feelings of hopelessness.

When I was in my midsixties, I stayed at a gay resort and as I ambled back to my room from the pool in my swimming trunks, I met a young man on the sidewalk. As we approached each other, he put his finger beneath my chin and slid it below my belly button. He smiled and said, "Delicious!" as he kept walking by me.

I was shocked by his remark. I thought, "Does he see what I see when I look in the mirror?" The answer is no.

I believed that since I am not attracted to someone with my body type, no one else could be either. I expected him—if he noticed me at all—to feel the same way about my body as I felt about it. I felt uncomfortable about exposing my body. I expected him to be as uncomfortable seeing my body as I was displaying it. I couldn't believe my body would ever be attractive to anyone else.

Oddly enough, I got over the shame of my body at clothing-optional resorts. Being with a group of naked people boils life down to the basics. You are a blank slate with no pretenses. Nothing is more authentic than being naked in the presence of others. Finding acceptance—without adornments and disguises—can be liberating. When you find that others welcome you as you are, it's possible to accept yourself as you are.

The gay men at clothing-optional resorts are no different from anyone else except they like to take their clothes off. If you put a group of gay men together, naked or clothed, sexual tension will be in the air you breathe. In a nude resort, sexual attractions persist but are not amplified. Sex happens, but it isn't the entirety of the experience.

For a larger gay man like me, trying to fit the queer men's definition of beauty is like the ugly stepsister trying to fit into the glass slipper. When compared to heterosexual men of the same size, bigger gay men are more likely to be ignored, treated rudely, or mocked. Many gay men say that their BMI is healthy, but they don't feel normal by gay standards.

The LGBTQ community's binding principle is supposedly diversity. But the politics of exclusion leaves many men feeling left out. Those who don't believe a hierarchy of body image exists in the gay community probably find themselves near the top of the pyramid.

Some gay men join gay "bear" groups because they recognize they can never fit the ideal. Bears protest being denied fun and loving relationships based on weight and size. But some big men have felt there is no place for them in the bear group because they aren't hairy enough, don't have the right belly shape, or aren't muscular enough. One said, "Not just any fat, hairy guy can qualify."

Overweight men are often their own harshest critic of their weight. They make comments like "Most of the fat-shaming I've experienced is aimed inward." It isn't just average-weight people who incorporate the stereotype that fat men are lazy, unmotivated, and undisciplined. All of us do.

Choosing not to date someone who is fat is one thing, but believing that fat people are lazy, unmotivated, and lacking in self-discipline is quite another.

Telling a large man he is fat is redundant. He knows. Body shaming is real. It happens in personal contacts, dating apps, and social media. Body shaming is not saying "You're not my type." It is when fat people are ridiculed, insulted, demeaned, and told they're ugly or lazy or unmotivated. These remarks come from those who do not understand how impossible attaining and maintaining the desired weight is for some.

When someone in response to our interest says "You're not my type," it may hurt, but it hurts much more when people shame us. Words become weapons if we believe that an insensitive comment is correct. Cultural change and the reduction of stigma occur only slowly, but we can't change culture through humiliation and insults.

To promote inclusion, we must first recognize the ways we exhibit exclusion. We must acknowledge that the LGBTQ community is not free from prejudice. When a person says he or she feels too fat to attend a gay pride rally that is supposed to be a celebration of diversity, we have a problem. When someone has the wrong body shape to be a bear, we have a problem. When a person feels it's necessary to respond to a ping on a dating app with a humiliating response, we have a problem.

We must also understand that sometimes the harshest judgments we make are those we make against ourselves. Those of us who struggle with our weight must advocate for ourselves. We must understand that we are just as worthy of loving and being loved as anyone else.

Many people believe no one will want them with the body they have. Mirrors are dangerous for men and women who feel marginalized. But the truth is not everyone sees us the way we see ourselves. Your body, as unappealing as you think it is, is delicious to someone just the way you are.

I've always been a big person. I have gone into stores to shop for clothes and find that none fit when I try them on. I have had a clerk smugly say to me, "We don't sell anything here for men who look like you!" I felt as if I'd been verbally kicked in the balls. People have recommended stores for big men where nothing was stylish or had any fit or structure. When I finally found a store for big men that had stylish, well-made clothes designed to enhance the attractiveness of larger men, and they fit me, I cried in the dressing room.

I have resigned myself to the fact that I will always be a big person. I know I'm not delicious to everyone, and I may not even be delicious to myself. But I don't need to be. I can accept myself as I am because I know that someone out there sees me in a way I cannot see myself.

The Illusion of Truth

Every story has a back story. In doing research for my previous book about my coming out at age forty, I was often asked the question I mentioned earlier, "How could you not know you were gay until you were forty?" It is a question I had asked myself many times. I had found some partial explanations in my father's death and growing up in small-town America, but I knew there must be more. I wanted to put my life in context of the culture at the time when I was still a boy growing up in Wakefield, Nebraska.

An old saying about propaganda goes, "If you repeat a lie often enough, it becomes the truth." Psychologists call this the *illusion of truth.* As humans, we tend to believe familiar things are true. If a statement is repeated often enough, it is perceived as true even if it's false. People not only believe these statements, but they defend them as true, and they close themselves off from the possibility they might be untrue. In the search for truth, it's impossible to evaluate everything. Most people aren't interested enough or don't have the resources to examine everything they hear, so the brain takes a shortcut to help organize information based on what we've learned.

Repeated enough, the lie becomes the illusion of truth. Our current politics are filled with examples. The good news is that truth will override beliefs. The bad news is it takes a lot of effort to scrutinize every piece of information you hear. My family might do that with baseball statistics but not politics. Growing up in the 1950s, I lived in an apolitical bubble.

All my family except my Grandma Olson professed to be Republicans, although I doubt any of them had given much thought as

Christmas photo of four generations: Grandma Olson (Elizabeth Geneva "Janet" Blatchford Olson), Grandma Martha, Whitney (Loren's first daughter), and Loren in 1974. (Courtesy of Loren A. Olson.)

to why they were Republicans. The only comment I remember hearing was "Democrats get us into wars, and Republicans get us out of them." It was never said with any passion; it was stated as a fact.

My Grandma Olson was the outlier. The family branded her as an "FDR Democrat" (referring to Franklin D. Roosevelt's brand of liberalism), not simply a Democrat. I suspect Grandma Olson had given a lot of thought as to why she was an FDR Democrat. She was a woman of strong convictions. Outliers always have to be prepared to defend their "deviant" positions, but their arguments are rarely heard. Perhaps the primary reason my family voted Republican was no more complicated than a wish to blend in and be accepted.

In my research, I went to the archives of the Nebraska State Historical Society, and I found this statement made by Nebraska's Republican senator Kenneth Wherry in an interview with the *New York Post* in December 1950: "Mind you, I don't say every homosexual is a subversive, and I don't say every subversive is a homosexual. But a man of low morality is a menace in the government, whatever he is, and they are all tied up together." Did the senator my family helped elect just call me a subversive man of low morality who was a menace to the government? In fact, he did. I wanted to know more.

FDR introduced the New Deal in 1933. It brought a rapid expansion of government. Gay men and women flocked to Washington, DC, where they lived without judgment or restriction. Then, World War II sent men from small-town America to far-off places, including Washington, DC. In contrast to the small towns they came from, no one looked alike, thought alike, or believed alike. The war thrust them into a world without the constraints of their youth, yet they understood that they would return to that restricted world after their service—if they survived. The war ushered in a period of sexual freedom and they thought, "We're all going to die. We might as well fuck! If it's with a same-sex partner, so what?"

President Truman followed FDR in 1945, and after having Democrats in the White House for twenty years, Republicans grew desperate to regain control of the White House and Congress. They latched on to the concept that the Democrats and FDR's New Deal were responsible for "sexual immorality," a theme they've returned to again and again over the years. If you repeat it often enough, it seems to be true. As early as 1947, Republicans in Congress warned of the threat posed to national security by homosexuals in the State Department.

Alfred Kinsey released his book *Sexual Behavior in the Human Male* in 1948 with its well-known Kinsey scale and the claim that 37 percent of males had homosexual contact to the point of orgasm at least once. The public was quick to reject the report because it was contrary to what had been taught for generations.

Dr. Arthur L. Miller, a physician from Plainview, Nebraska, served as a Republican US congressman from 1943 to 1959 in Nebraska's Fourth Congressional District (now merged into the third district), the same district as my hometown. My family would have voted for him too. Plainview is just fifty miles west of Wakefield, and the people looked, thought, and believed much the same as they did in Wakefield. Congressman Miller hated the New Deal—except for those parts that benefited farmers.

In 1948, Miller drafted a sexual psychopath law for Washington, DC, known as the Miller Act. Congressman Miller said, "I would like to strip the fetid, stinking flesh off of this skeleton of homosexuality." The Miller Act would have allowed the US District Attorney to initiate mental health commitment proceedings against anyone who demonstrated a "lack of power to control his sexual impulses." (Did he know women could be gay too?) The accused would remain under commitment until the hospital superintendent found that he had "sufficiently recovered." He needn't be found guilty of a crime or even charged with one. Miller believed that Russians venerated homosexuality and that communists had used gay men and women to advance their cause.

The Red Scare, a perceived threat of communism, began at the end of World War I. It intensified again in the late 1940s and 1950s. Republican senator Joseph R. McCarthy of Wisconsin became the crusader for the anticommunist movement and its overreach. Using gossip and intimidation, he charged anyone who disagreed with his political views as being disloyal. The political climate transformed into a conservative hurricane. McCarthy championed the idea that homosexuality was a psychological maladjustment that led people toward communism. McCarthy's invectives paved the way for policies that demanded gay people be purged from the federal government.

McCarthy and his evangelists considered homosexuals as "perverts" who are weak, cowardly, and godless. He believed their immoral behavior caused them to be security risks and vulnerable to blackmail. Anticommunist, antiliberal, and anti–New Deal factions in Congress consolidated America's homophobic culture into their rhetoric and platforms, creating the illusion of truth. The focus of the purge shifted from communists to homosexuals. Same-sex behavior was more accessible to track, and homosexuals were more numerous and less difficult to catch. A national hysteria set in as the nation became more disturbed by homosexuals than communists.

President Dwight D. "Ike" Eisenhower, in one of his first acts as president, on April 27, 1953, signed Executive Order 10450. It barred homosexuals from working in the government. It remained in effect in some form until 1995. The military developed an aggressive policy to exclude homosexuals from service. Even one event, based on circumstantial evidence, could result in a service member's interrogation. The interviews began, "Information has come to our attention that you are a homosexual." Interviewers asked with whom they lived, who their friends were, and what bars they frequented. If the interrogators weren't satisfied with the answers, they asked, "Would you like us to call your family to ask these questions?" Under this pressure, most resigned. Some committed suicide. My family liked Ike.

In 1957, Evelyn Hooker, an American psychologist, issued a report that found no difference in the mental health of gay and straight men. In her research, Hooker was one of the first researchers that did not rely on clinically identified people. Rational thinking was no match for oft-reported lies, particularly if no one reads the information.

Also, in 1957, the US Navy commissioned a study of security risks of service members. The report, called the Crittenden Report, found no security risk for gay servicemen and women. The report remained secret from 1957 until 1976. The Crittenden Report lay in the navy's vaults until several years after I was discharged from the military.

Stories of sex crimes filled the papers. These stories conflated homosexuality, sexual psychopathy, and child molesters, and they used the words interchangeably. Wakefield is about thirty-five miles from Sioux City, Iowa, where two children were brutally murdered in 1954. In an attempt to quell public hysteria, police arrested twenty gay men, who the authorities never claimed had anything to do with the crimes. The men were sentenced to Independence Mental Health Institute until "cured." I was eleven years old when this was reported in the *Sioux City Journal*, the newspaper delivered daily to our home in Wakefield.

Because the Vietnam War was so controversial, some heterosexual men who had been drafted self-reported as gay so they would be discharged from the military. One of my tasks as a US Navy flight surgeon was to interview these men to determine who was gay and who was simply claiming to be gay to get out of the military. The conditions for their discharge differed: the homosexual received a general discharge under honorable conditions while the liar received a dishonorable discharge. Nothing ever reported tied homosexuality to violations of security.

As I review this history from my childhood, I recognize so many parallels with life in the twenty-first century. Lies are often repeated and assumed to be true. Scientific evidence is available to controvert them, but sometimes it seems no one is listening. We live with an illusion of truth.

Is It Cheating If It's with Another Dude?

My curiosity about sex with another man began to grow when I was in my midthirties. This was prior to today's ubiquitous access to porn sites on the internet. I picked up a copy of *Blueboy* magazine at the local bookstore in Maine, carefully sandwiching my copy between copies of *Architectural Digest* and *Psychology Today* to avoid detection.

The magazine became my road map to explore the adult bookstores and theaters that showed explicit gay films in New York City. My curiosity continued to grow even though I was married with two kids.

Sometimes we don't want to want what we want. I told myself, "All I want is a blow job. I just want to experience it one time. It's not like I want to be gay." If I wanted to achieve that goal, I was going to have to look for it, but I had a lot of questions: "Who does what to whom? How is that negotiated? Where do I go to find it? What would be expected of me in return? What if I like it too much?" I had no one with whom I could feel safe asking those questions.

My first experiments with cruising—if you can even call them that—didn't go well. Having read the ads in *Blueboy* magazine, I thought my best chance for achieving my goal would be in New York City. I needed continuing education credits to maintain my license, so I began to search for medical education courses in NYC, even if I was only semi-interested. It would be easy to sell the idea to Lynn, and NYC was an easy flight from where we lived in Maine.

Times Square had once been the hub of New York's world-class theater. But it had deteriorated into one of the seediest areas in all New York City. It became home to illicit activities, dominated by the sex trade. Many of the area's theaters survived by becoming grind houses that showed sexually explicit films. Times Square became home to adult bookstores, peep shows, and arcades. Prostitution was rampant. The ads in *Blueboy* pointed me there.

After one day of lectures, I took a cab to Times Square. I wanted to check out the list of addresses I'd compiled from my research. The first venue I visited was an adult bookstore. The front of the store displayed magazines with nude models without caution. The models engaged in sexual activities I'd never heard of or had fantasies about. Toward the back of the store was a curtained-off area with a sign that said Video Arcade.

I entered the darkened space, and for a while I observed as if I were doing social research. After several minutes, I decided to enter one of the video booths. The only explicit porn I had watched before were scratchy pirated videos I'd watched with guys from my squadron on a previous deployment with the navy to Italy. All the officers crowded around as we watched low-budget, black-and-white 16 mm movies. The actors had conventional heterosexual sex, and they were projected onto the wall of the Bachelor Officer Quarters.

I opened the door to enter the bookstore video booth. A boy I estimated to be about fifteen jumped into the booth ahead of me. He said, "I'll do anything you want for twenty dollars." Frightened, I exited the booth without ever dropping a quarter in the slot. I wasn't sure what I wanted, but I knew that paying for sex with a kid was naughtier than I wanted to be. What had happened repulsed me, yet an atmosphere of naughtiness continued to pull me back in.

I decided to pull myself together by having my favorite chocolate almond chip ice cream cone from the Häagen-Dazs store. I had walked by it earlier that day. On my way to get the ice cream, I passed a movie theater on Broadway that was well past its earlier grandeur. It was on life-support, playing adult gay films. I paced back and forth in front of the theater. I watched other men walk up and buy their tickets without apparent reservation. Then they entered the theater without looking back. As an adult with very limited prior same-sex experience, I felt like I was flying on a trapeze without a safety net.

I screwed up my courage and purchased a ticket. I entered the seating area through worn wine-colored velvet drapes. I stopped short at the half-wall before the seats where I confronted big screen, man-on-man sex. It was 1975—decades before the internet made gay porn ubiquitous. I was thirty-two years old with a lovely wife and two young daughters. Part of my brain said, "You shouldn't be doing this." Another part whispered, "I'm about to unwrap the Christmas gift on the top of my most-wanted list."

I stood at the barrier in the back of the theater while my eyes, heart rate, and breathing adjusted. I watched as one man in the audience would sit down by another man. He either got up and moved again shortly or the two men walked together to a curtained-off area to the left of the screen. I was too nervous to sit down. For several minutes, I watched the movies, but I was more interested in the frantic activity of the men in the seats. Then I walked down the well-traveled steps to the men's room in the basement. Several men loitered around the perimeter of the restroom. It was as if they had come to explore the bathroom more than to watch the movie. One man stood out from the rest.

As I entered the room, he left, and I followed him. I continued to follow him as he returned to the men's room. When he entered a stall, I opened the door of the one next to him. Captured by the excitement but confused about the rules, I sat down and began to masturbate. He stood on the toilet in his stall and looked at me over the partition. His interest elevated my desire. As I sat there, I envisioned what might come next. Then his head disappeared.

As I sat there, trousers around my ankles, he flung open the door to my stall. Then he shouted with disgust, "Look at this motherfucker! He thinks I want to have sex with him." Humiliated, I gathered myself together and crept out of the theater. To calm my shame, I fled to the Häagen-Dazs store to get a double-dip chocolate almond chip ice cream cone.

I promised myself I'd never return, and for several years, I kept that promise.

Anonymous sex is an efficient, uncomplicated, and accessible way to get off, but it comes with risks. Before hookup apps, men who have sex with men searched for discreet sex in public restrooms or at rest areas on the freeways. They still do. Anonymous sex in public bathrooms and rest stops remains common. Hookup apps have displaced some of this. Whether in public restrooms or on swipe apps, hookups are usually a one-and-done affair. Participants yield little if any personal information. What little they do release is generally not true.

Everyone holds secret desires. We want things society tells us we shouldn't want. But passion can be an explosive device. It is ready to detonate its destructive forces when you least expect it. Sex in shoddy and dirty bathrooms doesn't help you to feel good about yourself. It tends to reinforce the idea that man-on-man sex is also sleazy and dirty. Promising yourself to resist same-sex desires and failing to keep that promise can make a person feel weak.

Many of the men who engage in anonymous same-sex activity are married men who are cheating on their wives. Or they are men who are uncomfortable with their same-sex attractions, but they feel that discreet man-on-man sex is a way of protecting their heteronormative existence. Anonymous sex places boundaries around the relationship. They exchange limited information. Sexual intimacy displaces any emotional intimacy. It's not cheating if it's with another dude, and it's not gay because I'm not part of "that scene."

Some men partition off these experiences as a moment of pleasure. They don't consider it a betrayal of their commitment to their spouse. Those who are conflicted about their same-sex desires may have a sense of shame about it. Although some express guilt about anonymous sex, many men dismiss it. That's what I did. It was as though it were not a part of who they are: "I'm not gay; I just want a blow job." In other words, I am not one of *those* people.

These men believe the stereotypes of what it means to be gay, and they don't want to be seen as "those people." Shedding the internal stereotypes of what it means to be gay or bisexual comes through getting to know gay or bi people you like and respect. This experience shatters the stereotypes. It allows you to accept who you are and discard the person you thought you wanted to be. Being with a man and being "gay" for a few days while out on the town feels very liberating.

When anticipation and opportunity come together, it can revitalize a man's confidence. It improves his sexual desire, sexual capacity, and sexual confidence. Anonymous sex is driven by a desire to restore an image of oneself as a desired and desiring sexual partner. Some men—although definitely not all men—have a great deal of guilt and shame about these behaviors, but once learned, same-sex desire cannot be unlearned. Two men—their eyes meet, and they sustain a glance for a bit too long. They communicate their desire. Game on. What we want can manifest itself despite our efforts to contain it. It does so in infinitely more harmful ways. Although some men may feel guilty about these encounters, the guilt is not universal. The guilt is experienced mostly by those who feel conflicted about their same-sex attractions.

We have no control over our sexual appetites. But rational humans have some control over how we respond to them. Whenever we pursue someone, we take a risk. We not only risk rejection, but we also risk exposure of our same-sex desires to the broader community. Sexual desire clouds our sense of reason. After I recognized that I could not contain my same-sex desires, I realized that I would return to those public venues.

Guilt is the feeling of "I've done something bad." Shame is the feeling of "I am bad." Public exposure changes our shame into humiliation. A fear of public exposure and ridicule keeps many of us in the closet. Guilt and shame are private emotions, and we wrestle with them inside. We cannot combat the fallout from public exposure. Humiliation is what I experienced in that restroom in New York City. I now know that my cruising in that theater in New York City simulated stalking. Had my prey whispered, "Get lost," I would have recognized the awkwardness of my behavior.

I returned from New York City feeling as if I'd seen the gay underbelly of society. When men say, "I don't want to be part of that scene," that is the scene to which they are referring. It seems dirty, sleazy, risky, and sinful. But isn't it partially that naughtiness that makes it so exciting? It would be hypocritical of me to say I didn't enjoy some parts of it. It would be unfairly judgmental to speak of those men as the dregs of humanity. But it's impossible to defend the immorality of sex-trafficking with underage boys and girls.

Prostitutes know that they must always get their money up front because the value of their services goes down immediately after the service is delivered. In pursuing the satisfaction of sexual pleasure, dopamine, the "pleasure hormone," surges in the brain in anticipation of sexual release. Rational thought is dismissed. Once the anticipation is satisfied in one way or another, dopamine crashes, making room for guilt and shame. This trip to New York City was like that. Anticipation was high and all I thought about was seeking pleasure. I put up a barrier against thoughts about Lynn and my kids. But on my way home all I could think was "What was I thinking? Look what you almost did. What a shit you are to risk everything you have always wanted and now have at home in Maine." On the way home, the value of the services went way down, reinforcing that partition in my brain between the two mutually exclusive things I wanted.

It took a long time and a lot more experience to resolve those two conflicting desires. It wasn't easy. It is difficult to explain the peace that comes with resolving it, and I can't think of any way to convey that to another person who is trapped in the same predicament. So many men remain stuck in that limbo. They want to leave, but they want to stay. As they choose one or the other, the one not chosen begins to have more and more appeal, so they swing back in the other direction.

Freedom comes with finally accepting the goodness of who we are, a freedom from guilt and shame. Once you have taken the chance of exposing yourself, the possibility of scandal disappears and the fear of being humiliated fades away.

I am what I am, love whom I love, and am a good person, so what do I have to explain? Nothing.

What Do You Call Men Who Have Sex with Men?

If you ask some men who have sex with men (MSM), "Are you gay?" they will respond, "Absolutely not." If you ask them, "Have you ever had sex with a man?" the response is apt to be "Well, maybe."

Most studies suggest that gay people make up about 4 percent of the population. Some researchers have reported that 10 percent of married men say they've had sex with another man in the preceding year. They also report that up to 10 percent of men who say they are heterosexual are having sex exclusively with other men. If these numbers are representative, it appears more straight men have sex with men than gay men. When Alfred Kinsey reported in the late 1940s that 46 percent of men reported sexual attraction to both genders, no one wanted to believe it was true. The public condemned Kinsey's report.

The mission of the Centers for Disease Control and Prevention (CDC) is to prevent and control disease. One of their goals is to prevent disease transmission among all MSM by changing their behavior. The CDC isn't concerned about how MSM identify themselves. Sexual identity—being gay or bisexual—is an abstract and ambiguous concept. Behavior is definitive. Sexual identity is what is in your heart, not what you do. The CDC uses the awkward label of MSM because they want to alter the behavior of a defined population.

As a term to describe male same-sex behavior, MSM has not caught on with the general population. Other terms are more familiar. But the CDC has a point. Behavior clearly defines who's in and who's out. Much depends on who does the labeling. One woman who interviewed me on a podcast said, "Anyone who's had a dick in their mouth is gay!" I wanted to ask, "Does that mean a woman who performs oral sex on her male partner is gay too?"

When I've written about bisexuality in the past, I've walked into wildfires. I've been accused of being an uninformed scientist, biphobic, and guilty of bisexual erasure. What most agitates bisexual advocates is when bisexuality is referred to as a conduit from straight to gay. They call that bisexual erasure. They see it as an attempt to wipe out the existence of bisexuals. Let me be clear: Some people see bisexuality as a stable and enduring identity. But some men self-label as bisexual when their sexual orientation is in a state of flux and before they are ready to identify as gay. That does not erase the identity of those whose bisexual identity is stable and enduring.

I briefly labeled myself bisexual while I was still married to my wife and having an affair with a man. It was the only term I could think of that could describe my behavior. Under similar circumstances, many other men have used the term in the same way. It is a compromise we found acceptable. It protected me during a time when I saw gay as too threatening. Perhaps that is not the way it should be, but that is the way it is. Where is there a place for those who believe they are too straight to be gay and too gay to be straight?

The Gay and Lesbian Alliance Against Defamation (GLAAD) in its media reference defines bisexual this way: "A person who has the capacity to form enduring physical, romantic, and/or emotional attractions to those of the same gender or to those of another gender. People may experience this attraction in differing ways and degrees over their lifetime."

The keyword is *enduring*. Bisexuals see their identity as enduring. My brief identification of being bisexual did not survive. I have no agenda to ignore, remove, reexplain, or deny the existence of bisexuality. Some may argue that I am bisexual, but I never felt at home calling myself bisexual the way I do when I refer to myself as gay.

Our culture prefers labels to be binary: you're either gay or straight. One man who felt caught between gay and straight emailed me after reading something I'd written on bisexuality. He was married and had a family. He described himself as "bisexual, leaning heavily toward gay." He justifiably felt erased when his best friend said, "People are gay or straight, and the rest are just seeking more and more attention."

After my correspondent had been married a few years, his same-sex attraction grew to cataclysmic proportions. He sought out casual sex with men that he described as "rub and tugs." He added, "I never saw this as cheating. I compartmentalized, rationalized, and denied." Later, he wrote he'd met a man who "rocked my world." He went on, "Are you comfortable being gay?" I told him I am, but it wasn't always true. Pleasure seekers become converts to a gay identity when they fall in love.

I hear stories like his over and over. Their same-sex desire intensifies a few years into their marriages. They begin to have casual sex with men, and they don't see it as cheating. "It's only about sexual pleasure." Sex is transactional: you rub mine, I'll tug yours. It's a one-and-done interaction with little or no honest exchange of personal information. Some MSM engage indefinitely in these casual sexual encounters without conflict, but others report a great deal of turmoil about it. Many exist in a kind of sexual purgatory.

Imagine you are in a jail cell and standing at the door looking through the bars. You are living the life that society told you was the only acceptable life to live. You have a wife and a family whom you love. By all external measures, your life is a success. Then you begin to acknowledge to yourself that you desire sex with men. You thought you were too masculine to be gay. You wonder how you can escape. You stand at the bars of that jail cell trying to figure a way out, but you're only looking straight ahead. You turned toward your religious faith, but it told you, "Don't look to the left or right. You will go to hell." After struggling at the gate for a long time, you look to your left and then to your right. There are no walls there, only ones you imagined. You discover you can escape, but only by changing the direction through which you're trying to escape.

You can stand at that gate, shouting, "Let me out!" for as long as you like. Or you can choose to walk to the left or right. You hope what you want will be somewhere down that new, unexplored path. You are afraid you will never be able to connect with a community that might accept you. You denied your identity for too long. You fear you will never find love. You wonder, "Do I want to date only men? Will a woman date me if I tell her I'm bisexual? Will both the gay and bisexual communities consider me an interloper? What am I? Where do I belong?"

Behavior, orientation, and identity do not always agree. Gay and bisexual identities are very complex. One man said, "I am socially heterosexual, but sexually bisexual." Gay is an identity. Bisexual is an identity. Men who have sex with men is a behavior. Sexual orientation does not necessarily correspond to sexual identity. You can have a bisexual orientation without ever having experienced same-sex behavior. You can identify yourself as a straight man while you have sex only with other men. A person establishes a gay or bisexual identity when he or she admits it to themselves, sees it as lasting, and announces it to at least one other person. When they have done that, they are prepared to accept the consequences.

I sometimes describe how I suddenly "became" gay when a man kissed me. I know that I didn't become gay overnight, but it sure felt like I did. I experienced an identity-quake as the tectonic plates shifted inside my head. It became impossible to continue to compartmentalize, rationalize, and deny. I had to reexamine my sexual identity, something I had avoided for years. To find integrity and authenticity I had to align my attractions, my behaviors, and my identity.

Can I Pray Away the Gay?

My family raised me to be a good Lutheran. At one time, I expected I would always be a Lutheran. When I was young, I never questioned what the church taught me. Every Saturday morning, when I was in the seventh and eighth grades, I attended classes that taught us Luther's catechism, a part of *The Book of Concord*, an authoritative statement of what Lutherans believe.

We memorized the catechism, including the three parts of the Apostles' Creed and each section's meaning. The explanation for each of the three parts of the Creed ended with this: "This is most certainly true." When we completed confirmation classes, we faced a public examination. My friends and I sat in the choir loft at the front of Salem Lutheran Church. As Pastor Carlson randomly called on each of us, we stood, faced the congregation, and declared, "This, I believe."

The church taught us what to believe, but it also taught us that we should not question those beliefs. Pastor Carlson told us that if we had any doubts, it was because we had a "weakness of faith." We also learned that men had an obligation to become the head of the family and to teach these beliefs "in a simple way to his household." I was a good Lutheran. The summer I graduated from high school in Nebraska, I traveled throughout Minnesota and Iowa as part of a team that held workshops for Lutheran youth.

Wrestling with the conflict between what religion teaches and who we are complicates our lives. As I matured, ideas shifted inside my head. I felt I needed to skip over some words of the Apostles' Creed that followed "I believe in..." No matter how much I wished for it, I couldn't make myself believe some of those words. When I couldn't reconcile these matters, I withdrew from the church.

When I came out, my mother didn't have trouble accepting that I am gay. What she feared was that she wouldn't see me in heaven because that is what her pastor told her.

Yet when I amputated the church from my life, I felt something was missing. I made several attempts to go back to the Lutheran church. I visited a large and growing Lutheran church in Des Moines. After the service, I wrote to the pastor, "What programs do you have for outreach to the LGBTQ community?"

He wrote back, "None. We're a family church." That was his entire response.

In other words, "There's no place for you here." They didn't want me even if I wanted them. After about twenty years, I visited a church I had driven past for all those years. I had been going to the YMCA in downtown Des Moines to work out. I typically went to the sauna after my workout. A Black man about my age had a similar schedule to mine, and we often ended up in the sauna together. Since I had never had a Black friend, I was eager to know more about him and his life. We spoke of many things, some quite personal. Then one day, he said, "We have to do something about the fucking queers in this gym." I was devastated, and I thought, "Apparently, there's no place for me here either." Not only had I lost a friend, I had for the first time directly experienced homophobia.

I left the sauna immediately, and I saw Rick, a gay man about my age that I had known only casually. But I needed someone with whom I could share my pain. I went to him and told him what had just happened. I then related my experience at the Lutheran church.

He responded, "It's not like that everywhere. Give Plymouth Church a try."

I went to Plymouth on the following Sunday. During the service, we sang a hymn that everyone was welcome. Everyone. Every time I sang it, I cried. "Here. Here is a place for me," I thought.

The statement of their belief was "We don't do dogma!" I looked up the meaning of *dogma*, and I found that it is a set of principles laid down by an authority as unquestionably true. "This is most certainly true" precisely fit the definition of dogma. When dogma proclaims absolutes of right or wrong, someone else has done your thinking for you. "No dogma?" I thought. "What a refreshing idea. No one will tell me what I must believe. I won't have to skip any words."

This isn't a critique of the Lutheran church. Dogma forms the basis of most religions, and dogma doesn't allow much freedom of thought. We are told to trust the principles laid down by authority: "This is most certainly true." Leaders of faith groups determine religious truths from the content of their holy books. Christians look to the Bible, Jews study the Torah, and Muslims use the Qur'an. But these truths are often interpreted differently by different people and in different times. Not all Christians, Jews, or Muslims believe the same things. Could it be that it's the same God, only with different names? If something is most certainly true, why can so many religious authorities interpret it differently? No matter what my church leaders say, I must follow my own conscience.

I receive a lot of emails from members of all faith groups. They are often similar to this one:

> I am a thirty-year-old man who only recently realized that I am gay. I come from a very, very conservative Christian background, so every sense of being attracted to other boys was shut down. Recently I met a guy who rocked me deeply to my core. I have come out to a few family members who've told me that Satan has found a breach in my soul and entered, and he is now trying to destroy me and my family. I am reading the Bible and praying that God can change me, but I know deep down that I don't want it to work. Do you think that I can be changed? —"Elijah"

I always respond to these messages with "I cannot counsel you about your religion. What I can tell you is that dealing with the conflict between religion and sexual orientation is often the most challenging issue we must confront when we decide to come out as gay."

One of the advantages of growing older is that we can think for ourselves; we recognize that reality is not as black and white as it once seemed. We appreciate nuance and ambiguity where we didn't see it before.

When people we love and respect tell us that same-sex attractions are because "Satan found a breach in your soul," it agitates us. We may question whether this is true, but we worry, "What if it is true? Can praying harder and longer fix it? Am I to blame for my disbelief?" We must untangle the conflict between who we know we are and who others tell us we are. Many LGBTQ people have abandoned their faith when they couldn't resolve this conflict in any other way.

Although many religions discourage independent thinking, we can decide whether to adopt the dogma as our personal belief. Our rational thought allows us to deconstruct our old value system. Then we can reconstruct a new one based on a broader range of information and experience.

A Roman Catholic monk who had struggled with his sexual identity for many years wrote to me:

> My ultimate goal is to get to heaven. When I started down the slippery slope of seriously acknowledging I was gay, I talked (prayed, if you like) to God and Jesus. I sought guidance from them. I believe with all my heart that I am in THEIR good graces. I was born gay. I can't change my gayness. Lord knows I have tried many times and never succeeded. I believe with all my heart and soul that no matter what my Church leaders say, I have to follow my own conscience. —"Bro. Joe"

In every situation in our lives where we face such conflict, we have only three options: fix it, put up with it, or get out. Resolving this conflict is central to relieving the anxiety Elijah feels. If and when he addresses it, the course he needs to take will become apparent. We are powerless to fix institutional beliefs, so the remaining choices are to put up with it or get out. Putting up with it means people you love—people who believe a breach in your soul will destroy the family—may reject you. Even if Elijah sheds the dogma, those he cares about likely have not. Therein lies the risk.

Most of us who are gay don't feel like the abomination that others tell us we are. We feel we are good people who just see the world differently. Believing we are sinful—as the dogma declares—creates much of the guilt and shame about who we are. Without resolving this issue, the shame and guilt will continue to control the way you see yourself.

Many religions preach that they have a lock on the truth, and any departure from their dogma is sinful. They try to maintain an iron fist over your spiritual beliefs. One young Muslim wrote to me that his religion did not allow masturbation or homosexuality. When I responded that not all Muslims share that belief, he replied, "Then they are not true Muslims." I cannot resolve this for Elijah or any of these other men. I can only tell him that rigid definitions of right and wrong do not dominate all faiths, and I can remind him of his capacity for rational thought. He can choose whether to accept that multiple avenues exist for being a Christian, a Muslim, or a Jew. This is most certainly true.

Some faith traditions support what is known as *conversion therapy*. Often through prayer and study of the Bible, these "therapies" attempt to change an individual's sexual orientation. Major mental health organizations have repudiated these practices; several states have outlawed them. Increasing evidence shows that conversion therapies are ineffective. They also may harm patients who fail to change and their families. Many of the former leaders of conversion therapy organizations have now become vocal critics of the ministry. They now claim it caused them psychological distress. Several former leaders have come out as gay.

I believe that Elijah's same-sex attractions are never going to go away. He may try to bury them again as he did for the first thirty-plus years of his life, as I tried to do, but that is probably not going to happen. The struggle will continue.

I believe we don't choose to be gay but that we can decide how we respond to those same-sex attractions. Elijah may decide not to respond to those desires—at least most of the time—but he will remain tormented. During moments of weakness and vulnerability, the struggle will be profoundly challenging.

Elijah will never be entirely successful in "praying away the gay," especially since he has experienced a new sense of authenticity that he has never experienced before. If he prays, he might be better off to pray to gain the strength to deal with the consequences of his desires. Hopefully, he can come to the same sense of peace found by Bro. Joe and many others.

Supporters of LGBTQ people and families have grown into the majority in the Lutheran church. God—if she exists—is still revealing her truths. This is most certainly true.

While I was writing this, I was working in Missouri, and a Benedictine monastery was only a few miles away. I had heard that the Basilica of the Immaculate Conception was beautiful, so I decided to see it and remain for the compline, the monks' last prayer service of the day. As I walked through the basilica, I began to feel a sense of peace. Later, as the monks entered the basilica and began to chant their prayers, the heaviness of a stressful day felt lifted from my shoulders. During the week I was there, I returned twice and experienced the same feelings.

I still don't know what I believe. I know I don't buy into the dogma. What I do know is that if churches, mosques, and synagogues preached about peace and love instead of dogma that fills us with shame and guilt, they might find their pews full again.

My Disappointing Introduction to Gay Sex

In the spring of 1968, my final year of medical school, I took a trip to Saint Louis with Lefty for a bachelors' party weekend of baseball. I had proposed to Lynn at Christmas, and we planned to marry after I graduated in June 1968. For Lefty, a party meant baseball.

Lefty had obtained tickets to see Bob Gibson pitch for the Saint Louis Cardinals. Gibson was at the pinnacle of his pitching career. He was a nine-time All-Star and two-time World Series champion, and in the previous season, he had pitched three complete games in the World Series. As if that weren't acclaim enough, he was also a Nebraskan.

Prior to the game, Lefty and I explored a gentrifying neighborhood near the Busch Stadium. Some stoneware in a window intrigued me. Lefty couldn't get into the store in his heavy electric wheelchair, but he agreed to explore on his own while I went inside. I entered the musty-smelling store and began to examine a piece of Red Wing pottery that I would have collected if I'd had any money. A handsome man about my age approached me.

The young man was educated and knowledgeable about the antiques. I enjoyed visiting with him. He asked me a few questions about myself, and I told him I was in medical school in Nebraska and in Saint Louis for the baseball game. As we talked, he had his thumbs hooked inside the pockets of his Levi's with his fingers extending below. He was standing unusually close to me, and he flared out his fingers and touched my crotch. I thought, "How clumsy of him!" and I moved away from him. He approached me again, and as we continued to speak, he said he and his friends were having a party that evening. He invited me to go with him. As he offered me the invitation, he touched me once again, this time with obvious intention.

I was flooded with a mix of feeling both violated and intrigued. "Do I call the police or ask for his phone number?" Believing I had invited this violation, even in some small way, was completely unacceptable to me. I was a soon-to-be-married man. I wondered, "Why did you come on to me?" I was twenty-five years old and had never met an openly gay man. I fled the store and ruminated all day about this young man and the invitation.

Was it possible to feel transgressed while at the same time welcoming this man's behavior? To continue affirming my heterosexuality, I had to ignore everything that suggested I might have been accountable for what had happened. If I portrayed myself as the victim and felt angry with the perpetrator, I was able to continue to maintain a façade of heterosexuality. It was several years before I could accept that I had unconsciously invited his approach. We blame others when our remaining defenses are ineffective.

At that time, my thinking was very black and white. There was no room for nuance or ambiguity. It was not until several years later that I discovered a new way to understand myself. I became familiar with Kinsey's *Sexual Behavior in the Human Male,* in which he described sexual orientation on a seven-point continuum from exclusively heterosexual to exclusively homosexual.

Viewpoints about Kinsey's research were as diverse as his description of sexuality. Opinions range from elevating him as a pioneering researcher who challenged moral hypocrisy to berating his work as pseudoscience intent on wrecking the family.

In 1971, when I was stationed in Sicily in the navy, the senior physician at the base's clinic invited me to go for dinner and drinks to Catania, about ten miles from base. We had several drinks with dinner, and he said, "Loren, I've had too much to drink to drive you back to the base. Why don't you stay at my place, and I'll drive you back in the morning?" Having had several drinks myself, it was a reasonable suggestion.

As we got to his place, he said, "My maid wasn't here today to make up the guest bed. Do you mind sleeping in mine?" I didn't think much of it until he stripped naked and got into bed. I left my T-shirt and underwear on as I climbed in beside him. I lay on my back with my hands pressing the duvet against the mattress. I knew that if I touched him even innocently, I would have asked to be initiated into gay sex.

After being discharged from the navy in 1973, I began my training in psychiatry. During my third year of residency, the chief of psychiatry supervised my psychotherapy training. Dr. Elkins had trained as a Freudian psychoanalyst in New York City. Although he was shorter than all the residents, his stature towered above us. He always wore a stiffly starched long white coat over his white shirt, rep tie, and gray slacks. His penny loafers gleamed like a polished apple. He was a brilliant man who had the rapid and abrupt speech of native New Yorkers, and he walked just like he spoke. No one ever questioned his authority.

The intent of our supervision was to disentangle our own emotions from those of our patients to preserve our objectivity. One day, Dr. Elkins said, "Tell me about your relationship with your father." I began to cry. I thought, "I don't want you to be my father. I just need someone to be my father." Then he said, "I think you have some work to do." While I sat there wiping my tears, he picked up his phone and dialed a colleague—no one ever refused his calls. He set up an appointment with a respected psychiatrist trained in the psychoanalytic tradition.

During the sessions with my therapist, I worked through many of the issues of grief and loss that had plagued me. I learned how to use those feelings to zero in on a patient's feelings to understand my patients' emotions.

Late in my therapy, I went to New York City to take a class on hypnosis. Lynn and I knew a guy named Ricardo through her interest in dog shows. Neither he nor I showed dogs, so we chatted casually as the dogs were groomed and sat together ringside kibitzing about the dogs and their handlers. He loved to dish about everyone with outrageous comments, and I enjoyed his often-bawdy humor. When I knew I was going to New York City, I alerted him to my plans, asked him if he wanted to go to dinner, and told him I would call him when I arrived.

I didn't have any clear expectations about how the evening would go, although I had some definite ideas about how I hoped it would go. I called Ricardo at the hair salon in Saks Fifth Avenue, and he asked me to meet him at the salon after I finished my meetings. When he greeted me in the salon, he took me to introduce me to his client, Peggy Cass, an aging actor who had no make-up on and sat under a hairdryer in curlers. Her career as a Tony-winning and Oscar-nominated actress had waned. But she had resurrected her career as the raspy-voiced, smart, and sassy guest on television game shows. Ricardo rode piggyback on her dwindling celebrity.

After Ricardo finished Ms. Cass, he suggested we walk to his apartment on West Fifty-Seventh Street so he could shower and change clothes before we went to dinner. He was a tall, thin man about ten years older than me. He dressed in bold-colored, stylish clothes. As we walked, his hands perpetually gestured to emphasize every phrase. He had a dramatic stage laugh designed to reach the second balcony, and he delivered a monologue with an occasional rhetorical question. He didn't pause long enough for me to respond. He touched me as intimately and frequently as the streets of New York City would allow in 1975. Unlike my experience with the antiques dealer in Saint Louis a few years earlier, this time, I didn't move away as he touched me. I wanted him to touch me. As he talked with his hands, one of them almost always held a cigarette. He came from a world where the stereotypes are true for some but unaccompanied by any shame or embarrassment. He felt no discomfort in calling himself a "flaming queen." I was thirty-two years old, and Ricardo was the only man I'd ever met who lived openly and comfortably as a gay man.

Upon arrival at his apartment, Ricardo asked, "Would you like a cocktail, sweetheart? I'm simply dyyying for one." His apartment was a single room with minimal furniture except for the large bed in the middle of the room. He had two little Pekingese dogs. As Ricardo mixed our drinks, he inquired, "Did you see my credits for the photoshoot I did for *Brides* magazine?" Then with that theatrical laugh, he added, "Oh, you probably don't get *that,* do you?"

Ricardo told me how he'd flown to Europe with a glamourous movie star, whose name everyone knew then but I can't remember now. He styled her hair on the flight before she deplaned to meet the paparazzi. I saw through how he tried to impress me, but it didn't matter. It wasn't difficult to impress a shy man from Nebraska who now lived on a farm in Maine. His intentions were obvious—and no different from mine when I'd called him.

We had several more drinks before going to dinner. We had wine with our dinner at an Italian restaurant around the corner from his building, and then we returned to his apartment. Perhaps Ricardo thought he'd remove any hesitations I had if he got me drunk, but those hesitations were gone when I made that phone call to him.

I had sex with Ricardo twice, perhaps three times—the night is blurred in my memory. When he woke me up, morning punished me for our previous night's drunkenness and sleepless frolic. He had to get to work, and I needed to shuffle to the hotel where my meetings were held. As I reflected on what had happened, I thought, "Well, now I've done that. Rather disappointing. Not what I'd imagined. I must not be gay." Some fantasies are better than reality. Later, my thoughts turned to "What am I going to tell my therapist?" I knew I would need to confess it.

During the next hour with my therapist, I revealed my experience as so many men before me have: "Oh, God, was I drunk! You'll never believe what I did." Silence can be a highly effective tool for a therapist, but his silence wasn't just a therapeutic device; it demonstrated his bafflement at what to say next. As the silence continued, I began to feel that what I'd considered a casual mistake, he'd interpreted as a grave concern and disappointment.

Finally, he said, "Have you ever read *Advise and Consent*?"

"No, I haven't."

"I recommend that you read it." Our session ended. I met with him a few more times, but we never addressed the topic again.

Fortunately, I hadn't read the book. The novel spent more than one hundred weeks on the *New York Times* bestseller list, won the Pulitzer Prize for fiction, and was adapted into a film. I hadn't seen the film either. *Advise and Consent* is a fictional account of a US Senate hearing of a controversial former member of the Communist Party. To silence the senator, the president used a photo of the senator's brief, wartime homosexual liaison. The senator decided there was only one way to maintain his honor and dignity, and he killed himself.

While I was seeing my therapist, psychodynamic theories dominated psychiatry. Homosexuality was attributed to a trauma caused by a distant father and a too-close mother. Distant father? Check. Too-close mother? Check. You may question, "What the hell was your therapist thinking?" But I know what he thought. He believed being gay was a deviancy, and he didn't want to see me as sick. I believe his recommendation to read *Advise and Consent,* however poorly considered, was meant as a warning to change my life or expect terrible consequences. And in those days, the outcomes could be very destructive.

In 1972, a year before I entered my psychiatric training, Dr. John E. Fryer testified in a hearing of the American Psychiatric Association. He testified as "Dr. Henry Anonymous," and he wore a face mask, wig, and tuxedo. Speaking through a microphone that distorted his voice, he said, "I am a homosexual. I am a psychiatrist." Dr. Fryer's testimony is credited as a critical factor in the removal of homosexuality from the *Diagnostic and Statistical Manual of Mental Disorders.* Ultimately, most other professional organizations came to the same decision. Up until then, defining homosexuality as an illness buttressed society's moral debasement of same-sex relationships. In one stroke of a pen, I was cured of being a pathological deviant.

Several times in the months that followed my visit to New York City, Ricardo called me at home. I really had no interest in a continuing relationship with him, so it was easy to express to Lynn my authentic annoyance with these phone calls. Each time, I felt like I was being stalked by a pesky and persistent telemarketer. I was no longer interested in what he was selling. Lynn never asked for further explanation, but I wonder if the calls planted some seeds of doubt.

Shortly after I finished my residency in psychiatry in December 1975, Lynn and I purchased a home built around 1795 by Captain John A. Given along with fifteen acres in Pennellville on Middle Bay on the coast of Maine. Pennellville had once been the location of the Pennell Brothers' shipyard, the most successful shipyard in the country. The Pennell brothers had designed, built, and launched wooden sailing ships made of the huge native oaks. The small farm had a beautiful old barn built like an inverted sailing ship. After the launch of its biggest and most beautiful ship in 1874, the Pennells fell on harder times. Many of the homes were left to deteriorate until purchased and restored by people "from away." I had a grandiose plan to restore our home to return it to its former grandeur. Lynn was less enthusiastic about the house but loved living on Middle Bay.

When Lynn and I and our two young daughters lived on our farm on the coast of Maine, we discovered one of the problems with small-scale livestock farming is that you tend to fall in love with your animals. You block off the thoughts that the reason you raised them was to fill your freezer. One of my friends, also a psychiatrist, said he preferred to eat other people's pets.

I purchased two six-week-old piglets. My first mistake was to name them: Sweet and Sour. My plan was to sell Sour to the other psychiatrist and to reserve Sweet for our own meat locker. By the time Sour had met her predetermined fate, we had grown attached to Sweet. I decided that Sweet should at least have an opportunity to leave some legacy of her brief time on earth.

I found an old Mainer who agreed to bring his Duroc boar over to breed our less pedigreed Sweet. After a few short weeks, she had six of the cutest little pigs. Following the instructions in *How to Raise Pigs on a Small Farm,* I learned that I needed to cut off the first teeth in the piglets' mouths when they were about two weeks old.

Sweet's name suited her. She was so docile that our daughters, age two and five, could ride her in the open pasture. By then she had grown

In 1976, Lynn and Loren purchased this home in Pennellville on Middle Bay on the coast of Maine. It was built by Captain John A. Given in about 1795. Loren's first psychiatric practice occupied the space to the left of the front door. (Courtesy of Loren A. Olson.)

The often-photographed barn on Loren and Lynn's farm in Pennellville, Brunswick, Maine. In the 1800s, the Pennell Brothers' shipyard was the most successful shipyard in the country. The barn was constructed as if it were an upside-down wooden sailing vessel. (Courtesy of Loren A. Olson.)

to six hundred pounds. Sweet insisted on having her ears scratched by everyone, including a photographer who had come to take the family's Christmas photo in our pasture. Sick of Sweet's interference in the photo-taking session, he threatened to have her made into a new camera bag.

When the piglets were a few weeks old, I climbed into the pen with Sweet and her precious piglets. I carried my side-cutting pliers in the tool pocket of my bib overalls. I was ready to perform a minor dental

Whitney, Lynn, age four, and Krista Lauren, age one, with newly arrived goslings. (Courtesy of Carolyn "Lynn" Severson.)

Loren and Lynn's daughters, Whitney, age four, and Krista, age one, on one of the family's many camping trips in Maine. (Courtesy of Carolyn "Lynn" Severson.)

procedure. As I picked up one of the little pigs, he squealed as if I were going to put an apple in his mouth and roast him. Sweet's maternal instincts detonated before me. She charged at me like an out-of-control locomotive. I saw a side of her personality I'd never seen before. If anyone was going to be served on a platter, it was me.

I dropped the piglet and went flying for the nearest fence and cartwheeled over it. Unbearable pain in my right shoulder immediately announced that I had dislocated it. I banged my arm against the fence to put my shoulder joint back in its socket. I experienced relief almost instantly as I felt it slip back into place.

It is striking how midlife punishes us for the indiscretions of our youth. Twenty years later when I was in my sixties, the pain and restricted range of motion in my right shoulder would prove to be the final legacy of Sweet's brief time on earth.

The viciousness of that expression of her maternal instincts led my wife and me to realize that we could not have her around our little girls. Shortly after Sweet raised her little pigs, she was sent to slaughter. We brought her home from the locker in several large boxes; a six-hundred-pound pig produces a lot of unfrozen pork. The smell of the fresh pork made both my wife and me feel queasy. Had the butcher frozen the meat, it would have chilled the reality that the pork chops my wife prepared were once a part of our beloved Sweet.

Our children sensed our uneasiness. As we sat down to eat, our five-year-old daughter looked at us and innocently asked, "This our pig?"

I answered, "Yes, sweetheart, it is."

She took a bite, thought for a moment, and then asked, "Does she hurt when I chew her?"

I picked up my phone to call my psychiatrist friend. "Can you use any more pork?"

We should have had it all, everything we aspired to. We were married with two kids, Whitney, who was nearly five years old, and Krista, still a toddler. I had completed medical school and my residency in psychiatry, and I had passed all my board examinations. I had been a flight surgeon in the US Navy, and I was discharged as a lieutenant commander. I had paid off all my education debts. I had established a successful psychiatric practice housed in the library of our sea captain's house on a small farm on the coast of Maine.

Lynn and I had accomplished our shared goals, everything for which we'd worked and sacrificed. We'd made our families proud. Why weren't we happy? I not only felt alone, I thought I would never not feel alone.

Although "homosexuality" had been removed from the *Diagnostic and Statistical Manual,* I had not successfully removed the idea from my head that being gay was deviant. But for me, Ricardo had been a commodity, something of use but not someone of value. Being gay turned out to be so much more than that.

Lord, Make Me Chaste—Just Not Yet

The following stories are all true, and yet none of them are completely true. They all happened, but they didn't all happen to one person. Some happened to me; but they didn't all happen to me. Some happened to others who told me their stories. Some have been created to put pieces of stories together into one story. These stories are about what is, not a commentary about what should be. Stories like these aren't unique—far from it. Variations of these stories happen countless times every day.

I masturbated for the first time on camera in the early 1990s when I was on an out-of-town business trip. While driving through a small town, I spotted a sign on a fifties-era motel that said Free Internet Access. As I went to the desk to check in, I could smell the curry dinner of the Indian family who owned and operated the motel. My room was clean but basic and generic. It was a step back to a time when most motels were individual mom-and-pop businesses. Newer franchised, cookie-cutter motels had stolen most travelers.

Sitting at a Formica-covered desk lit by a midcentury lamp, I signed onto the internet, slow and choppy because of the truckers who parked in the parking lot to gain free access to it. I signed into a site called Silver Daddies that I had only just heard about but never accessed. The person who put me on to Silver Daddies had suggested that the site was more fun with a webcam. I purchased one right before I left on this trip. I told the clerk I wanted it to visit with my grandkids. He looked at me with an expression that said, "Yeah, sure. That's what all you old men say."

I pulled the camera out of its packaging, plugged it in, downloaded the software, and signed into Silver Daddies. When I clicked on some names, the inch-square image of the person I'd contacted appeared at the bottom of the screen. After scrolling down the list of prospects and contacting a few, I turned on my camera and began to chat with a man whose age was listed as thirty-five. He was a Realtor in a small town in Georgia. He loved to golf and lived alone in his newly renovated older home.

He was blond with a receding hairline, sturdily built, and handsome. I found him extremely attractive, and I was surprised that he wanted to chat with me since I was several years older. I could see from his image that he was athletic. His profile said he was single. He told me he was not out to his family or friends. His online friends were his only connection to a gay community. He was bright, educated, and well-spoken, his Southern accent adding to his charm. I told him I was new to chatting on camera, and he took it slow and easy with me.

Sexual arousal comes from a combination of desire and opportunity. The slow pace heightened the anticipation, cranking up the pleasure-hormone level in my brain. Being hidden and secret added to the excitement. He was shirtless, and I found his body attractive in the ways that often catch my attention. He seemed sensitive and sensual, other things I found appealing. It eased my anxiety. The visual images of his home made me feel more at ease.

After we had chatted for a while, he asked, "Do you mind if I call you Daddy?"

"Uh . . . uh . . ." I hesitated. I'd never been asked that question before. I have two children who call me Dad, and I struggled to separate out an intensifying erotic conversation from the times my kids had called me Dad. "I guess not . . ."

He sensed my hesitation, so he quickly added, "It's okay if you don't want me to. I just like men who look like daddies, and I meant it as a compliment. I think you're very sexy, Daddy," he added seductively. Having a dad body wasn't something I aspired to, nor did I think of myself as sexy, so I found it hard to believe a handsome, young, physically fit man would find me appealing.

I responded, "I'm surprised to hear you say that. I've never been very comfortable with my body."

"It looks great to me, Daddy. I like men with a belly."

I found it difficult to accept his compliment. What does he see that I can't see? Is this genuine? Southern charm? Or just typical internet bullshit? It didn't matter. I loved it.

I apologized, "It's just the way I've always felt about myself."

"Can I ask you to take off your shirt, Daddy?" His approach was slow, gentle, and respectful. On a personal level, I liked him. On a physical level, I desired him. And his cautious approach to me caused my hormones to surge. I was shy, embarrassed, and uncomfortable. But I was also strangely excited by this introduction to virtual sex. I had connected with a man I could hear and see but couldn't touch, smell, or taste. I thought, "Will he click off the moment he sees me naked and he sees not only that I have a belly, but tits too?"

I sat on that hard, fake-leather chair, at a cigarette-burned desk, under a cheap desk lamp, and I slowly began to unbutton my shirt to expose my hairy chest. By then, I was ready to do anything my virtual lover asked. I would have even played golf with him.

Then he said, "Ohhh, Daddy." I began to fantasize about sneaking off to Georgia to spend a secret and secluded nonstop weekend of fucking.

Even after the sex was over, he wanted to continue to verbally "cuddle" with me. He seemed genuinely interested in me. His sensitivity and empathy for my anxiety endeared me to him. It softened any guilt I might have felt. Of course, I'd watched porn before, but this cam-facilitated fantasy was like a gift. It was more than the static images of penises I could find anywhere. It was a penis made hard because of me. It wasn't just seeing his penis become erect, but it was knowing I had been the one that had caused it to become erect. This was interactive sex, and it was safe.

His ejaculation seemed confirmation of his being attracted to me. And more than that, it helped me to feel that my body—at least to one other person—could still be attractive to someone else. There was a freshness about the sex that reminded me of the first time I had sex with a man. I couldn't contain the feelings, which were too strong to contain inside of me. The experience went beyond a private physical intimacy. Not only had I exchanged ideas with Georgia Boy, but I could see him and hear him speak to me. I listened to the affirming sounds he made during his orgasm. All of that had been missing in my previous online chatting. When it was over, I returned to rational thinking. I realized that this flat-screen experience is not life as we live it day to day.

As I've grown older, I have become aware of how things have changed for me sexually. As a young man, I worried about getting an erection in all the wrong places: in the shower after football practice, while being examined for school physicals, when giving a report in world history. As I've grown older, I worry instead, "Will I be able to get it up when I want to?" With aging, it usually takes longer to become erect, and it's even harder to remain fully erect. It's much easier for me to lose an erection. It also takes longer to reach "ejaculatory inevitability," the feeling you have when you're going to cum even if your mother were to walk into the room at that instant.

The first few times I experienced diminished sexual functioning, it created a chain reaction of thinking about aging and decline: "Is the time coming when I will no longer be a sexual man?" When I experienced these anxieties with my husband, they were transferred to him as well. He personalized them, feeling that I was no longer attracted to him. He didn't understand why I needed more warmup time, more time to build up some dopamine reserves in anticipation of reaching orgasmic eruption. Being fourteen years younger, he had not yet experienced any of the more significant changes in sexual functioning that come with age. Aging demands more romance. In some ways, cam sex rescued me from those worries. It added a dimension of prolonged anticipation, pursuit, the discovery of attraction, and desire. I felt successful again, and it improved my self-confidence. That carried over to my relationship with my husband.

In some instances, cam sex allowed for an emotional connection with another. Having others watch when I got erect provided the validation that I was still a complete man. That validation led me closer and closer to the payoff. It helped combat the negative self-perceptions of my sexual attractiveness. Aging had magnified all the body-image issues I'd always struggled with. The doubts of "Will I ever fuck again?" were answered with "You've still got it, old man."

It's a given that passion will diminish in all long-term relationships; an active sexual fantasy life can help compensate for that loss. Watching someone sexually exciting to me, who is feeling the same way about me, lights a fuse that explodes the fireworks. Through no fault of my husband, I had not felt those things in a while. Perhaps I thought I would never feel them again.

Cam sex is not exclusively a gay activity. For men—gay, straight, or bisexual—it censors out thoughts such as "Will my retirement savings be enough? How can I get my blood pressure or blood sugar under control? When and how will I die?" The risk and variety of sex on the internet invigorate men's sexuality. It makes old men feel young again.

It is easy to understand why cam sex is so popular with old men who often find themselves invisible. In the internet's expansive world, it is much easier to connect with people who appreciate old men. A subgroup of gay men—and presumably straight women as well—find a bit of a belly to be a sexually charged invitation just as many heterosexual men find women's breasts.

I began to see the idea of daddy in more of a metaphorical sense. It seems to represent characteristics that a significant group of young men finds in old men that they can't find in their contemporaries. Showing my silver-haired chest on cam usually grabbed the kind of attention I sought, while I could still hide the parts of my body I wanted to hide. But for some young men, I was the trifecta: a chubby old man, a hairy chest, and the ability to still get a hard-on.

Old men like slow sex. Some young men—and again, I presume women—like it too. They frequently enjoy kissing, cuddling, and touching, and slow sex contains no urgency to chase the terminal orgasm. Many enjoy some conversation both before and after sex. Slow sex expands the sexual experience. Young men I have spoken with say they are attracted to the wisdom and security of the older man. They typically accept that erections don't come as freely and predictably as they do with young men. They are more patient with men whose sex drive is lower, whose erections are less predictable, and who just don't cum as much as young men.

Most of these young men will say, "I'm not looking for a sugar daddy. I'm perfectly capable of taking care of myself." Older men in these age-gap relationships are reassured to find that they still have some sex appeal. They enjoy slow sex, and in many cases, that's all they're capable of. The availability of these young men as cam sex partners increases a sagging sex drive. The newness and risk add to the thrill. It may be their only outlet for a same-sex activity for many married men or those in conservative cultures. And cam sex carries a lower risk of compromising their lives in the process.

Cam sex also helped me discover hidden sexual desires inside myself. Falling in love with fantasy is a risk, and I needed well-defended, impervious boundaries to protect me from those possible consequences. Often, both men on opposite sides of cam sex share an agreement that these are one-off, short-term casual encounters. It isn't courting; it's a fantasy.

When things at home become strained—and they always do—cam sex can be a way of avoiding conflict resolution with a partner. Some partners develop parallel worlds of virtual friendships. It is easy to whip up a little on-demand sexual excitement to take your mind off the day's work. It's two strangers, irrespective of gender, connected online with no serious consideration of anything more than a one-off event—fast, efficient, done.

Some people say that masturbation is only for losers who can't get a partner. If that's the case, the world is full of losers. Most people masturbate, even when they are in a satisfying sexual relationship with a regular partner. Many people just want to get off or to watch someone else get off. Cum shots are the ultimate payoff. But people masturbate for a wide variety of reasons, and I don't have to list them because you already know your reasons for doing it. Live streaming on camera is available on demand. It is facilitated masturbation with a virtual partner.

Unless it is causing damage to your primary relationship or causing harm in other areas of your life, it is a safe and easy way to expand your sexual experiences.

Cruising is something you do before you know you're doing it. It's something about the way you look at a man that is different from the ways heterosexual men look at each other. I didn't know it then, but I know now that in the antique store in Saint Louis, with the flight surgeon in Sicily, and even with the sailor I got high with, I was sending an invitation I didn't know I was sending. I began to understand the pattern more clearly while visiting Washington, DC, in the mid-1980s after moving to Iowa.

When I first started actively exploring same-sex activity, we lived in a much different world. Cruising for a hookup partner was much more interactive. I had gone to one of the gay bars in the O Street area. I was still in the curious and questioning stage of my coming out. As I left to go back to my hotel, a man walked out ahead of me going his own way. When I reached the corner to hail a cab, the man stopped about thirty yards from where I was standing. He looked back at me as I looked at him. He stopped, leaned against a car, and lit a cigarette. He continued to look at me as I returned his gaze. Nothing more happened than my recognition, "Oh, this is how it all happens."

Meeting glances and holding them is an affirmation of some mutual interest. Your eyes might meet across a smokey, crowded gay bar. A smile was returned with a smile. You bought the guy a drink and asked the bartender to deliver it. If the prospect was interested, he'd walk over to thank you and the conversation would begin. I once heard that a person could walk into a bar and within thirty seconds know with whom he might be able to spend the night. Assortative mating is a mating pattern and a form of sexual selection that happens in most species of animals. It happens unconsciously and almost instantaneously.

The internet and hookup apps changed all of that beginning with the introduction of Grindr in 2009. A middle-aged man I'll call Topgun searched through Grindr from his hotel room. Topgun is married with children and has traveled out of town on business. As he sat on his hotel bed, he began to scroll through pictures of men in a grid on his cell phone. He checked the profiles of those that triggered his interest. While cruising electronically, Topgun received a ping on his cell phone, and his app told him the man was 989 feet away.

Topgun checks the message:
Bottomboy: great profile. woof.
Topgun: thanks
Bottomboy: yes SIR. you're welcome. i love your age group.
Topgun: even better
Bottomboy: i'm just looking to suck. i'd consider bottom if we click.
Topgun: i'm good for that
Bottomboy: yeah?

These two men have negotiated the terms of their encounter within moments. There's no "What do you do for a living?" question asked. No "Who's your team: Saint Louis Cards or Chicago Cubs?" It's sex—all sex, a no-strings encounter that is designed not to complicate either person's personal life.

Topgun: how late could you come?
Bottomboy: whenever
Bottomboy: (sends picture of erect penis)
Topgun: lovely
Bottomboy: thank you
Topgun: (returns a picture of his erect penis)
Bottomboy: uncut is my favorite
Topgun: thanks
Bottomboy: i wanna suck you
Topgun: i need it

After buying someone a drink in a bar, it's a bit more difficult to walk away if the guy has bad teeth. On the hookup app, you just swipe right and don't respond to any more texts about where and when the hookup might happen. You're off on a search for someone just a bit more perfect.

Topgun and Bottomboy maintained an interest, and the conversation continued:

Bottomboy: ok. can you host?
Topgun: yes. i'm in a hotel
Topgun: want to come now?
Bottomboy: ok
Topgun: i'll get in the shower
Bottomboy: i'll leave shortly
Topgun: room 307 [map attached]
Bottomboy: ok. i should be there by 10:15

Topgun prepared the bed and put the lube and condoms in the bedside table. He took his Viagra and jumped in the shower. He dried off, wrapped himself in the towel, returned to sit on the bed, and waited for the knock on the door.

Bottomboy knocked quietly on the door of room 307 at exactly 10:15 p.m. Topgun, excited but apprehensive, peered through the security window in the door. He thought, "So far, so good." Then he slowly opened the door. Bottomboy took a few steps inside. Bottomboy was a bit taller than Topgun, very tan, with long, curly hair that fell loosely to his shoulders. He wore beat-up cargo shorts and a faded blue-gray T-shirt. His sneakers had passed their best-if-used-by date.

Bottomboy stood in front of Topgun, his arms stretched out at his sides, and he asked, "This okay?"

Topgun responded, "Definitely."

With that, Bottomboy quickly pulled off his T-shirt and began to undo his belt. His shorts dropped to the floor as he slipped out of his sneakers and stepped out of his shorts. In haste, he removed his navy Calvin bikini briefs. Topgun did a quick inventory: "Tan, but no tan line; must enjoy the sun naked. About twenty years younger than me. Only one shoulder tattoo, nicely done. Fit, but not heavily muscled. A slight belly suitable for his age. Wedding ring. Nothing that's a deal-breaker."

Bottomboy grasped the towel from Topgun's waist and dropped it to the floor. They stood naked, facing each other, penises semierect. Topgun thought, "Not too handsome, but attractive enough. I might not have needed that Viagra."

Bottomboy said, "Sit on the edge of the bed."

Topgun thought, "I wonder what excuse he gave his wife to get away for an hour. My wife will never know. He isn't wasting any time. But I wasn't looking for conversation, either."

As Topgun moved to the bed to sit down, Bottomboy dropped to his knees. Almost before Topgun was fully seated, he moved to take Topgun's penis in his mouth. Bottomboy didn't just suck Topgun's penis; he attacked it like a hungry teenager might attack a Double Whopper.

He stopped briefly to say, "There's that penis I came for."

Topgun responded, "I'm already close."

Bottomboy proceeded to suck his penis, faster, deeper, hungrier. As Topgun's pleasure intensified, he placed his hands on the back of Bottomboy's head and pushed his head down even further on his penis. Topgun climaxed more quickly than he had in a long time. Bottomboy didn't stop until he was certain he'd swallowed all Topgun's cum.

Bottomboy got up from the floor and quickly slipped into his clothes. As he left, he said only, "Thank you."

Later that night, Topgun went to his phone to send Bottomboy a message to say he'd be back in town in another month. When he clicked on their earlier conversation, he received this message: "You have been blocked by this member."

This is not a story about steamy sex, forbidden romance, or a lurid affair. This also is not a commentary about morals or ethics; it is a story about what is, not what should or should not be. The story isn't about being gay or bisexual or coming out. Although these two are both men, the story could just as easily have been about two women or a man and a woman. These men may not think of themselves as anything but heterosexual.

The story of Topgun and Bottomboy is a tale of a transaction: there is an equal value given for every value received. It is just a deal made, with something exchanged for something desired. The commodity exchanged is sex, of course, but perhaps something more too.

Gay men on swipe apps are often good negotiators. In the story of Topgun and Bottomboy, no money was paid, and the terms of the contract had been negotiated and agreed on before they even met. They were clearly laid out in their early exchange of messages and during their initial in-person contact.

I once asked an online discussion group of older gay men, "Have you ever felt like it was hard to say no to sex or sexual activity (touching, oral, anal) with another man?" I received this response: "I have left if a situation takes an unexpected and unwelcome direction. Not a big deal for me. I explain that I'm just not comfortable with whatever is happening. Usually, it's just a case of learning boundaries. Most men I've met want to be respectful that way. If you can have this discussion before anything begins, it can save a lot of time and frustration on both parts."

In the story of Topgun and Bottomboy, they established the ground rules and expectations upfront. But there were other boundaries as well. Both were married men. They didn't exchange names or have any meaningful conversation. Bottomboy blocked Topgun from contacting him again. Both men were protecting their private lives from the intrusion of further emotional intimacy.

In my book *Finally Out,* I wrote a section called "Men with Rounded Corners," about gay men in intergenerational relationships. After reading this, a man from Europe who had read my book sent me this communication in an email:

> Between ages 18 and 24, I was not out as a gay man. I wanted sex without compromising my life, so I chose older, married guys to

> have sex with. I knew they were going to be hidden people, too, and that gave me peace of mind. Sex was intense and the risk increased the level of excitement for both of us. Sometimes, that was all it was.
>
> After I came out at age 24, I continued to search for married men, but it was different. I was there for sex, but also to be a listener if my partner wanted to talk. Men of different ages came to me for sex but also for the company. They knew that I would protect their privacy. Some of these visits became more frequent, and a couple of times, more lasting. I was there to ease our burdens of living a lie. They were looking for something outside of their marriage, and I offered someone to talk to, someone who would offer security, attention, and caring without disrupting their relationship. I didn't demand anything.
>
> I was not looking for a relationship. I was looking for real moments of affection, even if limited to small, very casual encounters, and arranged on the sly. I knew that both he and I would be true to ourselves, if only for a few moments.

Why do we make so much of sex, affairs, and cheating? If something is so wrong, why does it occur so often? I suspect that one of the answers lies in loneliness. Loneliness comes from expecting more from your social relationships than what you feel you're getting. That may mean we're expecting too much. Loneliness is a primal warning signal, much like hunger, thirst, and pain.

Sometimes the loneliness comes because we feel different from other people. When this happens, people isolate themselves from others, which leaves a lot of time to have negative, self-critical thoughts. At least some of the time, hookup sex isn't about sex as much as about loneliness. Even in a marriage, people can feel lonely, particularly if they feel "different."

Sometimes it's just about sex. Attraction, anticipation, and opportunity all come together to satisfy some need that is not being met. Sometimes it's because eroticism had died in their primary relationship, and it always does. It may be a wish to feel young again, to feel the intensity of sexual desire they felt earlier in life. It could be a wish to break some rules in a life that is always bound by following the rules. It might also be a wish to have a sexual experience they cannot have with a partner they love.

Willful ignorance operates in these circumstances too. Isn't that what "Don't ask, don't tell" was all about? In their almost nonverbal encounter, perhaps what Topgun and Bottomboy were seeking was a brief connection to experience a moment's pleasure with someone like them, someone who was different from other people but much the same as each other.

Maybe they just wanted to hang out with someone who wouldn't judge them for being who they really are.

The fact that these stories are so ordinary, but rarely spoken of, is what makes them worth examining. Then again, society chooses to be blind to them. When what we do and what we say we believe are at odds, perhaps we need to reexamine those values. It's as if we pray, "Lord, make me chaste—just not yet."

Society is guilty of willful ignorance: if we don't allow ourselves to see it, it doesn't exist. Many see masturbation, even with a fantasied partner, as cheating, but willful ignorance is why we don't talk about it. We value monogamy as a culture, and yet we're not very good at it. We say "once a cheater, always a cheater" and are quick to advise people to dump their partners—no nuance, no ambiguity. Willful ignorance is also why for many years, I didn't see the early clues of my being gay. And yet all these inconsistencies are apparent to anyone who chooses to open their eyes.

When I grew up in Wakefield, Nebraska, people couldn't see the lesbian couple. When I was in medical school in Omaha, Nebraska, my classmates didn't see the gay bars and cruising area in Omaha. In the navy, military lifers didn't want to see the rampant alcoholism. But I see them all now.

For many years, I was ashamed of who I was, but as an old man I can reexamine the values I once held. You may not hold the same beliefs I do, but it no longer matters to me. I am comfortable with the way I live my life, and I am prepared to deal with the consequences.

Dying for Someone to Talk To

Many mature men who question their sexual orientation fear that if they come out as gay, they will sacrifice everything they once valued.

For several years, I was affiliated with Prime Timers Worldwide, an international social group for mature gay men. I began giving talks primarily about how men's sexuality changes over their life span and how to accept those changes as a normal part of aging. The theme of these talks was that old men make better lovers. As men age, their sex drive diminishes, erections are more unpredictable, and ejaculatory volume diminish, but sexual satisfaction does not necessarily decrease *if a man understands these changes*. If a man does not understand these changes are normal, he may begin to believe his sex life is over. One man responded to my talk by saying, "I'm tired of being led around by my dick."

As I met more men who had come out later in life, I theorized that the process for coming out is different for mature men. I did some research that validated my impression (and paralleled my own story). I found that not much was written about that, which led to my writing *Finally Out*. The publication of the first edition in 2011 led to more talks about that subject and to a broader audience largely composed of people who'd been touched by that experience. It also led to more opportunities to speak on the subject on the radio and podcasts.

A few years ago, at an LGBTQ community center, I gave a talk about men who come out as gay late in life to a group of about sixty mostly gray-haired gay men. A man I'll call David sat near the back of the room. David appeared to be in his midfifties. Nothing about him gave any inkling that he was a gay man. He was a large, powerful, very masculine man with the calloused hands of a tradesman. His jeans, T-shirt, and work boots lent further support to that impression. His hair was thick, and his attempt to control it was only partially successful. His shadow beard seemed more a statement of rebellion than of style. He had a reserved and notably shy manner. He seemed to thoughtfully examine every word I said and clutch onto it.

My remarks engaged the group and led to an active discussion. As the comments wound down, David hesitated and then raised his hand. When I acknowledged him, he stood to speak. His voice quivered as he began: "I want to tell you guys something that I've never talked about before. Even my friends here don't know about this." He looked around the room as if to get their support. "I was married once, and I had a young daughter." His voice broke as he continued, "My wife and daughter were both killed in a car accident." He paused as if to gather strength, and then he said, "I know what I should have felt, but what I felt was relief." Then he sat back down.

The room fell silent, and it took me a while before I could think of anything to say. At first hearing, the story is horrifying. I thought, "How could he have felt relief in the face of such a tragic loss?" But the more I reflected on it, I thought, "I know exactly how you felt." Like many of us in the room who loved our wives and children, we understood that he wasn't relieved because he lost them. His relief came when the accident lanced an abscess on his soul that had festered deep inside him. The accident had punctured the painful decision of leaving the family he loved to come out as gay. The problem was not that he didn't love them. The predicament for him was how much he would hurt the people he loved.

After *Finally Out* came out, I promoted it through book readings, speaking, and radio and podcast interviews, and on social media. I heard from men from all over the United States and Canada but also from Europe, the Middle East, India, South Africa, and Australia. Many had never discussed their sexual conflicts with anyone. Some were in countries where to have done so would have risked their lives. Many of the men who were married had remarkably similar fears. With so many requests, it was difficult to keep up with the kind of friendships they wanted of me.

Many of these men delay a decision to come out because they don't want to hurt their wives, kids, parents, and even their in-laws. They had made their "for better or worse" vows in good faith. They had never considered any other life than the one they had. They expected to live to old age with their wives, surrounded by their children and grandchildren. They wanted nothing more than what almost everyone seems to want.

Still, they'd spent years feeling lonely. Whom do you speak with when you consider walking away from your dream for a life of uncertainty and social disapproval? Loneliness comes from trying to be someone you're not. Fitting in is not belonging. You can't tell someone, "I think I might be gay," and the next day say, "I take it all back." Even admitting it to yourself means you're acknowledging you believe you're a flawed man. When you say, "I think I might be gay," the person to whom you're speaking thinks, "He's gay. Otherwise, why would he say that?" Once you confess it, you've lost control over how that information is shared.

The internet has offered isolated men—many from rural areas or cultures with strong prohibitions against homosexuality—an opportunity to have anonymous conversations with others like them. If they are lucky, they will cross paths with someone who offers hope. But the fears and sense of isolation persist. Even if they find someone to chat with, that person may have no useful advice on how to solve their predicament.

Empathy spread through that room at the community center like the smell of a a pine-scented car air freshener. Although everyone had a different story, we all knew what David felt. Some knew they were gay early on but thought marriage might fix them. Others knew but struggled with varying degrees of success to contain their same-sex attractions. Others buried underground a more robust secret sexual life. Of course, some were jerks about it and betrayed their wives from the beginning. But those guys don't often come to my talks, and if they do, they aren't eager to share their stories.

You don't need to precisely experience what another person has experienced to feel empathy for them. Although my story is different from David's, the sense of loneliness and hopelessness that he felt resonated with me. I once had a thought, "If only my wife would become an alcoholic. I could leave and take the kids with me, and everyone would approve of my decision." It mortifies me to admit those thoughts, but I felt a sense of desperation to escape the torment I felt. I had a wife and two healthy children that I loved, a successful career, a new home I'd designed and built, and financial security I'd never known before. I thought, "Why isn't that enough?"

Life wasn't as good as I expected it would be, but I didn't know why. "Maybe what I have is what everyone has. Am I expecting too much?" Had the intense focus on my career excluded the possibility of taking a look at my sexuality? Or could it be that I fixated on work to avoid taking a more in-depth look at it? Being busy is a respectable excuse for not doing almost anything. I began to wonder, "Am I in the right place in my life? Have I been living my own life or a life to please others? Have I taken a good look at what I value?" I imagined that David had asked himself many of those same questions. David never mentioned he had considered suicide, but I've talked with so many others who feel trapped in this situation that I'm confident he likely did.

While most gay, bisexual, or questioning men maintain good mental health compared to other men, they are at greater risk for mental health problems. Gay and bisexual men seek mental healthcare more frequently than heterosexual men, but they are three times more likely to have attempted suicide and succeeded. About half have made multiple attempts.

Many people contemplate suicide when they first begin to have serious questions about their sexual orientation. For some, they can think of no other way to resolve the conflict. At whatever age a person first begins to question his sexual orientation seriously, that conflict has been implicated in the lead-up to many suicide attempts. When coming-out milestones are reached later, the first suicide attempt for gay, bisexual, and questioning men occurs at an older age.

Whether the person is young or old, one common theme underlies almost all successful suicides: a sense of hopelessness. We tend to believe that coming out is more accessible as more young people come out at younger ages. On the level of society at large, that may be true; on an individual basis, not so much. After one of my book readings, an older woman cried as she told how her grandson had recently visited her to tell her he was gay. She reassured him that it didn't matter; she would always love him. He then went home and told his father. His father responded, "I will not have a gay son!" Her grandson then went out and shot himself.

Most research on suicide has been done on youth, with an increasing emphasis in recent years on bullying. Gay boys know the code of masculinity even better than straight boys. The code is enforced by self-appointed gender police who threaten them if they transgress the norm. They remind nonconforming boys to "Take it like a man!" For older gay men, the more common mental health issues are related to the following: homophobia, stigma, and discrimination; social isolation; lack of trust in healthcare providers; lower income; alcoholism and illegal drug use; and HIV.

For those struggling with conflicts about sexual orientation, reaching out to someone can offer hope. Many older gay, bisexual, and men who have sex with men do not seek care from a mental health provider because they fear discrimination and homophobia.

Therapists who are knowledgeable and affirming provide helpful therapeutic experiences. It is essential to find a provider who is trustworthy and compatible. Patients have a right to interview a prospective therapist about their attitudes and training before committing to therapy. Good therapists will not impose their values on their clients. Counseling from therapists who focus on changing sexual orientation or encouraging hiding is not helpful and can worsen the situation. People who see religious counselors who consider homosexuality sinful have a higher risk of suicide than those who counsel with affirming religious groups. For some, medications may help.

Most gay and bisexual men can cope with coming out successfully if they have access to the right resources. Almost all the older men I have worked with or interviewed had magnified the potential negative consequences of coming out. It is also difficult for them to understand the peace that comes with living authentically. Here is a fairly typical response I received:

> I had a two-hour conversation with my parents tonight and everything went a lot better than expected. They told me they would love me no matter what. I think my mom was still in shock about me having an affair with a man. But it feels like a big weight has been lifted off my shoulders!

Suicide looks like a rational choice when faced with a seemingly impossible predicament, but many of the challenges that lead gay, bisexual, and questioning men to consider suicide are not enduring. Coming out is not an event, it's a process; the most significant challenges are often telling the people we love the most. Not everyone has to come out to every person in every circumstance. A supportive group of family and friends is essential. But when families are not accepting, some will need to develop a family of choice.

The It Gets Better Project provides an encouraging message of hope for young people faced with conflict about their identity. But that message of hope—the hope that it gets better—must also be shared with older men who feel a sense of loneliness and despair. If you're struggling with conflicts about sexual orientation, reach out to someone who can offer you hope.

In all my years of practicing psychiatry, I have come to believe that hopelessness is the common denominator in most thoughtful deliberations about suicide. While I had only fleeting thoughts about suicide, I can empathize with those who have seriously contemplated it. I know the feelings of hopelessness and that there is no one you can trust to share those feelings with. But there is.

I Knew I Would Have an Affair; I Didn't Expect It Would Be with Another Man

After fifteen years of marriage, I had never been unfaithful to my wife, and I had never thought of ending the marriage. Betraying my wife with another woman was even further removed from my mind than divorce. Those thoughts were contrary to everything I professed to believe. But there I sat at the kitchen table at our home just outside of Ames, Iowa, desperately alone, and I thought, "I cannot live like this, feeling this alone in my marriage."

It was Saturday evening, and I was home alone with our two daughters. Lynn had gone to Kansas City with a new friend she'd met while taking prelaw classes at Iowa State University. She had told me to expect her to be home on Sunday afternoon.

Before moving to Ames, my wife and I had lived for ten years on a small farm on the coast of Maine. We decided to move back to Iowa to be nearer our families. Although we made the decision supposedly to be close to our families in Nebraska, it was more likely an attempt to save our marriage.

Lynn and I had both grown up in small towns in Nebraska, where everyone looked alike, thought alike, and believed alike. In 1983, divorce had not touched our families, our friends, or even our community. One man, one woman, until death do us part. Life had to be impossible for me to break that vow.

I felt alone and abandoned. Every effort I had made to make our relationship better had reached a dead end. Of course, I accused Lynn of not even trying.

I was hungry for some intimacy, some touch, some connection, but I couldn't make it happen. I wrote, "Dear Lynn, I have made the decision that I must leave you." I put down my pen to allow myself to feel my overwhelming sadness and sense of failure. What should I write next? I wondered, "Would suicide be a better option?" But suicide and leaving Lynn and the kids was too desperate.

Having lost my own father when I was three years old, and although I was always a bit uncertain about how to be a father, I had been convinced that I would always be there for my kids. I would be interlocked in our two daughters' lives, and I would be the best father I was capable of being.

Then I thought, "I'm going to have an affair." I had not yet met the woman with whom I intended to have that affair.

As I sat there, pondering this thought that was too new to have a well-thought-out plan, Lynn unexpectedly walked in the door. I quickly crumpled the note, stood to give her a stiff hug, and said, "I'm glad you're back."

In the days that followed, Lynn and I spoke briefly about the strain in our marriage. Lynn didn't want to see a marriage counselor, so we agreed to each see our own therapists. As a therapist, I found it difficult to choose one for myself. You find out rather quickly who you think the best ones are, but by then you have worked with them as colleagues and, at a minimum, have a professional friendship. I called a psychiatrist in Des Moines, whom I had not met, but he had an excellent reputation. I expressed a sense of urgency, and he agreed to see me for a half-hour during his lunch.

I heard only one interpretation the psychiatrist made, "You're very angry with your wife." I reacted silently, as many of my own patients do. "This is not my problem. She is the one who needs to change."

When Lynn returned from her appointment, I was hoping her psychologist had fixed her. "What did your therapist tell you?"

"She said, 'You smile a lot for someone so unhappy.'"

Neither of us scheduled a follow-up appointment. I'm not sure why Lynn didn't reschedule. I didn't reschedule because I didn't want to accept how angry I really was. Always the good boy, I avoided conflict whenever I could. Without speaking a word to each other, Lynn and I had silently agreed once again to put all our conflicts on hold.

After our aborted efforts to resolve our conflict, I thought, "I can't fix Lynn, so I should focus on fixing myself." I decided to start going to the gym. I am a reluctant exerciser, and by 1983, I was in the best physical shape I was ever in. On alternate days, I ran four to six miles and biked about thirty miles. I weighed the same as I did when I graduated from high school. I hadn't grown passionate about exercising or losing weight. What I was excited about was having a legitimate reason for being away from the friction at home. Who can question the motivation for fitness?

One afternoon at the gym, I had completed my workout, showered, and was slowly dressing, mentally preparing myself for returning to the demilitarized zone at home. Standing thirty feet away from me in the locker room was a man I'd guessed as about ten years younger than me. I was forty-two years old.

He was slightly taller than me, dirty blond, slightly receding hair, slender but not overly muscular. He wasn't effeminate but not entirely masculine either. He smiled at me with a smile that a Cheshire cat would envy. When I looked at him, he did not look away as most men would do, so I invented reasons to search through the gym bag I had already packed before my trip home. When I looked back at him, he was still looking at me with an unwavering expression. I grew uncomfortable, but at the same time, intrigued. I busied myself again, artificially delaying my departure. I looked back at him, and his smile had impossibly grown even broader.

He nodded his head toward a door that exited the locker room. He then walked toward the doorway, and inexplicably I followed him, twenty paces behind. He confidently walked down a long industrial corridor to a small lockable men's room. It appeared not to be his first visit. By the time I entered, he was already standing at the urinal, cock in his hand, and he turned to show me he was hard. We didn't touch.

He asked, "Do you have a place?"

"Huh?" I responded, unable to understand his Spanish-accented broken English. Even if his English had been better, I'm not sure I would have correctly understood what he was suggesting.

He repeated, "Do you have a place?" As he continued to pull on his cock, I understood the intent more unquestionably.

"Uh, no."

"You come to my place? Tuesday, two thirty?"

"Where do you live?" He gave me the address of an apartment in Iowa State's graduate school housing.

"Yes. I'll be there."

We walked in different directions as we left the men's room. As I walked back to the locker room to get my gym bag, I thought "I am going to get my first blow job." When anticipation and opportunity meet, brain chemistries suffocate rational thought. I drove past the address on my way home to make sure I knew where he lived.

On Tuesday, I stopped my red Corolla in front of his place at two in the afternoon, a half-hour earlier than we'd agreed. I anxiously walked to his door and knocked. A woman with stylishly frosted hair, trim and casually well-dressed, answered the door.

"May I help you?" She also spoke with a Spanish accent, but I understood her easily. Her voice carried a tone that let me know that she had absolutely no interest in helping me.

"Uh, uh, uh. I think I have the wrong address." I was stunned to meet her, even though I, too, had a wife at home. We both knew I had exactly the right address.

The next time we met was an unplanned meeting at the gym. He was not happy with me.

"Why you come at two o'clock? I told you come two thirty."

"I'm sorry. I was excited to see you. Was that your wife?"

"Sí." He corrected himself, "Yes."

He told me his name was Roberto and that he and his wife were both graduate students in architecture at Iowa State. They had just come to Iowa from Argentina. He said his wife was scheduled to be a teaching assistant in a design studio starting at two thirty. He reminded me again that he'd been explicit about the time I should come. He explained that she was suspicious of him because he had told her before their marriage that he was bisexual and had had male lovers in the past.

I explained to him that I had never been with a man, and this was all new to me. In my mind, I didn't count my experience with Ricardo in New York City. We agreed to meet again. We began to meet regularly, at precisely the scheduled times.

Then one day, he kissed me in a way I'd never been kissed before. The kiss betrayed my unconscious desires. I knew I had too much interest, not only in the sex but in the romance. The kiss punctured the steel barrier I had inside my head that separated my conscious and unconscious minds. It left a hole that could never be closed again.

My wife and I were building a new home in Ames—likely another fruitless attempt to rescue our marriage as so many other couples chose to do to save their marriages. Another child was not an option. I'd had a vasectomy. I was excited to show an architect the house I'd designed. Roberto and I now had a place for our series of casual hookups.

Knowing that he would return to Argentina assured me this brief fling would eventually end. It put some boundaries around our relationship, after which I could return to my monogamish, heterosexual-like life. I would not be forced to make unacceptable choices.

One day, Roberto and I went to Des Moines. I lied to my wife that I was going to look for light fixtures for our new house. I had told her a little about meeting Roberto at the gym, that he was a graduate student in architectural lighting and I wanted his consultation. It was early November, so darkness arrived early. He was driving his old baby-blue VW Bug that had been turned over from one graduate student to the next. As he drove down Eighth Street in West Des Moines, I reached over and began to insistently touch his cock. He responded by touching me as well. Not being satisfied with feeling his cock through his jeans, I unzipped his fly. As we continued to drive down the street, I opened mine too.

Now with flesh on flesh, our arousal heightened quickly, like a spring on a sexual mousetrap. He pulled his car off the road into a deserted industrial site. We ran to a weed-filled, secluded spot, holding up our still-open jeans. We intended to satisfy our passionate sexual hunger. When I arrived home, I realized that I had lost my wallet while my pants were around my ankles.

I slept very little that night, and with an invented medical staff meeting as an excuse, I left the house early the following morning. I drove thirty miles back to Des Moines. I found my wallet still in the weeds with a few bits of evidence of our lovemaking.

Shortly after my wife, daughters, and I had moved into our new home, my mother and stepfather paid their first visit to our home. While eating dinner together, I received a phone call from the emergency room at the hospital where I worked.

"Dr. Olson, there's a young international graduate student here who says you know him. He has asked us to contact you. Do you know him?"

"Yes, I know him."

"He's been in a bicycle accident and has fractured his hip. He doesn't have insurance, and we need to transfer him to the university hospital in Iowa City."

Roberto's wife had returned to Argentina. He had no one. I replied, "I'll be right there."

With far too little explanation to anyone, I abandoned our dinner guests midway through the meal and left for the hospital. The ambulance waited, and with no further thought about consequences, I climbed in after they loaded Roberto's gurney on board. Every little bump in the freeway on the ninety-mile trip to Iowa City aggravated his pain. I lovingly held his hand and tried to do what I could to ease his discomfort. I gave no thought to the opinions of the attendants. On that trip to Iowa City, I realized that Roberto meant more to me than just a fuck buddy.

I spent the night helping to get Roberto registered and consent papers signed for his surgery. Although the staff at the hospital never questioned us, they sensed the nature of our relationship and showed no signs of disapproval. I rode back to Ames in the ambulance. I arrived just in time to go to work the next morning.

I visited Roberto several times during his stay in Iowa City. After his discharge, with his wife still in Argentina, I attended to him daily as much as I could. The emotional intensity of this special time together intensified our investment in each other.

When I had been seeing Roberto for about a year, his wife made another trip to Argentina. I stopped by to give him his Christmas present, a CD of Whitney Houston's album with the song, "Saving All My Love for You," an anthem for our affair with only stolen moments together.

Sometimes a moment I'd stolen to meet Roberto was frustrated by his family's needing him. Doesn't everyone who's having an affair feel cheated out of something they have no right to expect? As I handed him the gift, he said, "My wife's pregnant." I knew that ended any fantasy I had about our running away together.

One day when his wife had returned to Ames but was away at the university, I went to see Roberto. When he brought his infant son to me, I saw a look on his face that confirmed that our relationship would end. I could see that Roberto loved his son like I loved my daughters, and I loved that about him. But I understood immediately that his relationship with his son would always be a higher priority than his relationship with me. And my daughters would always be a top priority to me.

After visiting Roberto nearly every day through the winter, in the spring of 1985 I was rushing down a corridor in the hospital where I worked. One of the hospital social workers I didn't know well stopped me.

"Hey, Loren."

"Yeah?" I was eager to get to the psychiatric unit to make my rounds, but I assumed I could address her concerns and be on my way.

She pulled me to a quieter spot and whispered with a voice that felt more like an inquisition than concern, "Is it true that you're getting a divorce?"

"No, it's not," I said, and actually I didn't think I was lying. I didn't know this woman well but well enough to know that she was the last person with whom I would share any secrets about my personal life. "You bitch!" I thought, but with no change of expression, I asked, "Where did you hear that?"

"Your daughter announced it to the fifth-grade class in school yesterday. My son came home and told me." I was speechless. Then she added, "I just wanted to help stop the rumors—if they're not true." Her smirk belied her intent. She wanted to own that rumor, not stop it.

I realized then that the conflict with my wife had not been as discreet as I thought. I knew that I had to speak with our older daughter about it. Now an eighth grader, our older daughter was pulling away from the family as teenagers begin to do at thirteen years old. That night I picked her up from a movie she'd gone to with her friends. On the way home, I said, "Your mother and I are having some serious problems."

"Really?" I was surprised by her surprise. I had thought what one daughter knew the other would know as well.

"Yes. There's a possibility we might get divorced."

She began to sob uncontrollably. She was completely blindsided by my announcement. It was then—and remains to this day—the most painful moment in our relationship. I discussed with Lynn what had happened after the girls went to bed. I didn't talk with our younger daughter, Krista. I thought she'd already sensed intuitively more than I wanted her to know.

Although I had decided to end my marriage, Roberto was a long way from that decision. In early 1986, went to see a lawyer. I chose a woman feeling that somehow a woman might be more sympathetic to my situation. She was from a major law firm in Des Moines, and Lynn had chosen a lawyer from another widely respected firm.

I explained the situation to my lawyer.

She said, "Hmm. You're a doctor and your wife's a lawyer. The judge isn't going to like this one." The divorce dragged on for years and thousands of dollars.

I wanted to put some distance between Lynn and me, so I accepted a job in Minneapolis. I took my younger daughter—the one with such ability to sense the future—to Minneapolis with me to look for a place to live. On the long silent trip back to Iowa, she finally said, "Dad, if you move up to Minneapolis, we'll never see you." I hadn't wanted to believe that, but I knew she was right. I turned down the job I had just accepted and searched for one in Des Moines. I serendipitously found and accepted a job as medical director of psychiatry at one of the largest health systems in Iowa.

I called my lawyer and asked her if I could buy a condo in a new high-rise complex in downtown Des Moines. She responded, "The judge will know you have to live somewhere." About two years after first meeting Roberto, I moved to Des Moines.

I was still so over the moon about Roberto that I had ignored the early signs of his jealousy. That would later become a far more significant issue in our relationship than the birth of his son. My relationship with Roberto deteriorated quickly. With his wife back in Argentina, Roberto became more and more possessive of my time and grew increasingly jealous of the hours I spent away from him. We also became more realistic about the fact that he would need to return to Argentina soon. Roberto and I continued to see each other, and we commuted back and forth from Ames to Des Moines.

Roberto had a key to my condo. One night I came home late from a meeting at the hospital to find him in my apartment. He had been waiting and watching for me from the roof of the building. "Who were you with?" he demanded.

"I had a medical staff meeting."

"You're lying to me."

"I am not lying." He refused to accept my explanation. He became enraged and demanded I confess to infidelity I had not committed. Suddenly, he attacked me with his fists. I covered my face but did not strike back. After he stopped beating me, I demanded that he give me back my key, and I asked him to leave. He angrily threw the key across the room. As he stomped out the door, he slammed the door so hard it rattled the dishes in the kitchen cabinets.

As I looked at my bruised and swollen face in the mirror, I searched for the lies I would tell the hospital staff the next day.

I was so tired of lying.

A few weeks later, I had taken my daughters for a vacation at Lake Okoboji in northwest Iowa. We planned to meet my Nebraska family. While there, I received a phone call from the psychiatric unit where I worked. "Dr. Olson, we have a young international graduate student here who attempted suicide. He asked me to call you. Do you know him?"

"Yes, I know him. Tell him I'm not available."

With that, our relationship was over. He took a piece of me with him. I saved a piece of him for myself. As painful as the affair was for all of us, I discovered myself.

I Didn't Want to Betray My Wife Again

I don't like calling my ex-wife my ex-wife because it seems like I've wrapped her in yellow caution tape. Thirty-five years after our divorce, Lynn and I still love each other, although not in the same way we once intended.

If parents arranged marriages in America, our families would have put Lynn and me together. We both grew up in small towns in Nebraska, and we shared the same hardscrabble life as many in our rural communities did. Our parents believed that education carved a path out of the economic wilderness. They were right.

In 1986, after eighteen years of marriage, she confronted me with some entries I'd written in my private journal. "What's this all about?"

"It's true. I'm gay," I confessed. "I've been struggling with this for the last few years."

Lynn's reaction was less than I imagined it would be as I thought about it all those months before the tsunami hit. Perhaps it was tempered by suspecting it for a long time and at last finding the evidence that confirmed it. A more likely explanation is that she accepted some responsibility for the failure of our marriage. My being gay was not the only issue.

During the divorce, we fought about the usual issues divorced couples struggle with: alimony, child support, and visitation. We didn't do well when all we could think about was our own pain. When we began to recognize and empathize with the pain we each had caused the other, forgiveness became a possibility and then a reality. It didn't happen immediately. It took some work. But both Lynn and I were committed to having the best possible outcome for our children.

It's often difficult for people to understand that many of us who came out in midlife or later still love our wives and kids. People accuse us of being liars and cheaters. Both things are true. But as couples therapist Esther Perel said in an oft-viewed TED Talk, "Everyone says that it's wrong to lie about an affair, but that's precisely what most people would do if they had an affair."

Although I had struggled with same-sex attraction for several years, I had never been unfaithful to Lynn until I was thirty-two. That first time with Ricardo was an unmitigated disaster, and I felt it confirmed that I wasn't gay. In my early forties, I tried it again with Roberto. That's what I'd written about in my journal, about which Lynn questioned me. It was then I knew I had to scrub myself of the shame and guilt I felt.

In 2007, twenty years after our divorce and while I was writing *Finally Out*, I called Lynn and asked her if I could have a conversation with her about our sex life. By then we were once again on friendly terms. Our rapprochement began when our first daughter got married. We agreed to set aside our differences to prepare for the wedding, and we rediscovered we still liked each other.

She responded, "Sure. You pick up some Chinese, and I'll have some wine for us."

As she poured the wine and I opened the Chinese dishes, I asked, "Did you ever feel I wasn't totally present when we made love?"

"No. You were an attentive lover."

"So you never had any questions?"

"No. We were both young and inexperienced. We thought it was as good as it gets."

"I felt the same way."

"Now we have both had other experiences, and we know it wasn't."

I've heard from many men with stories similar to mine who make comments like "The sex was good; it just didn't blow the socks off of me the way that I expected. It wasn't my wife's fault either." When I had my affair with Roberto, I experienced physical and emotional intimacy I hadn't known before. I didn't even know it existed. It didn't happen with Lynn, and it hadn't happened with the Ricardo disaster.

I often hear that coming out is a lot easier now than in 1986 when I left my wife. Back then, hardly anyone dared whisper, "I think I might be gay." It may be true that it is easier in a more global way to come out in 2021 since being gay is much more openly discussed. Still, on a personal level, it remains complicated and painful for both the gay man or woman and the spouse.

When I was considering coming out, I had two equally undesirable choices confronting me: I could live an inauthentic life while remaining married, or I could leave my marriage for a life I couldn't even imagine. Everywhere I looked, I could see only potential losses: loss of the family I dreamed of, damaged relationships with my extended family who loved Lynn, professional repercussions, financial losses, and, worst of all, becoming a "noncustodial parent."

At my daughter Whitney's high school graduation party, I felt like a guest among the people I had once considered my family. I was invited in by the man Lynn would later marry. Although he was quite gracious to me and I liked him a lot, I resented that he was the host of the gathering—a role I knew should have been mine. After I quickly gulped three glasses of wine, I realized I couldn't stay any longer. I cried all the way back to my barren apartment in Des Moines.

I'd been warned in medical school, "Medicine is like a jealous mistress." When I commuted the thirty miles from Brunswick to Portland during my residency, it seemed on every trip I heard Harry Chapin singing "Cat's in the Cradle." The words from that song echo in the head of every hard-working father who's heard his kids pleading for him to come home.

I would cry every time as I wondered if my profession was sending a "We'll get together then" message to my daughters, a promise that would be broken repeatedly by the demands of medicine.

My kids visited on the traditional Wednesdays and every other weekend. The keyword is *visited*. I had difficulty adjusting to the role of the noncustodial parent. One day, I'd cooked a slow cooker beef roast for our Wednesday night dinner. Upon arrival at home, I discovered I had not put in the meat. We had frozen vegetables cooked for ten hours. Another time, I took them to a movie after having bought a pound of sugar-free gummy bears. I didn't know they caused gas. We tried to restrain our farts, but it became impossible. Then farting became a contest.

Because I felt so guilty about leaving the girls, I tried to overcompensate by making each of their visits a special event. But I started running out of rodeos and Ice Capades. I had six pieces of furniture in my condo including their trundle bed. They never felt like it was their home. It didn't really feel like my home either.

One day when I drove them home, their mother met us wearing a sweatshirt I'd given to one of my daughters. We'd purchased it when we made a college visit in preparation for her leaving home. I lost it. "I'm paying you all this money, and you have to wear clothes I've bought for her!" She let me know she wasn't exactly living like a queen. But we needed those angry moments to help us affirm our decision to divorce. Fortunately for all, we didn't cling to our anger and resentment forever.

During our divorce, guilt kept me from demanding certain things that I had a right to claim. I rationalized that since our daughters felt more at home with their mother, they should spend their holidays with her. The fight over the sweatshirt was a proxy for all the resentments I felt, even though many of them were of my own creation. My daughters would tell you that the divorce was much harder for them than my being gay.

I don't think that my being gay added much more to the pain of tearing our family apart. I hate that I hurt them. I hate that I hurt their mother too. No one marries with the goal of having it end this way. And yet for many of us, it does. It wasn't as if it were a choice between pain or no pain. The pain was inevitable. It was a choice of which pain hurt the worst.

I left my marriage at the beginning of the HIV/AIDS crisis. I knew few gay people. I didn't know how to begin dating as a middle-aged gay man. I worried about how my daughters would introduce me to their prospective boyfriends. Once again, I had magnified the negative and minimized the positives. Whitney and Krista had plenty of boyfriends, but not one ever made my sexual orientation an issue.

I expected it would be emotional when I was interviewed on WOSU public radio with Karen A. McClintock. She wrote *My Father's Closet*, which was about her father, who had remained closeted for decades. I had read her book before the interview. At times, I wanted to defend McClintock's father against her criticism of him, but I wondered, "Am I defending him, or am I defending myself?" I identified with him when McClintock wrote, "He was just a kid trying to find love in all the ways he'd been taught to do it."

My tears began to flow when McClintock wrote, "Dad, I always wanted more," because I knew that my daughters felt the same way. The truth is I wanted more of them too.

I never intended to break my vow to their mother or to walk away from my children. Yet I have never second-guessed my decision to come out. I feel a sense of sadness that I could not give Lynn the dream she wanted. I feel even sadder that what I had to give my children was never enough. But all of us have evolved into much more complicated individuals than we anticipated. We have expanded our world to include a new definition of family.

Lynn and I reached rapprochement in our relationship through forgiveness. You may be thinking, "You son of a bitch! Why should she forgive you? You inflicted terrible pain upon her. She didn't do anything wrong." It's understandable why you might feel that way. Lynn accepted that a refusal to forgive me wouldn't hurt me. It would, however, interfere with the happiness and health of her future relationships.

Anger can be used in healthy ways to solve a problem. Lynn dealt with her anger with me by channeling it into a new career as an attorney and greater self-sufficiency. I focused mine on my profession. We must also grieve, though we can't until we dispose of the anger, resentment, and shame we feel. Lynn and I both expected more from the marriage than it could realistically provide. Lynn and I had to grieve the loss of what was, even if it was only a fantasy.

With the anger and grief under control, Lynn and I engaged in more in-depth conversations about our relationship than we ever had. Other couples have expressed a similar experience. The fear of loss from being honest had been removed. All that could be lost had already been lost.

Finding empathy for the pain the other has experienced is difficult but crucial. My difficulty with sexual attraction was an internal struggle. Lynn accepted it had nothing to do with a failure on her part. I had never blamed her. She no longer blamed herself, and her self-esteem improved. We grew able to set aside emotions and address how our marriage had not met—indeed, it could never meet—either of our needs. We talked about how unrealistic our expectations were.

After my affair with Roberto and after I came out to my wife, Lynn hoped to remain married. But I knew—and she later recognized—that love isn't loving if it's forced. We agreed to end a marriage that could not have worked for either of us. But I had been thinking about my future long before she was forced to consider hers.

Divorce doesn't always end in acrimony. As I worked on writing this, I treated Lynn to lunch for her birthday. Although we divorced in 1986, we still talk, correspond, and get together for special occasions. We visit to catch up on our lives and the lives of our kids and grandkids. I must be honest, it took a few years to gain rapprochement. It involved negotiation, compromise, and, most of all, forgiveness. It also helped that we received the support of our new spouses.

We come out to align our sexual desire and our sexual identity. But we also come out for those who remain isolated and suffering, as I was before I made my decision. We come out for those who may face the sobering thought that suicide is the only option to end their pain. We want them to know that there is hope for a new life.

I still love my wife, and she loves me, just not in the way we intended.

Outed on the Front Page

When I separated from my wife, I moved to Des Moines. I had accepted a job to become medical director of psychiatry at Methodist Hospital. I had financial obligations for large alimony, child support, and two house payments. I couldn't risk being "out" professionally. I needed that job.

One morning as I walked onto the psychiatric unit, I was met by an excited social worker who said, "Loren, we need to talk." She held my hand as we walked toward a private conference room. "Loren, Dr. Lorde has found out you're gay. I don't know how he knows. But he's on his way to report you to the administration."

Her anxiety became my anxiety. I didn't know how she knew I was gay, but obviously I hadn't hidden it as well as I thought. At that time, it was still risky to be an out gay physician. And I really needed that job.

I had been hired as medical director of psychiatry at Iowa Methodist because they were having some problems with psychiatrists on the psychiatric unit. Two of the primary admitters to the unit couldn't stand each other. And their behavior toward each other was beginning to impact patient care. As medical director, it was my job to solve the problem.

When I left my wife in 1986 to come out, I didn't think anyone but she and a couple of others knew I was gay. I had been living with my family in Ames, Iowa, a small, conservative college town. I decided I could not continue in the position I held there in the local clinic, so I took the job in Des Moines.

I immediately call my vice president and said, "Sharon, I need to come talk with you." I was nervous as hell on the long walk to her office. When I sat down with her, I began my confession. "Sharon, I need to tell you something." After a beat, I said, "I'm gay."

She responded, "Loren, we knew that when we hired you." If you've ever had anesthesia before surgery, you know the feeling that you have right before you go under. That was the feeling I felt when she responded to me.

"How did you know?"

"I can't tell you, but it doesn't matter." Then she asked, "Why is it so many older men are coming out these days?" I had no answer.

Her comment soothed my anxiety as I realized that they hired me based on my merit. That feeling of security has never left me.

I was still cautious about to whom I revealed my budding sexuality. My position placed me on a committee of physicians. We were tasked with developing criteria for admitting people to a new health maintenance organization. I knew little more than the names of some of the other physicians on the committee.

It was 1986, and in the preceding year, more cases of HIV had been identified than in all previous years combined. The HMO had concerns about the financial risks of insuring those who were or might become infected. At one of our first meetings, the HMO representative said, "I think we've developed a question on the application to identify the homosexuals so we don't have to insure them."

Her remark paralyzed me. I couldn't find words to respond. Another physician on the committee known for his blunt and obnoxious behavior said in a stage whisper, "What's the question? Do you like to take it up the ass?" A few physicians nervously tried to stifle their giggles.

If I had only felt secure enough to respond, "I'm gay. Do you not want to insure me?" But I needed that job. Even though they'd hired me knowing I was gay, they didn't have to keep me if enough people raised a fuss about it.

I worked seven days a week for the first two years. I wanted to protect my job. I missed only one day for the Register's Annual Great

Bicycle Ride Across Iowa, known to serious bicyclists across the country as RAGBRAI. It was coming through Des Moines. Doug, whom I'd only recently met, and I wanted to watch the ten thousand bicyclists pass through downtown Des Moines. I called the hospital to tell the staff I'd been up all night with diarrhea, and I wouldn't be in. I thought, "Who will ever ask for more information about diarrhea?"

Doug and I climbed into my Jeep with its hardtop removed and drove to downtown Des Moines. We sat at a busy intersection as the bicyclists began to pass through. The next morning when I arrived at the hospital, the staff showed me a copy of the July 28, 1988, *Des Moines Register*. Across the entire front page was a picture of Doug and me sitting in my Jeep watching the parade of bicycles.

Handing me the *Register*, one of the nurses teased, "Diarrhea, Dr. Olson?" Initially, I was horrified. I was outed by the *Des Moines Register*. On the entire front page. Wearing short shorts and a tank top. With my boyfriend who was dressed the same.

Then the staff started laughing. I laughed. By then, having dealt with Dr. Lorde, my position was secure. It was time for them to meet Doug.

Everybody Already Knows

The second hardest thing I've ever done was coming out to my kids. The most difficult was to tell them that I was divorcing their mother. When I thought about walking away from them, I felt so much sadness, shame, and guilt. Those feelings bound me to my marriage. I had made vows I believed in. I couldn't conceive that being a responsible father could run side by side with being gay and divorcing my kids' mother.

I had struggled for years internally with this decision before the divorce became a reality. When I finally made the decision, the struggle for Lynn was just beginning. *Dyssynchrony* is a medical condition where the activation of different parts of the heart is improperly synchronized. Although in medicine it is referring to a disturbance of heart rhythms, a lack of synchrony in our hearts fits pretty well with a married man's coming out to his spouse. Their hearts are not synchronized.

Australian psychiatrist Dr. Saxby Pridmore described what he called *predicament suicide*: when an individual *without a mental disorder* completes suicide to escape intolerable circumstances. Predicaments are problems that have no right solutions. There are only bad choices and worse choices; no good options are available. When married family men or women consider coming out, they face a predicament. They cannot find an honorable escape. They begin to feel hopeless that a respectable resolution is possible.

Gay men who say they've always known they are gay criticize those of us who came out late more harshly than anyone. A young gay man once challenged me: "If you so-called mature men had any balls, you wouldn't have found yourselves in that situation. Losers! That's what you are. And selfish. You hurt other people because of your dishonesty with yourselves and others." Some of what he said is true.

Another gay man in his midtwenties offered a softer critique: "Why would anyone come out at forty? You're too old for sex." He'll understand his mistaken answer to that question in about fifteen years. Coming out is so much more than a passport to sexual freedom. It is a process of shedding the shame and guilt we have felt.

Except for loving another man, I had always followed the rules. But no rules govern a decision on how to inflict pain on the people I loved. I had lied to my wife, my kids, my family, and my community. It began with the lie I told to myself. I thought that is what they wanted. I know that is what I wanted. If we all kept lying, no one had to change anything. But I was tired of lying. I had betrayed their trust, but I also broke faith with myself. I wasn't the person I intended to be. When we consider coming out, we magnify the negatives and minimize the positives. We make endless lists of pros and cons, and the list of cons is always much longer.

We have two types of thinking: either fast and emotional or slow, deliberate, and logical. Logical thought sometimes gets it wrong. Impulsive decisions are often as good as—and frequently better than—a decision made after endless deliberation of pros and cons.

When I considered coming out, I overthought it. But I was not thinking about the pros and cons. I searched for a way to come out without hurting anyone. But it isn't a decision of pain or no pain. It is a decision about which pain will be the least unbearable. Some of my decisions haven't turned out as well as I've hoped, although coming out is not one of them. Some decisions turned out much better than I could have imagined.

In 1987, when my daughters were sixteen and thirteen, I chose to come out to them. I chose a perfect flip-flop, shorts, and T-shirt day. A cool breeze eased the intensity of the July sun. Only an occasional fleecy cloud drifted across the sky. It was a Wednesday. I know it was a Wednesday because the court dictated that I could be a father only on Wednesday and every other weekend.

We loaded a picnic lunch in my Jeep Wrangler. I had removed the hardtop. We cranked up the radio and headed to my sailboat on Saylorville Lake, the wind whipping our hair. The only storm in the forecast was inside of me. After we had loaded our gear into the boat, I sailed it to the farthermost end of the lake until the rudder began to drag. I set the anchor and pulled out our picnic lunch.

I hesitated, then I said—every coming out story begins in the same way—"I have something I need to tell you. I'm gay."

I don't remember which one said, "Oh, Dad, we knew that already." It was probably Krista, who'd already sensed in the fifth grade that her mother and I were headed for divorce. But I do remember that the other one didn't challenge her response. The two of them didn't keep secrets from one another, so I knew they had already discussed it.

"How did you know?" I asked.

"We don't want to tell you. Can we eat now?"

Although their mother and I had not yet reached the rapprochement we now enjoy, I knew their mother hadn't told them. But who? How did they know? I've never found out, and now it doesn't seem important to know. Children are so sensitive and intuitive that they often recognize marital discord even before their parents are willing to accept it. Our kids always know more about us than we think they do.

From that moment on, I felt confident the only issues I had to deal with were the same things every noncustodial parent has to deal with. Thirty-five years later, my initial assessment has been true. My being gay wasn't the issue; not being there to kiss them goodbye as they left for school in the morning was a far bigger issue.

My divorce was not final until a year after I met Doug. Doug—more resolute than I—had been great about my need to split my time between him and my kids. He also was supportive of me as I worked out the burdens of alimony and child support.

After Doug and I had been dating for several months, we made plans for a future life together. The time had come to introduce Whitney and Krista to Doug. I asked him to join my daughters and me on my first vacation as a newly divorced father. We all felt nervous about the arrangement. He was still living with a roommate, and my apartment was so sparsely furnished that it was no place to entertain. I had little time off that first year in my new job, and I wanted to spend it with my kids. But I also wanted to spend it with Doug. It may not have been my best decision to throw them together the first time for a full week.

A few days into the vacation, Krista, my younger daughter, had a disagreement with Doug. She came to me and spurted, "It's just like having a stepmother!" I felt caught between my daughters and Doug. Unfortunately, I failed to recognize her genuine distress.

I was amused by Krista's comment, so I wanted to share it with Doug. With a laugh, I said to him, "Krista said, 'It's just like having a stepmother.'"

Doug, far less amused, responded, "I'm no fucking stepmother!" In all the fairy tales, the stepmother is always characterized as an evil person. Perhaps if she had just said "father," or even "mother," I wouldn't have been so amused, and he wouldn't have taken it so badly. But by the end of the vacation, in unguarded moments, they even appeared to like each other.

Doug and I saw each other nearly every day after we met at La Cage, a small gay bar in Des Moines on my forty-fourth birthday in 1987. By Thanksgiving of that year, we had begun to make plans to live together. It was time for Doug to meet Mom. I decided to invite both Doug and my friend, Bruce, to go to Nebraska to spend Thanksgiving with my mother and her husband, whom all of us called Grandpa Marvin.

As we sat down at the table, Bruce and I sat on the ends of our side of the table with Doug in the middle. Lefty and his wife, Sylvia, and Sylvia's mother, Thelma, were also at the table. Directly across from Doug, Bruce, and me sat my mother and Grandpa Marvin. The smell of tension competed with the smell of the turkey. As we began to visit, my mother would address a question or comment to me, and then she would turn to Bruce. She failed to make eye contact with Doug.

Doug is never easy to ignore, and he became more and more animated. He once said, "I'd never want to go to a party if I knew I wasn't going to be there." By the time we'd finished the last of the Mogen David wine, Doug was fully integrated into the table conversation. At the end of the meal, my mother and Doug were in the kitchen, chatting while they picked the meat off the turkey and put away the gravy.

Doug didn't ask for a place at the table; he took it. He showed up as himself. He always shows up as himself. Unlike me for much of my life, he doesn't compromise to fit in. He is who he is; take him or leave him. And most people take him. Doug is one of those people that can say the most outrageous things. For example, he might say, "That's a nice dress, but the color is all wrong for you." But the most amazing thing is, he doesn't seem to offend anyone. If I said some of the things he gets away with, I'd be asked to choose a pistol for a duel.

Doug wasn't just fighting for his place at the dinner table. He was making a statement: "I'm planning to have a place in Loren's life, and that means I will have a place in yours too." When we're not granted a seat at the table, sometimes we have to seize it. And for Doug, it worked. My mother grew to love Doug like a son, and Doug loved my mother too. Doug was not content to be treated as my plus one whose place at the table had to be squeezed in. He insisted on having as much space as anyone else. None of us want to be the companion of an invited guest in other people's lives. Doug was not going to accept being tolerated; he wanted acceptance. Yet he wouldn't compromise himself by trying to fit in. Isn't that what we all want?

So often I've heard the stories from men who ruminated endlessly about coming out only to discover that the person to whom they came out already knew or suspected. In every circumstance where I came out, the response was "I know. It doesn't matter"—except for my wife.

For the spouses of a person who comes out, it shatters their sense of identity and security. It may undermine their belief in their sexual desirability. Most will say that restoring their ability to trust after having been lied to is their most difficult challenge. It damages their ability to trust in future relationships.

Someone once asked me, "What was the aha moment when you knew you were gay?" I told him about an instance when my sexual desires and my sexual behavior solidified into a concrete sexual identity. I understand now that it wasn't as sudden as it seemed. It was a process that had been going on for a long time. As I've mentioned, for many of us who battled with same-sex attraction, we labored with a conflict about what we desired and how we behaved long before we were ready to accept a gay identity.

After I realized that my physical, romantic, and emotional attraction to men was more than a passing curiosity, I finally accepted that I am and always will be gay. I thought, "Okay, Loren, now you understand yourself. What are you going to do about it?" I knew I could not put the tiger back in the cage. Once we say, "I am gay," a cascade of events begins—some I did not want.

When I met Doug in 1987, he was twenty-nine. It seemed like quite an age gap at the time. I said to Doug, "There's fifteen years' difference in our ages. Do you think we can make this work?"

He responded, "I've always liked older men." We rarely discussed it again.

Family and friends were supportive of our relationship. Although we heard occasional and predictable comments about Doug's marrying a rich doctor or my grabbing a young trophy, the age discrepancy left my mind. Mostly. Although there was a significant disparity in our ages, we enjoyed many of the same interests. We were emotionally and sexually compatible. Physically we were a match. The only thing that did not seem to match was the number that represented our ages. At the time, I wasn't aware that a lot of couples have a similar age gap, and they have enduring, long-term relationships.

I don't spend any time regretting things—what a supreme waste of time that is—and I don't regret my decision to come out. Lynn and I are both stronger people now than we were before. We had once hoped we could find that strength in our marriage, but it was a false hope. I've always made my decisions with the best information (and intuitions) I had at the time. Why should I regret a decision when I've made the best one I could at the time? However, I am not indifferent to the pain I have caused others.

First you come out to yourself. Then you come out to at least one other. Next you make the decision about how widely to share your story. There will be consequences, but the ramifications are likely to be less than you anticipate.

We must ask ourselves, "Am I ready to take the next steps?"

Coming out is like having an orgasm. Everyone can tell you how great it is, but you really can't imagine what it feels like until you've experienced it. Once I stopped lying to others, I felt a great freedom. I felt free to live my life as I chose rather than the life others told me I must live. But once I stopped lying to Lynn, her pain had just begun.

A Husband or a Dog? Don't Make Me Choose

Doug and I had been dating for about a year, and we decided to move in together. Doug lived in an English-cottage-style home with a half-acre of gardens that he had lovingly restored.

I said, "I want to get a dog."

"No dogs!"

"But I've always had a dog."

"I won't discuss it. Dogs destroy gardens. No dogs!" Doug has always been passionate about gardening. When he moved to Des Moines, he restored the garden in the home in which he lived, the one we eventually shared. As he showed me the garden for the first time, he made it abundantly clear that I should never step off the walk. If a plant was in the wrong spot, it wasn't a weed, it was simply a plant that hadn't found its proper home, and he transplanted it. My suggestion that composting it would lead to the plant starting a new life fell upon deaf ears.

He was equally passionate about animals, especially cats. Cats can walk through a garden and not damage anything. Dogs, on the other hand, treat a garden as if it is their garden. One of the cats once caught a chipmunk. Doug rescued the chipmunk from the cat's mouth and held it in his hand.

"It's dead. Why bother?" I asked.

He ignored me as he kept stroking the chipmunk. Suddenly, it lifted its head and scampered off to hide in the hostas.

Once I was driving about fifty miles per hour and we hit a blue jay, which hurtled off into the ditch.

"Stop!" Doug screamed.

"What's the point? It's dead."

"Stop!" he screamed louder. Doug can be very insistent.

I stopped the car and backed it up to where the bird had been flung into the ditch. He gathered it up in his hands and we drove on. He soothed the dead bird in his hands. And like the chipmunk, it looked up as if to ask, "What happened?" I stopped the car and he released it into the woods.

Once Doug found a starling on the front stoop. It was so young it wasn't completely feathered out. Doug named it "Baby M," and brought it into the house. He boiled eggs to feed it as if he had hatched it himself. It thrived. After a few days, he put it in a box back on the front stoop. As the young bird called for its mother, the grieving mother starling returned to feed it. Eventually, mom and Baby M flew off together.

After we had been together for a few years, Doug and I decided to buy a farm, where we raised Belted Galloway cattle: we often had fifty-sixty cows in our herd. Doug knew if one was missing. Cows would often isolate themselves from the herd to give birth. Doug would go look for and find the missing cow. We also raised sheep, and Doug became the midwife. If a ewe was struggling to give birth, Doug would wash his hands, reach inside the ewe to find the lamb's legs, and assist in the delivery. He always seemed to have a sixth sense that connected him to our farm animals. But early in our relationship, I didn't know this yet.

Clearly, Doug felt differently about dogs. He had never grown up with the same attachment to them that I had. As a child, a dog was my constant companion. Dogs always accepted me in ways that I never felt accepted by humans. For my dogs, I didn't have to pretend to be someone I was not. They didn't care if I was the best little boy in Wakefield. I didn't have to convince them that they should love me. They shielded me from the loneliness I always felt. They cuddled with me when no one else would. Dogs were my safety net, and I didn't want to live without that safeguard that protected me from life's inevitable pain.

Doug and I had the same discussion over and over, always ending the same way, and I wondered, "If he tells me I can't have a dog, do I want him for a husband? Do I have to choose between a husband or a dog?" I dragged Doug to the Animal Rescue League several times, but he wouldn't even look at their dogs, much less pet one.

One Sunday morning, as we waited for the ARL to open, a family pulled into the parking lot, and a boy about ten years old tearfully exited their car, carrying a Shih Tzu mix adolescent puppy. The boy had to give up his beloved pet.

Doug went over to the boy, took the dog out of the boy's arms, looked at me, and said, "Do you like her?"

"Yeah . . . ?" I hesitated. I was afraid to like her too much only to be disappointed again.

Doug looked at the boy and said, "We'll take her." I was gobsmacked. Then it became clear to me. The reason he would never touch a dog at the ARL was because he knew how vulnerable he was to falling in love with one of them, putting his garden at risk. His compassion for every living being is one of the things I love about him.

One day, before I left for the hospital to see my patients, I dropped Doug off at home. When I got home later, Doug excitedly met me and said, "You have to see this!"

I followed Doug out to the garden, and Doug knelt with the dog he'd named Gert after his favorite aunt. Dirt went flying as together they dug a hole in the garden. It was a day of surprises.

Another time when we returned home from work, we found that Gert had torn Doug's favorite thing, a cowhide rug beneath the cocktail table, into pieces about two inches square. Doug's only comment was "Gert, you must be exhausted from all that."

Two men competing for one dog didn't work, so we went back to the ARL and found Cassie. She was a three-pound bundle of attitude and was built like a Chihuahua with the coat of an apricot poodle. Cassie once got drunk on about three tablespoons of beer at a balloon festival. Our relationship secure, Doug and I bought a farm and moved to the country to raise sheep and cattle. I wasn't forced to choose.

One Valentine's Day, Doug was asleep on the couch. We had watched the sheepdog trials at the Iowa State Fair, and I decided a Border collie would help us work our sheep. While Doug was asleep, I called the phone number of a sheep farmer who also raised Border collies. They had a litter about six weeks old, so before Doug got up, I left to go see them.

If you want a working dog, you get one from people who work their dogs. After the breeder demonstrated that his dogs work his sheep, I picked out a puppy and I returned home, uncertain about Doug's response. By the time I returned home, Doug was in the garden. I walked up to him, placed the puppy in his arms, and said, "Happy Valentine's Day."

Doug didn't speak, but the look on his face said, "You son of a bitch! We don't need another dog." He took the six-week-old Border collie puppy in his arms, the momentary scowl melted, and he became the Madonna looking at the Christ child.

Jeb was the smartest dog I'd ever known. Although Doug's immediate reaction was less than I'd hoped for, Jeb became Doug's constant companion and I believe Doug's best friend ever. Jeb knew Doug's darkest thoughts and all his secrets. If Doug had to choose between Jeb and me, I have no doubt Jeb would have won.

As our herd of cattle and our flock of sheep expanded, so did our dog family. Coyotes had devastated our sheep, so with Doug's agreement, I went to buy a Great Pyrenees puppy. I answered an ad from a breeder who had a litter of fourteen. I picked out one, and one picked out me, so when I got home, two bundles of white fur fell out of the pickup, Pam and Prudence.

The Pyrenees are an independent breed; they trust their own judgment more than their owners'. No one ever really owns the Pyrenees; they share the role of masters of the estate. Pam and Prudence bonded with our sheep, stood guard against the coyotes, and rarely stepped off our 240-acre farm.

One winter, Pam was running on the ice and tore an ACL (a knee ligament) that required surgery. As we waited in the emergency veterinary clinic, the owner of a golden retriever, also with an ACL tear, anxiously waited for the veterinarian. When the veterinarian told the owner the price of the recommended surgery would be about three thousand dollars, the owner began to sob, "But I don't have that kind of money!" Although that amount was a stretch for us, I knew that if we'd had the money, Doug would have wanted to pay for the other dog's surgery too.

Pam got the surgery, and her rehabilitation included confinement in the house with three-times-daily walks on a leash. She decided she preferred the warm house to the cold barn and became a house dog.

Prudence was shot by a neighbor, which resulted in a Hatfield-and-McCoy feud with them that we never resolved—another story for another day. Her treatment required a three-month stay in the Iowa State University Veterinary Hospital. Doug drove sixty miles each way to visit her several times a week, and with each visit, he delivered a pot roast. Hungry veterinary students who subsisted on a diet of ramen noodles looked on while Prudence dined.

Our dog numbers grew to five when we adopted a male Maremma, a livestock-guard dog named Guido. Maremmas are an Italian breed, similar to the Pyrenees. Guido hated me for a long time after he arrived, apparently believing I was Doug's predator rather than his partner.

Note to reader: be cautious when adopting a dog named Guido.

Gert and Cassie lived to be eighteen years old. One Sunday, Gert crawled into my lap and made some strange, undoglike sounds.

"What's going on?" Doug demanded.

"I think she's dying."

Gert, the hole-digging, rug-eating first dog, died in my lap that afternoon. Cassie, who at the end was blind but didn't know it, also lived to be eighteen. After Gert died, although we still had four dogs, it left a hole—time to go back to the ARL. Reggie entered our lives that day, along with a massive multicolored rooster who was named Pet of the Week. Every farm needs a rooster to crow the sun above the horizon. That rooster hated Doug. Each time Doug entered the barn, that rooster flew at him with spurs aimed to gouge out Doug's eyes. This adoption was decidedly less successful than our others.

Reggie had the attitude of Cassie and the independence of the Pyrenees. He had been found as a stray, a life he seemed lured to return to. The only creature on the farm he bonded with was Jeb. They were inseparable, except once.

I waited at my office in Des Moines to go pick up Doug at the airport at about ten at night. I knew Doug would want to see Jeb and Reggie more than me, so I'd taken them along. As we left the office for the airport, Jeb took off in one direction, and Reggie took off in another. The streets surrounding my office were always busy, even on a Sunday evening. I was frantic!

I decided I had to pick one dog to follow. Jeb was more reliable, so I went after Reggie. Reggie ran twenty yards ahead of me before he stopped to look back to see if I was following. Then he ran another twenty yards before checking on me again. Suddenly, he was gone as he disappeared between the buildings.

I was in tears, thinking, "Jeb, Doug's best friend ever, is gone. Reggie is going to be killed by a car. Doug will hate me for letting them out without a leash. I wouldn't blame him if he does." I gave up on chasing Reggie. Chasing him only drove him farther away. I went back to the car, where Jeb—always the perfect dog—sat waiting patiently for my return. We got in the car and began circling the area to find Reggie.

I had all but given up on finding Reggie again. As I sat crying in a church parking lot contemplating a tragic welcoming for Doug's return home, Reggie ran out from between two houses, sauntered up to the car, and looked at me as if to say, "Where have *you* been?" Reggie jumped in the car with Jeb and me, and we were off to unite our family at the airport.

Reggie is the only surviving member of our canine family. Gert and Cassie lived to be eighteen years old, while Jeb, Pam, Prudence, and Guido all lived to be about twelve. We have a drawer full of ashes that we'll spread with our own ashes when the time comes.

The farm, cattle, and sheep are all gone now too. Reggie, Doug, and I have all retired to a townhome in suburban Des Moines. Reggie seems to believe the entire subdivision is his farm. He welcomes every person, much like a country wife whose coffee pot is always on for

Doug and Loren with Jeb the Border collie; Pam, the Great Pyrenees; and their rescue dogs, Gert and Cassie. (Courtesy of Loren A. Olson.)

everyone. But he challenges every dog that enters his territory, no matter how large, as if he were a Pyrenees pursuing a coyote.

Every afternoon at about five, Reggie comes and sits in front of me as if he were a statue. He stares me in the eye as if to say, "Daddy, it's time," as if he too knows the words to "Cats in the Cradle." He sits there motionless until I say, "You want to go for a walk?"

At the word *walk*, he springs into motion, running from one end of our home to the other, spinning his wheels on the wooden floors. He grabs one of his toys, runs to the door, and drops it. Then he sits there as I gather the leash, harness, and plastic poop bags. Every day it's the same. It's always as if it's his first time.

I laugh, and I clap my hands. It's always like my first time too. I love that little guy, just as I have loved all my dogs.

Doug and I still love each other, too, but it hasn't always been as easy as loving our dogs. Doug and I both grew up with the expectation that loving humans can hurt us. Dogs can hurt us too; Guido comes to mind. But unlike humans, once you've gained the trust of a dog, they will never hurt you. Doug and I are cautious about whom we give our hearts to, including to each other. Love always comes with the risks of being hurt. People, like dogs, always leave us before we're ready to let go of them.

I Did Drag Once and That Was Enough

Adjusting to a new life as a gay man was fraught with danger. After leaving my wife in 1986, my first gay friends were a group of men I met in a support group for gay fathers. In those days, being a "gay father" almost always meant you'd had children with a woman to whom you'd been married. I had joined the support group to help with the transition from straight to gay. My closest friends from the group and I were all in our early forties and beginner gay men.

Halloween is a special holiday for LGBTQ people. It has little to do with its historical roots and customs. For gay people, Halloween has more to do with celebrating our roles as society's outsiders. It is a way to find humor in life's absurdities and misfortunes. It also has a lot to do with having fun. My new friends and I decided if we were going to be gay, we'd jump in with both feet, and that meant doing drag for Halloween. The plan was for us to meet in drag for dinner and then move to the gay disco in Des Moines, Iowa. Although we were outsiders, we wanted to make a statement by eating out in a restaurant.

I went to the Salvation Army to shop for a dress. I'm a big guy, so choices were limited. I found a pale blue, floor-length dress and some costume jewelry. I went to the Theatrical Shop for a platinum wig, false eyelashes, fingernails, and makeup. I stopped at Hy-Vee grocery store for two pair of the aptly named "queen-size" control-top pantyhose. I had no idea why I needed two pair, but I always follow directions.

I had started dating Doug, who was about two-thirds my size. He had found a black-and-white sequined majorette outfit and an ostrich feather for his hair. He made some tassels for his cowboy boots. He completed his costume with a baton, although he'd never held one in his hands before. He nailed it.

I put on my pantyhose, dress, eyelashes, makeup, and fingernails. I thought, "I can do this." When I finished, I looked in the mirror and there, staring back at me, was my mother. I looked exactly like her. That was not the look I was going for. Drag queens don't look like anyone; the point is to take it over the top and be outrageous. I looked like my mother getting ready to go to an Order of the Eastern Star gathering. It was not a promising start for a fun evening.

When Doug and I met our friends for dinner, I was put to shame. My friends had taken drag to the next level. They had hired a professional drag queen to do their hair, makeup, dresses, and accessories. I looked like someone who'd shown up at the wrong party.

When we got to the disco, I began to drink beer, as much and as fast as I could. Then, I had to pee. I remember standing at the urinal, trying to extract my junk from those two pairs of pantyhose. My fingernails became weapons producing jillions of runs in my pantyhose. My wig was askew, and the eyelashes were more off than on. As I stood there with my dress hiked up to my waist, I looked behind me. My semibeautiful gown was dragging in a blend of fluids on the floor of the men's room. I wanted this night to be over.

By the end of the evening, I realized I don't have to do drag to be gay. I vowed never to put on a dress again, and I haven't.

After that, Doug helped me recalibrate my new gay wardrobe. He suggested I make it more suitable for a man in his forties. He implied that to be gay, I didn't have to look gay. I threw away my blue-and-white striped jeans and some too-short green shorts.

Becoming gay had a steep learning curve.

Cowboy up: Gay Men in Rural America

Several old men wearing seed-corn baseball caps sat around in the feed store in Saint Charles, Iowa, drinking Folgers coffee out of Styrofoam cups. Although Doug and I never heard this conversation, I imagine it went something like this:

> "Have ya seen what those two sissy boys that bought the old Palmer place are doin'?"
>
> "Isn't that the darndest thing you ever saw!" (Good Baptists don't say "damn.")
>
> "They're gonna raise some weird-lookin' cattle with a white stripe around the middle."
>
> "Those cattle belong in a zoo. They look like Oreos." (Everyone chuckles.)
>
> "They even bought a Russian tractor, 'stead of a John Deere."
>
> "Well, I'll be. Never saw such a thing."
>
> "And they've never farmed before!"
>
> "They're plannin' on sellin' grass-fed beef." (Heads shake all around.)
>
> "That meat'll be as tough as a fourteen-point buck!"
>
> "Well, they won't last long out there."

Doug and I purchased our farm in Saint Charles, Iowa, in 1990. Saint Charles is a town of a little over four hundred people about thirty miles south of Des Moines. And yet it was a world away from where we'd been living. Saint Charles' claim to fame is as the site of the oldest of the covered bridges made famous by the book and movie *The Bridges of Madison County*. I drove by the Imes Bridge each day on my commute to my job in Des Moines. Doug and I stood out from the rest of the people in Saint Charles for several reasons.

Saint Charles could be any town in rural America. These small towns are often characterized as friendly and overly nice. But small towns in rural America are rather insular. They welcome visitors but can be inhospitable to interlopers who stay too long and threaten their way of life. People don't lock their houses, and they leave their keys in the car. But they also have a loaded shotgun under their beds. Life centers around church and family. They are overwhelmingly traditional, and the community quickly identifies, judges, and shares any deviances from those expectations. Democrats are as closeted as gay people.

People in Saint Charles knew who Doug and I were before we knew them. No one ever asked us about our relationship. Still, whenever we introduced ourselves to anyone, the townspeople knowingly raised their eyebrows, moved their eyes to the side, and said, "Oh, you must know Tom and Dan." In twenty-five years of living there, we never met Tom and Dan.

Having grown up in a small town, I was a bit nervous about living there. I fully expected to come home to the farm one day and see FAGGOTS spray-painted in white letters across the length of our long red barn. But it never happened. Willful ignorance is a powerful force in rural America. If you pretend not to know the truth, you can avoid making tough decisions based on that information. If we didn't make a fuss about being gay, most of Madison County tolerated us. Some even accepted us.

When the Realtor called to tell us about the place, he said, "I think I've found the place for you. It's a bit further from Des Moines than you wanted. And it's quite a bit bigger than you wanted. But it has everything else. It's 240 acres, about one-third in old-growth timber, another third in pasture, and the rest tillable. It has four ponds and a creek." We drove by the farm the following morning. Even though it was Easter Sunday, and we hadn't even been on the property, I called him back and made an offer. We had fallen in love with it.

Several days after signing the contract, we drove out to walk the property to see what we'd just bought. The farmer who was renting the pasture for his cattle was there. I said to him, "We just bought this place. But we've never seen most of it." He was a big bearded man wearing a ball cap, torn T-shirt, jeans, and cowboy boots. He spoke like a movie cowboy.

"Just climb in the truck. I'll take ya around."

Doug and I grew more excited as we surveyed the property. The farmer stopped his truck on a hill looking to the south. There was not another farmhouse in sight. I said to him, "The Realtor said there are four ponds on the place, but we've only seen three of them."

He pointed into the distance and said, "That there's yer other pond." Doug and I looked at each other in surprise. We suddenly realized that we owned eighty acres we didn't know was ours.

"That there pond needs fishin'. A lot a' bass in it. Ain't been fished in quite a while. So many in it they don't get very big."

Doug and I both grew up in the country. We envisioned a return to a quiet and simple life filled with rustic pleasures. In many ways, the farm was precisely that. We moved a 115-year-old farmhouse to the farm from fifteen miles away. It had recently been inhabited primarily by raccoons. People thought we were crazy, especially when they discovered we were going to raise "Oreo cows," as they called our Belted Galloway cattle, which were black with a white belt around their middles. Only my mother seemed to think our farm was perfect.

The house sat on the site as if it had been built there over a century before. While we renovated the house, we lived in the barn. With three dogs and two cats, we lived in a room about twelve by fourteen feet. We had a shower, dial-up AOL, a microwave, and a portable outdoor toilet. When I woke up in the morning, I could shut off the alarm, put on the coffee, and turn on the shower without getting out of the queen-sized bed that filled most of the space. We learned how happy you could be with only just enough stuff. Our grandkids still think of it as the place they'd like to live someday.

Top: Loren and Doug purchased this farmhouse while it was still occupied only by racoons. They moved it fifteen miles to their farm in Madison County, Iowa. Some people are still asking why. (Courtesy of Loren A. Olson.)

Middle: The home after it was moved to the farm near Saint Charles, Iowa, during a two-year renovation while Doug and Loren lived in a small room in the barn. (Courtesy of Loren A. Olson.)

Bottom: After the renovation was completed, most people stopped asking why. (Courtesy of Loren A. Olson.)

We lived a quarter of a mile back from the infrequently traveled gravel road that ran by the place. The dogs alerted us if anyone was coming, but hardly anyone ever did. The only regular visitors were the UPS man and the two women who were Jehovah's Witnesses. We tended our garden naked. We got caught only once, and that neighbor stopped at the far end of the driveway to allow us time to grab the clothes we always kept nearby. We raised most of our food and heated our home with wood. Our only option to dine out was Annette's Bar in East Peru. We always ordered her homemade pork tenderloins, the size of a dinner plate.

We swam and fished for the bass in our farm ponds. When we fished, Doug and I stood about twenty feet apart, using the same rods, the same gear, and the same bait. He stood there with a beer in one hand and a cigarette in the other. He pulled in fish after fish while my bobber rarely dipped below the surface. Then he'd look at me and say, "My arms are so tired from pulling in all these damn fish."

After our first winter with cattle, the cows began calving in April. A surprise winter storm emptied twenty inches of snow on the farm. We had to check the cows every two hours for new calves because they need to get up on their feet quickly and suckle or they will die of hypothermia. We lived in our red Dodge Ram pickup truck for three days, sleeping in naps, eating Ho Hos cakes, and drinking whiskey—a slug of whiskey for us and one for the calves to get them moving.

A few days later, Doug stopped at the feed store for some grain. One of the guys asked with a smug look—obviously expecting we'd had a disaster—"Hey, Doug. How many calves did ya lose in that storm?"

"None. How about you?" The conversation shifted quickly. Doug's star had risen.

For most of my teen years, I wanted to escape from my hometown of Wakefield, Nebraska. It wasn't that something drew me away. I wanted to flee from something, not go to something. I knew that I was different from most of the people who lived there, and—with the arrogance of youth—that included feeling superior to them.

The Des Moines Register | TUESDAY, MARCH 16, 2010 | METRO EDITION

IowaLife

JOHN GAPS III/REGISTER PHOTOS

Loren Olson, left, with husband Doug Mortimer in a barn on the farm they share near St. Charles. Below, Olson writes at a table in the couple's dining room.

Finally out*

* but not without fears

St. Charles man, other gay seniors prepare to face futures that include discrimination

By REID FORGRAVE
rforgrave@dmreg.com

Dr. Loren Olson nervously clutches a lectern at Des Moines University. It's lunchtime at the osteopathic medicine school, and students filter into the lecture hall to listen to Olson talk about a book he's writing. The 66-year-old could almost be a grandfather to these students: sweater vest and thinning white hair, ample belly and friendly laugh.

The book's title is scrawled behind him: "Finally Out: Unlocking the Closet in Mid-life and Beyond." It's filled with psychiatric research on mature gay men who come out later in life, a subject Olson — a semi-retired psychiatrist who lives on a farm near St. Charles — knows plenty about.

The members of this group are increasingly visible, but their situation is vastly different than that of younger gays. Gay seniors, after all, didn't grow up in a society at all accepting of homosexuality, and some who have been out for decades are now encountering discrimination when they move into nursing homes.

But first, Olson, true to his psychotherapy background, wants to tell a story from his childhood:

Olson was a 10-year-old in small-town Nebraska. His father had died years before. One day, Olson was about to mow the lawn. He tried to get his gas-powered mower running. It wouldn't. He called his mother at the factory, where she worked as an office manager, and told her he couldn't start the mower.

"Of course you can," his mother replied. "You're a man, aren't you?"

Half a century later, Olson's standing in front of these students. He closes his eyes, opens them. This moment, and many more like it, kept him closeted — through college, through

OUT, PAGE 3E

Story in the Iowa Life section of the *Des Moines Register*, March 16, 2010. (Reproduced by permission of John Gaps III, USA Today Network.)

Growing up in a rural environment, anyone who thinks they might be gay feels like they are the only gay individuals. Like me, most LGBTQ people in rural environments feel alone. Being gay in rural America is difficult, as it implies stepping outside of the heterosexual matrix.

Urban gay men have been the subjects of most research done on LGBTQ men and women. Many see gayness as inseparable from city life. The research emphasizes that escape from the country is the only possible option for living an authentic life. The city is their way out, and they run away to a new life in the city. The city plays a central role in the lives of many rural gay men. Most of them explored their same-sex desires and had their first same-sex experience in a city or college town far from their hometown. And if they came out at all, they came out in the city.

The city is intriguing, exciting, and liberating. Gay people view the city as a place where there is sexual freedom, affirmation, and, most important, inclusivity. When LGBTQ men and women discover the existence of gay culture, it sets them free. They see the city as a gay paradise and the country as a gay desert. But the city plays an ambivalent role for rural gay men.

In rural space, traditional gender roles and codes are difficult to transgress. Many struggle with the choice of gaining a new gay identity while sacrificing their homespun rural identity. Maintaining two distinct social identities is an impossibility in a rural community. Rural gay men and women must weigh the option of stepping away from their straight, traditional, gender-defined home and into the transgressive urban gay world. They may lose friends, jobs, and happiness in the process.

A brief visit to the dreamed-of urban gay life can be overwhelming and problematic if you don't know the rules. Gay people in the country misjudge those in the city. They find that their own identity does not resonate with the lives of urban gay men. Although in the city one can explore alternative sexual practices, some think of gay life in the city as "a bunch of homos in dresses," men who are flamboyant and effeminate, something they cannot or do not wish to recognize in themselves.

Country gay men see roughness, manliness, and earthiness as essential, so they "butch up" or "cowboy up" to guard against appearing effeminate. Having never seen the great diversity within the larger gay community, they see gay life in the city as monolithic. They think, "I don't want to be a part of that scene. That life just isn't for me." Willful ignorance operates in cities as well as in the country.

Are rural life and being gay incompatible? Are we less queer if we choose to live in the country? Just as country folk misunderstand city life, city people don't know life in the country. The country for gay men is not idyllic, but neither is it as abysmal as urban gay folklore suggests. Urban gay people misjudge the rural life and often discount the positive aspects of living in rural spaces. It is less oppressive than many imagine. Although prejudice exists, not all country folks are homophobic and intolerant. Many of them are "homo-naïve." The lives of rural gay men may be quite straight and traditionally masculine in all respects other than their occasional same-sex encounters. They may have wives and families and embrace masculine norms. Many compartmentalize all aspects of their sex lives and remain forever discreet.

When we study gay life, place matters. Many LGBTQ people live in rural America. Due to the rules of conformity, rural regions can feel oppressive. Rural gay people feel restricted because everyone knows each other. They also know if you need an extra hand, someone is always willing to help—that is, assuming you've followed the rules. Country people see the city as indifferent to the needs of others.

Dating can be problematic for gay men in the country. With a limited population, the pool of sexual partners is limited. Country boys often seek sexual partners with men like them. If you're straight and have only occasional sex with other straight-appearing guys, it doesn't threaten your masculinity. You're not gay if the guy you're having sex with is someone who doesn't seem gay at all. *Doing* gay things and *being* gay are not the same thing.

It used to be different. Men could go to the city to porn stores with glory holes, a hole in a wall through which they could give or get an anonymous blow job. The wall protected them from being identified by their partner, but it also served to protect them from seeing themselves. They also hooked up in the darkness of a park or bathhouse, or they found men with whom to have sex in public restrooms. But those places also created anxiety for those who didn't know the rules or who feared being exposed as "one of those."

The world of hookup apps has changed all that for them. In the city, gay dating apps have a grid of men, some of whom are located very few feet away. In the country, these apps have large blank squares with no photo and little information other than "must be discreet." The nearest prospective partner may be one hundred miles away. In remote areas with low population density, sometimes pop-up gay bars have been set up to give gay men a temporary reprieve.

Developing a gay identity means discovering who you are today and who you expect to be tomorrow. Men who are still closeted and struggling with their sexual identity frequently have a harder time with country living. Their fears of the reaction of the community isolate them and make them lonely and invisible.

Being an out gay couple in a rural environment was much easier for Doug and me than it would have been if we were single. We weren't thought of as a threat. Single gay men who are out are like the attractive new divorcée attending a cocktail party who makes the wives nervous. As a couple, we were "settled." We had a circle of friends, all straight, who included us as they would with any other couple.

Because Doug and I didn't think like traditional farmers, we could implement innovative strategies on our farm. We were on the cusp of the grass-fed beef movement. We sold small breeding herds of our Oreo cattle throughout the United States.

At the feed store, I can picture those same old men having this conversation:

> "Those gay boys just sent a load of those weird cattle to California!"

"It figures. California." (Heads nod in agreement.)
"Did you hear what they got for them!"
"Can you believe it?"
"Maybe they're on to somethin'."

Our presence as a successful gay couple in that rural Iowa countryside was an innovation too. We were no longer just two sissy boys with crazy ideas. We were a different kind of man. When we learn to know each other as real humans with different stories to tell, stereotypes disappear. Acceptance becomes a possibility.

Is There Cake at a Gay Wedding?

On my forty-fourth birthday, I entered a gay bar called La Cage in Des Moines, Iowa, to begin my new life as a gay man. I had left my wife and family a few months before. As the new medical director of psychiatry at a large healthcare system, I knew that I had to hide my gay life. With alimony and child support, I needed that job. It was 1986, and it was still risky to be out as a physician.

It wasn't hard to hide my gay life because I didn't have any. I had only just discovered it, and it was as yet unexplored. I chose a barstool with no one on either side of me with the same care men take when choosing which urinal to use in the men's room. At the opposite end of the bar, playing a video game alone, sat a handsome blond man who appeared to be in his late twenties. I found him attractive but felt superglued to that barstool.

It must be noted here that Doug's memory of this event is somewhat different. He would say, "I was trying to decide between you and a Canadian built like a lumberjack. I would never play a video game." I don't remember any Canadian man of any size or shape, but I do rather like the idea that if there was one, I won. What I do know is unquestionably true: when I first saw Doug, I thought, "How the hell can I meet that man?" My lack of experience in this new world paralyzed me. I spoke to no one except briefly to the bartender. I finished my drink and left a generous tip for him even though I had little money to spare.

As I was about to get up, the young man I had been watching came over and sat beside me. "Hi, my name is Doug." We shared a very heterosexual handshake.

"You from here?" I asked.

"Nope, I'm from Arizona. Just in Des Moines for a while."

I thought, "Damn! No potential here, but I don't want to be alone tonight on my birthday."

After a few minutes of the kind of conversation that was endlessly repeated in every gay bar, I steeled myself for the big question. "Want to come back to my apartment?"

This was a significant risk. So far, I had enough money to furnish my apartment with only a cooler for a refrigerator, an old oak desk, and an air mattress for a bed. The sheets on the bed popped off every time you sat down on it. I had one piece of art. I had made monthly payments on a large watercolor of an unquestionably masculine rooster painted in shades of blue. I coveted that rooster's attitude.

Doug and I spent that night together, and as he got dressed to leave in the morning, I asked, "Can I have your phone number?" I gave him enough time only to arrive home before I called him to ask, "Can I see you again?"

Doug planned to return to Arizona. He loved the desert, and I had sunk my roots deep in Iowa soil. As we continued to date, I kept pressing him for a commitment. Once he said to me, "If I'm here in the morning, you'll know I'm still committed." I needed him to say the words he couldn't say. Doug understood my alimony obligations, child support, and college expenses. He also respected the time commitment I'd made to continue to be active in my daughters' lives.

Doug and I dated for a year before we moved in together. Twenty-three years after we met, the Iowa Supreme Court found that limiting marriage to a man and a woman violated the equal protection clause of the Iowa Constitution. Over and over, we heard from friends in other parts of the country, "Iowa? Of all places?"

I knew that we loved each other, and we shared the same values of love, commitment, and family. Still, I never imagined that two people of the same sex would be able to marry—in Iowa, or anywhere else. Doug and I had never expected to grapple with a decision about whether to marry. He and I can spend four hours considering a paint color for the bathroom. Then we repeat the entire discussion the next day as if the first discussion never occurred.

Living in a relationship outside of tradition caused us to do more soul-searching about getting married than if we'd been a heterosexual couple. We'd already resolved the essential precondition for the decision: "Are you willing to make a long-term commitment to this relationship?" We were.

For Doug and me, marriage meant asking our family, friends, and colleagues to seriously examine our relationship. We were asking them to put it on an equal footing with their heterosexual marriages. It meant asking people to examine their own barriers to approval. It said, "You can no longer pretend we're just roommates who sleep in the same bed." We were ready to state our love and commitment publicly. We were about to plow new prairie in Iowa.

Doug and I have been together now for thirty-four years. All of my six grandchildren have never known me as anything but coupled with Doug. I had once overheard one of my granddaughters, who was about nine years old, say when they all visited, "I didn't know grown men slept together." But that was the only comment I ever heard from them suggesting they questioned our relationship. Though Doug had been a fundamental part of my grandchildren's entire lives, thoughts about the potential impact on my granddaughters slowly eroded my wedding planning excitement.

I worried Krista's three daughters would be taunted when they returned to school in their small conservative Ohio town when they told their friends their grandpa had just married a man. I worried less about Whitney's three children who were much younger and lived in Seattle.

I called Krista to discuss my concerns. "Will you be coming to the wedding?"

She responded, "Of course. We all want to come to the wedding."

"What will you tell the girls?"

"We'll tell them that two people who love each other very much are getting married." I was ashamed of how much I can underestimate my children.

Later, Krista called my three granddaughters together and announced, "You know we're going to Iowa soon."

"Yes."

"We're going because Grandpa and Doug are getting married."

One granddaughter responded, "Oh? Who are they marrying?"

"They're marrying each other."

After a beat, my granddaughter said, "That's weird." She thought for a while longer, and then she added, "Will there be cake?" In a child's mind, the only thing that mattered about this weird wedding was "Will there be cake?"

For the wedding, we decided to have cupcakes instead of the traditional wedding cake. At the wedding, my granddaughter said, "Cupcakes! Best idea ever. I had five of them."

I responded, "Perhaps that's why there weren't any left for me."

The questions about sex did not escape my granddaughters. Before the trip to Iowa for our wedding, Krista had "the talk" about sexuality with the two oldest granddaughters, who were nine a nd ten. On the way to the wedding, it was all still very new to them. On the long drive to Iowa, the girls in the backseat were unusually quiet, except for some whispering.

Then came, "Mom..." Every question a parent dreads being asked begins precisely like that.

"Mom... do you really have to do that every time you want to have a baby?"

"Yes, sweetheart, that's the way it happens." A long and dangerous silence followed.

Then, "Will Grandpa and Doug be doing that?"

Thinking quickly, their mother responded, "No. They don't want children." It was too soon to tell them the truth.

While my daughters and my grandchildren accepted without a hitch my announcement that Doug and I were getting married, one relative asked, "Who will be the bride?" I had expected this question from someone because it's one that most gay couples have heard. It feels like

Doug had just placed the wedding ring on Loren's finger at a private ceremony in the courtyard of Plymouth Church, September 26, 2009. About thirty-five family members and close friends witnessed the ceremony. (Photo courtesy of Byron Gustafson.)

The cupcake table at Loren and Doug's wedding reception. It was the first same-sex wedding for most of the 350 guests. The reception was at the Iowa State Fairgrounds where Doug and Loren had displayed their Belted Galloway cattle for many years. (Photo courtesy of Byron Gustafson.)

A family night out in Des Moines, Iowa, at a sushi restaurant about 2015. From left: Loren, Whitney, Doug, and Krista. (Courtesy of Loren A. Olson.)

an extraordinarily personal question, as if you're being asked, "Who will be the pitcher and who will be the catcher?" I stumbled a response, but what I intended to convey was this: In same-sex relationships, there are no socially (or sexually) defined roles. Each couple negotiates those roles. Heterosexual couples should be so lucky.

My family member had no experiential framework upon which to build an understanding of same-sex marriage. But just a few months earlier, neither did Doug nor I. Those of us who are gay have resolved many of the issues regarding the nature of our relationships. Still, we often forget that others are just beginning to examine the essential meanings of same-sex marriages.

As Doug placed the wedding band on my finger, I realized that my coming-out process was starting all over again. I knew that a shiny new wedding band would be evident to my patients who were always asking, "How's your wife?" Coming out as a mature gay man is complicated and never-ending. With my patients, I always avoided answering personal questions, so my generic response was always, "We're doing fine."

People often asked if anything changed in our relationship after we were married. After the ceremony, Doug's brother and best man gave me a hug and said, "Brother-in-law, welcome to the family."

Shortly after the wedding, I received a note from my cousin Jerry Koester, the Koester family genealogist. He wrote, "I need all of Doug's information so I can get him included in our family history." Marriage changed the line in the family tree from a dotted line to a solid one.

Legislation and judges' decisions do not dismantle stereotypes and prejudices; that only happens when others begin to understand the essential meaning of gay relationships. Gay marriage can be legislated, but understanding and acceptance cannot be.

My former wife, Lynn, Doug, my daughters and their husbands, our grandchildren, and I frequently spend holidays and celebratory events together. This did not happen immediately or simply. But now I often refer to Doug as my grandchildren's "bonus Grandpa," and we both refer to the grandchildren as our grandchildren. We celebrate our lives together in ways I once could not have dreamed were possible.

This accommodation in our blended family required that all of us examine our inner contradictions, remove partitions within our brains, and smooth out the frictions both within and between us. I don't believe every gay couple needs to marry, but I do think that every gay couple deserves the right to make their own choice about it.

Without Intimacy, Your Partner Will Look Elsewhere

Larry is a medical professional in his midfifties who lives in a small Southern town. He was depressed before reading *Finally Out,* and after reading it, he felt desperate for some change in his life. He wrote me this email:

> I've been married for over thirty years, and I have two sons and a daughter. A couple of years ago, I had an affair with a man. Will my wife ever get over it?
>
> My wife and I have hardly had sex in the last ten years, and when we have, she always says something like, "Ok. But let's hurry up and get it over with." It makes me feel like she thinks I'm raping her. I've always wanted more sex than she does.
>
> Two years ago, I started going to the gym. I met a man there that I started confiding in. I've never had close friends to talk to like that. One night when my wife was out, David and I went to his place after working out. We talked about many personal things, and the next thing I knew, we were having sex.
>
> It felt so good to feel wanted. David wanted me as much as I wanted him. I had had two same-sex experiences before I was married, but it was just sexual pleasure. With David, it was so much more than that. It reignited all the same-sex attractions that lay dormant for many years. David erased all the shame and guilt I felt about those past experiences.

> Will my wife get over it? Will I ever get over it? I'm not ready to define my sexuality.

Almost everyone wants a soul mate, the person of our dreams, someone with whom we can build the expected life and have a family. We want to find a place where we experience love, romance, emotional intimacy, and sex. We also want to share these things with a sense of integrity and authenticity.

I was sympathetic toward Larry because I'd experienced something similar in my life with Lynn. When I was about fifty years old, I began to feel a decline in my sexual drive. Relationship therapist Esther Perel said that at the heart of an affair are a yearning for emotional connection, a wish to recapture lost parts of ourselves, and a desire to bring back vitality. When we don't find it in our primary relationship, we look elsewhere. That's what I was looking for when I met Roberto.

Larry and I had both gone through similar experiences. Even though an affair went against all my values, I found the intimacy I sought with another man. I wanted to have it both ways. I enjoyed the traditional family life I'd built with my wife, but I wanted to hold on to the fantasied life with my male lover. I hadn't fallen out of love with my wife. But I had fallen in love with a gay man, and falling in love converts a casual fling into a dilemma about love, not sex.

Why do gay men marry women? Many of us had a strong need to conform to expectations. And it's true; we didn't have the courage to break free of the need to please others. Many of us genuinely loved the women we married and wanted to have what everyone else seemed to have. We wanted children. We wanted to share our lives with another, and we thought that was possible only with someone of the opposite gender. Others thought that marriage would cure them of their same-sex attractions. Of course, some wanted to hide their sexuality behind a woman's skirt.

Even after men begin to recognize and admit that they have same-sex attractions, they remain married for many reasons: children, elderly parents, extended family, friends, and social networks. Larry stayed in his marriage for all those reasons, and in addition, he realistically feared losing his patients if they discovered he is gay. Men like Larry and me hate the thought of letting go of the shared history we have with our spouses.

Larry and I were also "good boys." We attempted to prop up our self-esteem by getting approval from others. We hid our same-sex attractions to avoid disapproval. I once asked Larry why he felt the need to always say, "I'm sorry," when he corresponded with me because he had nothing to feel sorry about. Larry didn't feel the need to say, "I'm sorry," with his lover. He felt accepted even when he showed up as himself, not some role he assumed.

Larry said he'd experienced some difficulty with erectile dysfunction. He'd received some treatment with testosterone, which helped, although he felt it almost made him too horny. Larry was at an age where his sex drive had diminished, and his erections became more unpredictable. His wife's negative responses to sex added to his difficulty in getting and staying erect. When men do not understand this natural evolution of their sexuality (diminished desire, lower ejaculatory volume, and unreliable erections), they frequently begin to beat up on themselves. They begin to believe they are losing their manhood.

But David, Larry's lover, did something important with Larry. He told Larry he didn't care if he had an erection, removing the pressure Larry had placed on himself. David invited him to relax and slow down sexually. He made touch reciprocal. He suggested to Larry that he learn to value touch more than performance. He taught Larry to know his body in ways he'd never known before. Larry began to experience new and exciting sexual feelings. When desire combines with opportunity along with an element of risk, it sends pleasure hormones in the brain to new levels, and Larry began to feel like a new man.

At first, Larry wanted to stay in a mixed-orientation marriage, a marriage where one spouse is gay and the other one straight. He prayed about it, went to counseling, and had tearful conversations with his wife. But he also realized his marriage wasn't and could never be the storybook marriage they'd imagined and hoped for. He didn't want to return to a pretend life anymore. And yet, he didn't want to let go of all the ways his marriage defined who he was.

Why do women marry men who have same-sex attractions? Women marry men who question their sexual orientation for the same reasons men marry them: a wish to conform and a desire for a shared life and children. Some women who were told about their husband's same-sex attractions before marriage are homo-naïve. They think either their spouse will outgrow the attraction or that they can fix it. Some women have had bad experiences and want an antimacho man. Some are repeating dysfunctional patterns from earlier life experiences. Most of all, they marry these men because they love them.

When women discover their spouse's secret, they experience a blow to their heart and to their self-esteem. They feel used, cheated, fooled, and humiliated. It damages their sense of trust. They are pissed off and want to make their betrayer pay. The biggest issue is always the deception. The lies are a bigger infidelity than the sex.

Spouses in these mixed-orientation marriages are mismatched in the timing of their discovery. The husband has been thinking about it for some time, but as one woman expressed, "My life has just turned to shit while the world is celebrating his coming out." His values have shifted away from those they once shared. If the wife's identity is too closely tied to her spouse's, she may begin to wonder who she is. Both Larry and his wife had problems with self-esteem. That bound them together as two misfits who didn't deserve and probably could never have anything better. Larry, in his affair, had begun to question that; his wife had not yet come to believe that.

Couples' counseling was not effective for Larry and his wife. He believed that their therapist was far more aligned with his spouse than with him. He felt ganged up on. Larry said they had gone to a Christian therapist recommended by a mutual friend, and he felt the therapist had focused on Larry's "sinfulness." Larry advocated for a postmodern understanding of marriage while she was bound by more traditional values. Neither Larry's wife nor their couples' therapist was open to considering Larry's use of porn or masturbation to satisfy some of his same-sex desires. An open marriage was out of the question.

The therapist recommended that Larry try to regain his wife's trust by being totally transparent and reporting his whereabouts to his wife 24/7. He felt like a misbehaving child who had just been grounded. This created an imbalance in the power dynamics in the relationship. If maintained, it would have changed Larry's resentments into hatred. Larry began to consider suicide as his only option to escape his predicament. (Suicide rates are higher if the therapist labels same-sex behavior as sinful.) We all need to keep some parts of our lives separate and private. Trust comes through integrity demonstrated over time. It is not developed through suspicion and spying.

As mentioned earlier, couples in mixed-orientation marriages have only three choices: fix it, put up with it, or get out. Most studies indicate that about 80 percent of these couples end up getting out of the marriage sooner or later. For Larry and all the men in this situation, letting go of their same-sex attraction isn't going to happen. Some couples in mixed-orientation marriages that remain together deal with it by developing some change of rules allowing for more openness. But even then, this can only work if there is an expectation of honesty.

Paul, a retired military chaplain who'd been through this earlier in his life, wrote this:

> I never seriously contemplated suicide, though I did call a suicide hotline on one occasion. "Coming out" for me posed an indescribable, overwhelming predicament of losing my marriage, my military career, and my ministerial credentials, the very center of my life and devotion. I feared it might also result in losing my family, whom I hold closer to my heart than words can tell. Thankfully, there were serendipitous and unsuspected friends and a loving family along the way who reached out with helping hands and extraordinary life support.

To put up with a mixed-orientation relationship means pretending to be someone you are not. A sham marriage works for some who wish to sacrifice their authenticity and emotional intimacy for approval from family, friends, religion, and social networks. But it means returning to a dark place in the relationship.

The choices Lynn and I had were to fix it, put up with it, or get out. Same-sex attractions, once ignited, can never be extinguished, so neither she nor I could fix it. That left the choices to put up with it or get out, a predicament that has undesirable consequences and can lead some people to think about suicide. Although some couples seem to manage a mixed-orientation marriage, Lynn and I never had any serious discussions about that option. For a short time after Lynn confronted me about my same-sex attractions, she wanted to remain married. But in my head, I was already out of the marriage. I knew that remaining married would mean more lies and betrayal. The lies I had told could never be untold, and I was sick of lying.

AOL

Almost everyone believes that cheating is wrong. Even though I cheated, I'm not the cheating kind. But most of us who get caught cheating don't see ourselves as the cheating kind. It's only others guilty of infidelity who are the real cheaters. Transgressors rationalize their offenses as unintentional, temporary, excusable, or justifiable. My husband, Doug, was no exception. Neither am I.

Inside my head, a voice screams, "Don't say more. What will they think of you?" We are told, "Don't cheat." But then there's this caveat, "If you do cheat, don't talk about it." But I hate hypocrisy, not only in others but especially in myself. I have been told it would be unprofessional of me to talk about my personal life, but being old and almost retired gives me that freedom. I hate the thought of portraying myself as someone with all the answers but who couldn't figure things out for himself. I no longer feel threatened by the loss of anyone's approval.

As uncomfortable as this is, I would be a hypocrite if I didn't own up to my own philandering. What we want to do, what we say we do, and what we do are often quite different. Doug and I, like most people, valued monogamy, but the truth is we weren't very good at it.

On a hot August afternoon about ten years ago—the day made hotter by our disagreement—I aimed my flamethrower at Doug about how much he had once hurt me. Doug shot back, "How do you think I felt when I read your message to Roberto!"

"What message to Roberto?" I asked.

Doug answered, "I saw your messages on AOL."

"Doug, I haven't been on AOL for fifteen years! I have no idea what you're talking about." I remembered that Roberto, my first boyfriend, had surprised me with a message from Argentina shortly after I signed up for AOL. That was all I remembered.

Doug continued, "I read your messages while you were in the shower."

I was indignant. "And you're *still* pissed off about it? How am I supposed to remember?"

Doug fought fire with fire. "Well, I fuckin' remember it! You said you wondered what it would have been like if you were with Roberto instead of me." It's true. I had had those thoughts.

I answered, "I don't know what I wrote. I never wanted to be with him instead of you."

"It sure didn't sound that way to me," he said as he stomped away.

I thought about how easy it is to amp up a conversation online. Doug's accusations weren't the first time I'd been accused of dalliance. It was the same allegation Roberto made before his fists came at me and blackened my eyes when I ended the relationship. I didn't deserve to be assaulted, but I wasn't as innocent as I claimed to be.

I couldn't just leave well enough alone. "Now you know how I felt when you wrote to someone, 'I can call you on Sunday morning at ten. Loren will be at church.'" Doug and I shared a computer, so it was inevitable that we'd expose our private conversations if we failed to shut it down.

Doug responded, "That was Pieter from Holland. I've told you about him."

"If it was Pieter, why did you have to wait until you knew I'd be gone to church to talk with him?"

Then Doug dropped the final bomb. "Before you left for Vegas in April, I saw a text message from Alan that said, 'Can't wait to see you.' Who's Alan?"

I felt like I was on black ice and skidding out of control.

Justice is never served by retaliatory responses. I had to stop wanting to hurt Doug back every time he hurt me. What I had written to Roberto was wrong. Doug had a right to feel hurt by it.

We need rules, values, and ideals, but we must accept that our humanity makes us fall short in honoring them. The world is full of people and things. Every thought, feeling, and experience is a part of the brain's calculations. Desire mobilizes making choices. While thinking ushers in feelings, feelings don't necessarily give rise to rational thought. Our emotions spark access to unconscious forces we can't understand, and passions overwhelm our powers of reason.

The anonymity of the internet allows for a premature, two-dimensional familiarity. Men armor themselves against this kind of intimacy in their personal relationships, but on the internet they drop their breastplates and share their most intimate secrets. It feels good to shed the weight of that protection. I learned about the people I chatted with, and they learned about me. I also unmasked some mysteries about myself.

I make no excuses. Wondering how life might have unfolded had we taken back roads instead of the freeway isn't unusual. I revisited those fantasies about Roberto when I wanted something that I wasn't getting from the life I was living. But when I reminisced about Roberto, I romanticized an unrealistic future with him, and I edited out all the bad parts.

Falling heels over head in a whimsical fling creates a dilemma. We exaggerate the assets of our illusion and devalue its liabilities. If Michelangelo had created his statue of David based on an online chat, he would have sculpted a Brillo pad with an elephant's trunk. In online chat rooms, factual knowledge of the mythical lover isn't necessary or even desired: "I want to believe you are who I want you to be, not who you are." In chat rooms, our playmates are like artists' jointed mannequins fleshed out by our imagination. It didn't matter to me that the man on the other end also transformed me into something I wasn't.

Doug and I both had online friendships, and we talked with each other about a few of them, but only a few. Neither Doug nor I set out to break our commitment to each other or wreck anyone's home, including our own. But we explored a world of men who were seeking no-strings connections.

It was in a chat room where I first met Alan.

To resolve the conflict with Doug I had to do two things: one, I had to own my transgressions, and two, I had to accept that I had contributed to some of Doug's. When someone betrays us, we don't want to accept any blame.

Over a few years, I had become self-absorbed. I started the research for my first book. I got up at four in the morning and wrote for a couple of hours before starting my full-time job at eight. Saturdays I spent in my office working on it. After the book was published, I went on a book tour throughout the United States and Canada. Because we had livestock on the farm, most of the time Doug could not travel with me.

In the middle of this chaos, I was sued for malpractice. Regardless of how illegitimate I thought the claim was, I was afraid a jury might disagree. For another entire year, I spent exhausting Saturdays at my office reviewing medical literature and years of medical records. Often, I checked into a gay chat room to distract my mind before I went home.

After I completed my deposition, the case against me was dismissed immediately. The plaintiff's lawyer even asked if I would consider being an expert witness as her case continued against another physician. I had paid dearly for that freedom with every Saturday and many sleepless nights. I was distant, preoccupied, and irritable. At the time, I hadn't recognized that Doug had paid a price too.

If you believe monogamy is consummate, none of this matters. Rules are rules. Black is not white. No compromises. No ambiguities. But life can be very disquieting. When stress depletes us emotionally, our vulnerability skyrockets. People in substance-abuse recovery say that staying clean and sober isn't difficult for much of the time. But they add that some days you get the "fuck-its," the days when consequences don't seem to matter. As I look back, I can understand why Doug felt I was absent from our relationship. I had treated him like a distraction. I wasn't the husband I intended to be.

In about 2008, I spoke in Miami to present the results of the research I did for *Finally Out*. It was there that I heard the young gay man accuse all men who come out later in life as, "Losers! That's what you are. And selfish." He was expressing his point of view toward me—and other gay men who come out later in life after having had mixed-orientation relationships or marriages. And the audience was more supportive of his remarks than mine.

In the evening, the hosts held a cocktail mixer. Feeling defeated, I stood alone on the edge of the crowd. Near where I stood was a tall, slender, strikingly handsome Black man. His yellow cotton sweater, linen pants, and sockless loafers were sophisticated and elegant. He oozed self-confidence without arrogance, but he spoke to no one.

After a few minutes he walked over to me and said, "I hate these mixer events."

I replied, "I do too." Silence hung between us.

"Do you have plans for dinner?" he asked.

"No. No plans."

Then he said, "Let's get out of here." I was relieved to have some excuse to leave.

Although it was early May, the temperature was in the high eighties, and it was extremely humid. By the time we got to the restaurant, I had sweat through my clothes. I thought I must smell like a locker room during twice-a-day football practices in August. He, on the other hand, smelled like a just-bathed, freshly powdered baby.

I had never been unfaithful to Doug in our twenty years together, but as I talked and laughed with this young man, I began to consider it: "I'm out of town. I don't know anyone. The best-looking man at this event asked me to have dinner with him." His interest in me helped lift my sagging ego for the first time since arriving in Florida, maybe even the first time in a long time. After a lingering dinner, it cooled off a little and was getting dark.

"I guess it's time to head back to the hotel," I said.

He replied, "Yes, we can sit by the pool and have another cocktail."

When we arrived back at the hotel, gay men from the conference filled the pool. I inhaled the sexual tension. My sexual desire climbed like the jet planes taking off from Miami International a few miles away.

He slid our chairs closer together and put his hand on my knee. I put my hand on top of his to send an RSVP to his tacit invitation.

After we drank our cocktails, he said, "Let's go to my room."

Later that night, it didn't end well. When I left his room, he wanted me to spend the night. Guilt crept into my mind, but I challenged those thoughts with "It didn't mean anything." Then the rationalizations began. "Doug will never find out. We aren't married. Lust is human and I'm human. If I have sinned with lust, what's the difference if I sin with sex too?"

In the morning, I went to the pool. As I spoke with a man my age, we both saw my one-night-lover across the pool.

He leaned in and said, "Damn, he's beautiful. They say he has a ten-inch dick too." He tainted him with a racial smear hidden in what he considered admiration.

I responded with, "Oh? I didn't find it all that impressive." I heaped shit on an already offensive remark. I was reconstructing my boundaries.

Trying to remember when I first met Alan is like trying to remember when I first started getting gray. I know it happened, but the exact moment doesn't leap out at me. We had chatted online for several months and also spoke on the phone before we met for the first time. As we chatted online, I found him to be warm, sensitive, and intelligent. His pictures confirmed he was exactly the kind of man to whom I am attracted. I was new to the idea that younger men had serious attractions to older men, so I felt flattered by his attention but skeptical anything would come of it.

I never hid the fact that Doug was in my life. I also never brought him up. If anyone ever asked about him, I responded, "I prefer not to talk about it." I suppose a more accurate explanation was that I didn't want to think about it. I was resolute about partitioning off these two parts of my life.

In April 2011, I had a commitment in Las Vegas, and Alan said he would meet me there. As I pushed the button to call the elevator in the Blue Moon, a clothing-optional hotel, the door snapped open. I saw a tanned young man wrapped in only a small white towel. I realized the pictures he'd sent me of his gym-fit body weren't enhanced. He appeared to be in his early thirties as his online profile had stated. He was shorter than I expected. His head was shaved as a tribute to his mother during her chemotherapy for breast cancer. He carried an ice bucket and his room key. He was headed away from the room.

I entered the elevator and almost at the same time I said "Alan?" he said, "Loren?" We greeted each other warmly but with some apprehension, like two boxers circling the ring after the starting bell. We were eager to engage but assessing our first moves. He reversed direction, grabbed my luggage, and pulled it to our room.

As we entered the room, he went directly to his suitcase. He pulled out a paper and handed it to me. He said, "I thought you might want to see this."

I scanned the paper until I read, "HIV negative." It felt good to be cared for in that way.

He began to unbutton my sweat-soaked shirt, and as he did so he pulled me toward him to give me a soft kiss on the lips.

I said, "I need to shower."

He responded, "You can do that later." I dismissed any conscious thought about the wrong or rightness of what I was doing. I couldn't say no when my body blared "Yes. Yes. Yes!" But I wouldn't have been in that room if I didn't want what he wanted. I thought, "You want me to fuck you? I'm going to fuck you in a way neither of us will forget."

On our final night together, Alan asked me if he could treat me to dinner at Aureole, an upscale restaurant in the Mandalay Bay Hotel, one of the finest and most romantic restaurants in Las Vegas. He had already made reservations. When the maître d' led us to our table, Alan was disappointed that it was near the kitchen. He didn't want anything to spoil this evening. The dinner felt like a proposal of marriage. I felt like he was inviting me into his soul.

As we returned to our hotel, I thought, "I can satisfy us sexually, but I can't give you everything you want from me."

Few torments are greater than when love is not shared in equal measure. I was reminded of the words from Neil Young's song "Old Man," in which he expresses his indifference to how deeply his old man cares about him. But I had to use all my strength to keep it from meaning too much to me. Alan and I grappled inside a too-small space but with no possibility of expanding it.

Most of us hope to find a place where we experience love, romance, emotional intimacy, and sex, but all with the same person. I had found that with Doug when I met him over thirty years ago. I assume he had found that with me. Most of the time. Monogamy implies that a perfect marriage exists and that all our emotional and sexual needs can be met at home with one person. The preachers promise, "If you find the right partner, you'll never stray."

As a relationship matures, sex becomes routine and predictable. That doesn't mean sex isn't good; it means it doesn't blow your socks off the way it once did. Novelty, risk, and unpredictability with an outside partner act as catalysts to elevate the sex drive. They promise to restore dwindling sexual desire and fading sexual function. Anticipation amplifies the sex drive and is nourished by opportunity.

Months after our August disagreement and my trip to Las Vegas, on a speaking tour, I texted Doug from Oklahoma City and said, "Set a place for me at dinner. I'm coming home."

He asked, "You're leaving early?"

I responded, "Yes, I want to come home."

Perhaps Doug thought I had run off to Oklahoma in search of a better man than he was; perhaps I really had. But my decision to end my trip abruptly confirmed for both of us that what I wanted was to be with Doug. Doug and I needed to find a balance between anger and reason to propel our relationship forward. I thought, "How did we get ourselves into this mess?" But the question I needed to ask was "How do we get ourselves out of it?"

Some say that gay men and women are incapable of sustaining a monogamous relationship. I believe that gay and bisexual people are more honest about the difficulties of being monogamous. But Doug and I had never discussed how difficult it might be. We focused only on our relationship, ignoring that a world existed full of temptations. We had misguided notions about how our life together would unfold.

Regardless of my intentions, my behavior had consequences, and the effects were what mattered. I deeply regretted having hurt Doug. But he couldn't resolve his injury by chatting with Pieter, and I couldn't resolve mine by chatting with Roberto or meeting Alan. We needed to wake up to the fact that an internet lover has as many faults as the one across the room from us. Guilt about my past indiscretions played over and over in my head, but that didn't shut down desire.

On the five-hundred-mile trip home from Oklahoma, we began to talk. We chatted about the lies we tell and why we tell them. For the first time in a long time, he seemed eager to see me. Something began to shift in my relationship with Doug, and I hoped it would be a permanent change in our lives. But we weren't there yet.

A Blue Christmas

I don't think there's a lonelier place on Christmas Eve than a moderately priced residential hotel like the one I spent a few nights in a few years ago. Some things are worse than being alone for the holidays. I knew that I could not withstand a Christmas at home with Doug. So a few days before Christmas, I decided to check into a hotel. As bad as it would be to live alone in a cheap hotel over the holidays, I knew that I would feel shunned if I stayed at home.

When I checked into the hotel, the only other person I saw was the desk clerk. He looked as if he'd volunteered to work because he, too, had no one with whom he could spend the holiday. If there were other guests, I hadn't seen them. "If anyone else is here, they must be losers like me," I thought.

I brought a half-filled suitcase—I never unpacked—and a small cardboard box with a few dishes. Before checking in, I stopped at Walgreens to buy a cheap bottle of wine, a wine opener, and a cinnamon-scented red candle.

A few nights before, I had gotten very angry. When Doug falls asleep, he's dead to the world. His head falls back and to the side. His mouth opens slightly. He inhales quick breaths and burbles his lips as he exhales. One night, he lay on the couch as if he had fallen asleep while we watched television. "Typical," I thought.

I stirred as if preparing to go to bed, and I watched him: mouth closed, breathing unchanged, head erect. He was feigning sleep, a garbage defense. I knew he was avoiding going to bed with me, and it made me angry. I crept upstairs, knowing that if he came to bed, I would be so angry I wouldn't be able to sleep beside him. But if he didn't come, I would also be pissed. Either way, it was going to be a long night.

Later, as I lay in bed, bitterly awake, I could hear him rustling around downstairs. The more I lay there, the angrier I became, so I threw on my robe, stomped down the stairs, and confronted him.

I began my interrogation, "What the hell is going on?"

"Nothing. You're overreacting *again*."

I sat in my recliner for a while as he ignored me. He avoided eye contact by feigning an interest in a television program. The program hadn't engaged him enough earlier that evening to hold his interest.

"Of course! You *always* make this my problem," I bellowed as I stomped up the stairs again. My thoughts flew like bats through the darkness. I ached for a shouting match to clear the air. But what I got was always a stealthy, silent rebuke. I wanted to yell and scream, throw a vase against a wall, plow everything off a shelf. But those things happen only in the movies. My whole world was taciturn. I was raised to be rational, always disciplined, always in control.

Anger is madness. It is a blitzkrieg—frantic, frenzied, and furious. Anger hungers for payback, and paybacks didn't suit a good man. Anger is to return pain for pain. I once asked my sister if anyone in our family ever got mad. She replied, "I remember once being so angry with you that I went to bed for two days with a migraine." I never knew. It was the Olson way of dealing with conflict.

A few nights that winter, I became so angry that I left the house to sleep in my car at a rest area on the highway between the farm and Des Moines. I loaded myself with Ambien and wrapped myself in a blanket. I needed to protect against hypothermia during a chemically induced sleep. It began to feel more and more hopeless. A few days before Christmas, I had told Doug that I would move out for a while.

Doug had spoken many times about his passion for Adele. Her music had blown the top off the charts in 2011. Her song "Hello" describes the pain of trying to make amends with someone you've wronged, only to be rebuffed. It could have been our song.

In an effort to try to make some connection, I decided to buy Doug for Christmas the CD set of her concert, *Adele Live at the Royal Albert Hall.* I dropped in briefly at the farm on Christmas Eve to deliver it to him. When I handed it to him, he refused to accept it. I threw the CD on the floor and left the house. A few months later, I found the CD unopened. I played it on my laptop, listening carefully to the lyrics from Adele's song "Someone Like You."

Tears rolled down my cheeks, and my eyes swelled as I lay there listening to Adele sing about love that doesn't last. Two days before Christmas, Plymouth Church held a Blue Christmas service for all who had experienced a loss that sucked the joy out of Christmas. As I entered the large room, I felt as if the others were asking, "What's he doing here?"

I chose a seat against the back wall of the room. I didn't want to look anyone in the eye. From the moment Pastor Angie opened the service explaining why we were all there, I began to cry. As the service progressed, my tears turned to sobs. Everyone there had experienced an emotional punch in the gut. I was so preoccupied with my own pain that I had nothing left to feel empathy or compassion for anyone but myself.

After the service, I couldn't move from my chair. One of the lay ministers came and sat with me. "Is there anything I can do to help?" he asked.

"I can't talk about it." I was too ashamed to talk about what had brought me there. He gave it his best shot to find some comforting words. His words failed, but I was grateful for his hug.

I returned to church for the traditional eleven o'clock service on Christmas Eve. It was filled with reunited families and college students. I sat in the back so I could leave quickly and unnoticed. I drove back to the hotel over streets that were icy and empty of traffic. I could see families and friends inside some of the homes, celebrating the holiday together. When I arrived at the hotel's parking lot, I saw only one car, as frozen and lonely as the desk clerk to whom it had to have belonged. I was relieved he wasn't at the desk when I arrived.

I walked down the silent hallway to my generic room. The outdated décor looked like every other moderately priced hotel room I'd ever spent the night in. Every wall was covered in shades of beige.

I lit the candle, opened the wine, and began to drink right from the bottle. I was too emotionally drained to continue to cry. I was filled with self-pity. Like an ocean, the loneliness extended off to a horizon beyond which I could not see.

I woke up on Christmas morning with a hangover, wearing the clothes from the night before. I had a stiff neck from sleeping on the couch without a pillow. I looked at the candle that I left burning on the table before I fell asleep. The candle was completely melted, and the wick burned away. The dinner plate I placed under it had collected the wax as it melted. The plate had prevented the candle from burning into the table. I thought, "I am that spent candle."

I continued to stay at the hotel through the holidays, but I knew that I had to move back home. During the entire time I stayed there, I didn't turn on the television. I spent the time thinking about what I needed to do to end the sense of hopelessness and despair. I had to examine my role in the stalemate.

Our inability to forgive each other led to anger and bitterness in my relationship with Doug. It also bled into all our relationships with others. We brought anger and bitterness into every relationship and experience. We were so wrapped up in our past that it decapitated any joy from the present and amputated anticipation of any joy in the future.

Emotions cannot be shut down selectively. By shutting down our anger, we shut down all feelings. Our relationship was emotionally constipated when it came to resolving anger. We needed an emotional enema that would cleanse us of the shit that we'd been holding back. We could not find a midpoint between slinking away and flinging feces at each other.

We weaponize our anger by dredging up old hurts, even ones we'd forgiven. Healed memories are not forgotten. My inability to deal with my rage wasn't Doug's fault nor was I responsible for his failure to deal with his. Anger can only be constructive when it solves a problem. We weren't seeking resolution but an advantage over the other.

It is ironic that both Doug and I had a fear of losing each other. But our fears of losing led us to behavior that pushed us away from each other. When you are so afraid of abandonment, you create the circumstances for which abandonment will occur. My early life experiences created a mindset that caused me to withhold emotionally to prepare for the expected loss. "Do I love Doug? Or am I just afraid of being alone?"

Although we have difficulty knowing when a problem begins, it is much easier to recognize when and where it ends. Doug and I were like two sumo wrestlers, locked in a tight grip, as we searched for an advantage that would allow us to throw our adversary to the mat. This sparring had gone on for weeks, perhaps months. Although we grew weary, neither of us would surrender.

To hurt and be hurt is human. Doug and I had hurt each other. Although we continue to love each other, we will hurt each other again. We have no control over how others can hurt us. We do have control over whether we hurt them, but we weren't done hurting each other.

Sometimes Love Hurts

I drove my best friend, Bruce, home after my husband and I had eaten dinner with him. When Bruce opened the door to get out of my Camry, I shivered as premature winter cold rushed in. But the brisk temperature outside stung less than my frigid relationship with Doug.

As Bruce stepped out of the car, I said to him, "I don't know what's up. Something's really wrong between Doug and me right now."

For a moment, Bruce sat there half in and half out of the car, considering how to respond to my comment. Then he stepped back into the car and closed the door against the cold. He deliberated for several moments before he responded.

"Do you think he could be seeing someone else?" It was a question I thought I'd never be asked.

"Oh, no!" I said dismissively.

Doug had made it very clear the first night we met that he was monogamous, very monogamous. He emphasized *very* to make it clear that monogamy was absolute. Doug's integrity was one of the things I loved about him after we met. We both believed monogamy was like a reinforced-concrete foundation for long-term, committed relationships.

Then I added, "That can't be the problem. But I don't know what it is." I continued to ponder just how and when the killing frost had entered our relationship.

Bruce considered his response carefully. "One night, while you were out of town, we'd had a lot to drink. Doug told me he's been seeing someone by the name of Rick."

In the muddled thinking of his alcohol-induced lunacy, Doug had been loose lipped and spilled this deeply personal secret. He regretted it for a long time. I felt as if Bruce launched a cannonball at my midgut from close range. The revelation pulverized my soul and flung fragments of it in all directions. In this moment of insight, I knew that what I had so vigorously denied was obviously true. The something-really-wrong problem had been exposed. I sat there, stunned and silent. Bruce—like all keepers of secrets about affairs—had been thrust into a no-win position. Either he broke trust with me, or he betrayed Doug.

Bruce broke the silence and continued, "I think the two of them have been spending a lot of days together while you're at work." I worked thirty-five miles away in Des Moines, while Doug's work was on the farm. During the winter months, the farm demanded much less of his time.

Early life experiences forewarned me that I would always lose everyone I loved. My fear was so strong that I found evidence for it even where it doesn't exist. I thought, "Doug will leave me, and I will be alone again."

Although I had promised Bruce not to act, how could I not react? I called Doug.

"Who's Rick?" I blurted out when Doug answered his phone. Doug sputtered, totally ambushed by my question, and then I added, "I'll be home. We need to talk."

I had Rick's name and phone number because I had met with him once before. I called Rick, and a woman answered. She asked, "Who's calling?"

"I'm an old friend of Rick's. I want to surprise him." When Rick came to the phone, I said, "This is Loren. We need to talk. Now."

"Uh, uh . . . I'm leaving soon to go to Lowe's. I can meet with you then."

Rick's voice sounded as if he were shielding his phone so his words wouldn't escape as he spoke. Doug had already alerted him that I had discovered their affair. I arranged to meet Rick at Caribou Coffee. I had met him at the same coffee shop a couple of years before. Although I frequently forget names, I usually remember voices and faces, and I always remember people's stories.

Puffs of memories of our earlier meeting wafted into my consciousness. He had asked to meet me because of my work with married men tormented by their same-sex attraction. Their stories are as familiar as an old pair of slippers. The only clear memory of his appearance was that he had a goatee. I remembered thinking when I met him, "Why do all these married men who have sex with men think they need a goatee?" The first time I met with Rick, he had not yet met Doug.

Rick, like most of the men who corresponded or consulted with me, wrestled with the moral and ethical dilemma that threaten to capsize these men's lives. They ask, "How can I stop these feelings? Is it wrong to stay married if I can never love her like she deserves to be loved? Will I lose my children's love once they find out?"

When I met Rick this second time, I would not have recognized him because of his apprehensive expression. I found him neither as handsome as I feared nor as disgusting as I had hoped. He was in his midfifties, shorter than me, and still wearing the goatee. What surprised me most about Rick was that he was nothing like the men for whom Doug had ever expressed any attraction.

Rick ordered a latte and came and sat on a barstool at a tiny round table across from me as he had the first time we met. But this time, he fixed his eyes on his latte, not on me. He did not remove his felt hat, wool scarf, or coat, as if prepared for a rapid retreat. Smells of freshly brewed coffee and chatter from other coffee-drinkers filled the room. His latte remained untouched.

I began, "I understand you've been seeing Doug."

"Yes." He whispered his penitent response.

"And you have been having sex with him."

"Yes."

"And I think it's become a little more complicated than that."

"Yes." He looked like a puppy being disciplined for peeing on the carpet.

I tempered my words carefully. "I know you've been seeing a lot of each other. I understand how these things can happen. I am not without fault. But you must stop seeing Doug." Having just learned of the affair, I had very few facts.

"Yes." He crawled out the door, never having tasted his latte. I felt like I had just fought with a marshmallow. Each time I punched, I met no resistance.

After meeting with Rick, I shortened the thirty-five-minute trip home by several minutes. My mind was not thinking about the surly constables that frequently patrolled the road between Des Moines and the farm. When I arrived, Doug looked like a trapped wild animal ready to gnaw off his leg to escape.

"So, who's Rick?" I asked again.

"He's just a guy I've had coffee with a few times." He answered with a submissive demeanor strikingly similar to Rick's in the coffee shop. He fidgeted on the sofa, head down, occasionally glancing up. His eyes were wide and his pupils dilated.

"How did you meet him?"

He responded slowly and with cautiously chosen words. "We chatted online a few times. He told me you'd met with him before. He's afraid to come out. He needed someone to talk to, so I agreed to meet him for coffee."

"Apparently, he expected more than that," I replied with caustic sarcasm.

Doug insisted, "He's just a very good friend." Then he asked, "How did you find out?"

"That's not important." I wasn't ready to show my hand.

I didn't know who else might have known. But I did know if Doug thought Bruce had betrayed him, Doug would not forgive him. I would be forced to choose between Doug and my best friend.

Days later, when I returned home from work in Des Moines, we sat in the living room. After he got up to go outside, I noticed that something had fallen from his pocket. I retrieved it and discovered a cell phone.

When he came back into the house, I asked, "What's this?"

"It's a cell phone."

"Whose is it?" I insisted.

"It's mine," he muttered.

"But your cell phone doesn't look like this one."

"It's a prepaid one." He attempted a pivot. "I got it so you couldn't track my phone calls."

As I sprung up and exploded out of the room, I screamed, "If Rick is 'just a friend,' why do you have to hide your phone calls from me?" I took the cell phone out to the driveway and backed over it with my car. I left it flattened in the driveway before speeding out to a yet-to-be-determined destination.

Several weeks later, Rick accidentally sent me an email intended for Doug. He was writing in response to an email from Doug that challenged Rick about his lies to Doug. In his email, Rick admitted to other sexual partners. He attempted to justify each one by suggesting there were mitigating factors. He said, for example, he'd only met the priest in the hotel room because the priest wanted to chat with him. He flogged himself with an effusive and over-the-top confession laced with contrition and denial.

After professing his profound guilt for his weaknesses, Rick then wrote, "Loren's only crying crocodile tears. As bad as I have been, I will never be as bad as Loren." I assumed Rick was referring to Doug's discovery of my relationship with Alan in Las Vegas because anything more would have been pure bullshit. Apparently, Rick believed he could get off the hook if he could paint me as something worse. He went on to speak of their plans for a life together. Fuck buddies don't make plans for a future together.

It felt like I had discovered the black box amid fragments of human remains following a plane crash. I printed a copy of the letter and showed it to Doug. Now confronted with his lover's words, Doug could no longer claim that he and Rick were just friends.

One of the first questions in negotiating a hookup is "Do you have a place?" It was the first question Roberto had asked me years before.

It was long after I learned of the affair that I allowed myself to think about how Rick and Doug must have spent time together on the farm. With me thirty-five miles away in Des Moines, no place could have been more safely secluded for their "must be discreet" encounters as married men so often insisted in their hookup app profiles. But I never asked.

I didn't want to create visual images that I couldn't unsee. Some details are best left unexplored. Probing didn't answer my questions; it only provoked more questions. Mining for the sordid details would only cause me more pain and more sleepless nights.

People intoxicated with love should keep their mouths shut, but their starry-eyed intemperance inhibits their capacity to do so. Doug began to reveal the painful details of his affair. As the spring thaw arrived, their relationship thawed as well. Doug was obsessed with solving the mysteries of Rick's lies. Doug revealed how he had Sherlocked evidence Rick had been cheating on him throughout their entire relationship. Rick promised more than he delivered, and Doug felt used.

Alan called me from New York City. "Are you and Doug having problems?"

"How did you know?" I responded.

"I chat online with a guy from Minnesota. He's had sex with Rick, and Rick told him about you and Doug." It felt like I was back in Wakefield, where everyone knew everything about everyone.

Doug told me he'd consulted with a therapist who told him, "Run away as fast as you can." He had arrived at an emotional crossroad with his heart and head choosing different directions.

My emotions were gnarled and twisted. Oddly, I filled the gap as Doug's only confidant. Of course, we had other friends, but sharing details of an affair thrusts them into the middle of it as it had with Bruce. Life on the farm had been like living on an island. Until now, most of our off-island trips we'd made together. Neither of us had personal friends not shared by the other. Sometimes relationships fail because they become too all-encompassing where we expect all our emotional needs to be met by one person.

Doug had no one with whom he could talk about his pain in discovering the truth about Rick. Doug thrust me into the role of being his counselor. I began to feel like a captive and begrudged confidant. I didn't like the role but I thought, "It's this or nothing. And I'm not ready for the nothing. If I can just hang on, maybe it will change."

Initially, I felt reassured that Doug allowed me to peek inside his emotional vault. I could empathize with what he was going through, but I couldn't share my own turbulent emotions. I hoped in the process, we could restore some basis for a relationship. But I wanted to feel like his husband, not his father-confessor.

I was angry with Doug for clinging to the buffoon and even angrier at Rick for exploiting Doug's feelings. It's an old story. The lover is promised they will someday be the number one priority, but they always remain number two—or number three or four. It was safer to be angry with Rick than with Doug. I had no one with whom I could comfortably share my agony. Or perhaps I was just too ashamed about my own behavior to want to confess it to anyone.

Through the summer, Doug became more vocal about his anger with me. What he knew and what he imagined about my relationship with Alan had hurt him far more than he'd ever talked about before. I began to see how Doug's fear of losing me had contributed to Doug's affair with Rick. I needed to make some amends of my own. That would also mean being more honest about some of the things he didn't know about me. Learning about Alan had led him to imagine that I had betrayed him each time I went out of town. He was partly correct.

A few months later, we planned a winter vacation to Palm Springs. Doug was to go a few days ahead of me. Before I left for Palm Springs, Doug called me to tell me he wouldn't be there when I arrived. He was going to Los Angeles to visit a friend from his days in the air force, and he would return the following day.

When I arrived in Palm Springs, I took a cab to the resort. I stopped at the desk, introduced myself to the innkeeper as Doug's husband, and said I wanted to check-in. He told me he thought Doug was still in our room.

I wheeled my luggage back to the room to discover that Doug had already left. Housekeeping hadn't yet cleaned the room. I noticed two wine glasses in the sink. I went into the bathroom, and on the floor were two sets of beach towels, side by side. I searched the room for lube, condoms, and any other evidence I could find, but the room had been carefully policed. I felt as if I had walked in on my mother having sex with the local butcher.

I undressed and went to the clothing-optional pool. I felt beyond naked. I tried to avoid tears, and I sat as far away from everyone else as I could. I thought, "Why do I feel like I am the one who doesn't belong here?"

My thoughts spun like a hamster on a wheel. When I went to bed late that night, more drunk than tired, I slept on top of the spread. The sheets seemed too contaminated to sleep between them. Each time I started to slide into sleep, I would snap awake and visualize what I thought must have happened where I lay on the nights before I arrived.

I had not yet spoken with Doug, so the following morning, I called Doug. "The room hadn't been cleaned when I arrived. I know you weren't alone in the room." I slipped the noose around his neck. I had nothing more to say, so I hung up.

"I know you were here with Rick," I said when Doug returned to Palm Springs. I tightened the noose. It hadn't been hard to learn the facts. I had gone to Rick's employer's website and learned that Rick was scheduled to attend a convention for his professional organization in Los Angeles at the same time we were to be in Palm Springs.

A short time after we returned from Palm Springs, Doug told me he wasn't seeing Rick anymore. I wanted to believe that. But at the same time, I hadn't forgotten the disappointments I'd had before when I had believed their relationship was over. Betrayals compound like interest in a savings account.

Having been divorced before, I knew what to do. I called the banks and changed our bank accounts and credit cards. I changed the beneficiaries of my investments and my life insurance. I picked up the divorce papers from my attorney, and I took them home for Doug to sign.

"I've filed for divorce. I decided to serve these papers to you myself instead of asking the sheriff to do it." A long silence followed. Then I said, "It's so sad."

He looked at me as if he were on emotional life support and responded, "Yes, it is." As he watched, I walked into the kitchen, took off my wedding ring, and lay it on a shelf by the sink.

We continued to live together during the ninety-day waiting period. A few days later, I came home from work. Doug was sitting on the sofa in the den. His cell phone rang.

"Aren't you going to answer that?" I asked.

"No, I'll just let it go to voice mail." he answered with some edginess in his voice.

"Let me see that phone," I demanded. When he showed me the phone, it was another prepaid disposable cell phone.

"If it's over with Rick, why do you need a cell phone to talk with him?" I don't remember his response, but I was indifferent to his answer. I know it was something about not having any friends because I felt the same way.

I grabbed the phone and left the house again, driving down the road past my breaking point. I thought of throwing the cell phone in the pond. I considered searching his call history. I realized I was totally helpless to impact Doug's relationship with Rick. I knew the Doug I had been living with recently was not the Doug I had lived with and then married. I wanted the old Doug back, and I'm sure he felt the same about me.

All relationships have rules, and one of the rules Doug and I had was monogamy. Monogamy was to a relationship like enamel is to teeth; it should protect us against vulnerabilities. Everything we wanted should be at home. Every couple brings different values to the relationship, but monogamy was one we shared. We didn't realize how difficult it would be.

I was done. I knew that if Doug wanted a relationship with Rick, I did not want a relationship with Doug. I returned home and gave him the phone.

"Here's your phone," I said without equivocation, "I can't stop you from contacting Rick. You've made your choice. I will *not* live this way any longer. I want you to get out. Take the cats. I'll keep the dogs." If this were the "it's this or nothing" moment, I was prepared for the nothing.

Silence stretched out between us for a long time. Then Doug said, "I will try to make it work." Trying is always a half-assed commitment. He recognized it too.

After another long pause, he said, "No, I *will* make it work."

Something shifted at that moment. I recognized that man as the one I had known. It felt like being rescued from a riptide. I thought, "Can I learn to trust Doug again? Do I even want to try? How will I know if it is safe to trust again? Could Doug and I establish a new relationship with each other? Am I willing to invest in a new relationship with the same person?"

Affairs grow out of wondering "Is that all there is? Will I ever love again? Can I find the passion I once had? What would life be like if I had made different choices?" Affairs are about lust, sex, and a taste of the secretive and forbidden. The excitement of the forbidden fuels desire; the incompleteness sustains it. We become vulnerable to an affair when we thirst for an emotional connection with someone special.

But we are not only looking for someone. We are looking for the person we once were. We want to feel alive again. We think our relationship has failed when it doesn't provide all of those things all of the time.

Lovers are like the wizard behind the curtain; spouses are like the UPS man, functional and predictable but dressed only in brown. Spouses are real. Sometimes they are weak and fail us; sometimes we are weak and fail them. In affairs, we believe that we have finally found someone who understands us like no one else ever has. No matter how much we are told to walk away as quickly as possible—and we know that we should—our heart often interferes, at least until the curtain is slashed. Then we realize the wizard is not who we thought he was but someone we have created to meet our own needs. Doug and Rick had done that. I had done it with Roberto and Alan. Doug and I had done it with each other.

"Is it realistic to believe that one person can provide for all our needs?" When marriage originated centuries ago, it had little to do with love or religion. Marriage was a pledge to produce offspring so that a man's children got his cows. Wives were property and required to stay home while men had the freedom of concubines, prostitutes, and male lovers. Even in these relationships, rules still applied.

"How had I been so stupid to miss all the early signs of Doug's infidelity?" I could have learned the signs in any issue of *Cosmopolitan*. I had been preoccupied with my own life and not our life together. Distance between us had grown. We searched for reasons to be apart rather than to be together. Our conversations had narrowed to the minimum necessary. Sex became sporadic and perfunctory. He wasn't present in our relationship. But neither was I. He had recognized my infidelity early on, and then used it to justify his own. My idea that my indiscretions were of lesser consequence unraveled.

Should sex outside of a committed relationship be a deal-breaker? Our society expects that. How often do we hear, "Once a cheater..."? But it depends on who and what you believe. When Doug and I had agreed on monogamy, neither of us thought that would be difficult. While the exposure of our secrets shattered our idealistic expectations about relationships, it had not imploded our love for each other.

I knew that some changes were necessary. Rules needed to be examined and possibly modified. I couldn't control Doug's behavior, but I could change mine. We were both flawed. We had inflicted serious pain on the person we loved. We knew that we weren't the men we'd become; we weren't the men we were meant to be.

We weren't on firm ground yet, but we could see the shore in the distance. We knew it would take a long time to discover each other again.

Betrayer and Betrayed

I should be an expert on betrayal. I've been both the betrayed and the betrayer. How did Doug and I get to a place in our relationship where we both felt alone, helpless, and desperate for something more? Perhaps we expected too much from each other from the beginning. Boundaries around a relationship can be too loose, but they can also be too tight. Sometimes we do wrong to get out of difficult situations only to find that we've created an even more difficult situation. Our relationship hadn't died, but it was on life support.

We have no control over how others hurt us. The ones we love—parents, lovers, and children—inflict the worst suffering. A betrayal of trust by someone we love inflicts excruciating pain on us. It disrupts our inner world, and it bleeds into our outer world as well. It's difficult to concentrate on anything other than our own pain. We do have control over how we hurt others. Unfortunately, we don't always exercise that control. But we do have the power to apologize to those we hurt and to forgive those who have hurt us.

Doug and I, as all couples do, brought to our relationship different personal, religious, and cultural values, although the differences were small. Disagreements about these values ignite conflict in a relationship. Age and social class contribute to tension around the rules of sexual behavior. Value conflicts arising from religious or cultural traditions are the most difficult to resolve. Religion and culture have created the false narrative that instinctual drives like sex can always be controlled by rational thought.

Sometimes affairs are the death knell of an already dying relationship. Some couples stay together clinging by their fingernails. Others are bound together in bitterness. Doug and I needed to figure out what had worked before but wasn't working now.

I believe that infidelity is defined by a loss of loyalty, not what one does with one's penis. The primary issue in our affairs was both Doug and I had neglected each other because we spent too much time and emotional energy thinking about someone else. Our partner's needs did not receive the degree of attention each needed.

Lies about an affair are more destructive than sex. Lies destroy trust—and trust, once lost, is difficult to reestablish. Trust can be restored only with significant behavioral change over time. When Lynn and I went through the crisis in our lives caused by my coming out, I couldn't make a commitment to her that I would change. Continuing to deceive her would have been an even greater betrayal. "I'll try" suggests a half-hearted effort and an expectation of failure. Doug and I, on the other hand, recognized that change was needed, and these changes were ones we could make.

Marriage isn't for everyone, and neither is monogamy. And yet, the two words are often fused. French film director François Truffaut said, "Monogamy is impossible, but anything else is worse." We are told that some moral principles are common sense. But people disagree across different ages, societies, and cultures about those principles. Our brains aren't designed exclusively for rational thought, and marriage seeks to regulate parts of the brain that can't be controlled. Loyalty in marriage anchors stability and security, but can it compensate for the lack of awe and mystery that fuel desire?

Heterosexual couples have a long tradition of marital vows that include "forsaking all others." Gay couples lack that tradition. They may be more comfortable than straight couples at negotiating these rules. Discussions about other sexual partners often come up early in their relationships. But marriage doesn't guarantee fidelity. Estimates vary widely, but some claim that 30 to 60 percent of married couples cheat at least once and that about 70 percent admit they'd cheat if they were guaranteed they'd never get caught. And who begins an affair believing they will ever be caught?

The brain's most important work is managing the systems of our bodies that keep us alive and well, but we must engage our unconscious as well as our conscious mind to satisfy our needs. Many of us wrap our identity in our marriage, but too often we conceive our identity as how we think rather than how we feel.

Relationship and sex columnist Dan Savage popularized the term *monogamish* to describe committed relationships where an occasional outside sexual experience isn't a deal-breaker. He suggests that consensual nonmonogamy may be more realistic in relation to how our brain works than absolute monogamy. Relationship therapist Esther Perel also advocates for no-fault affairs.

Good sex fades even for couples, but emotional intimacy diminishes only if you allow it to fade. Sex can provide intimacy, but it can't substitute for it. Doug and I weren't looking for sexual partners. We were looking to find ourselves again, the persons we were when we committed to one another, the hope of experiencing the vitality of our younger years. But if you are the one missing in your relationship, an affair with someone else isn't going to make you present. Some people believe that hurting another person is incompatible with loving them. I would argue that loving someone means you inevitably will hurt them.

Lynn and I hurt each other. We raged about the pain we'd experienced at each other's hands. When you feel you've been betrayed, the most common emotions are anger, distrust, and hopelessness. Lynn had a right to be angry with me. I had my own reasons to be mad at her. Perhaps we deserved some unkindness toward each other. But what were the pros and cons of hanging on to those resentments? The endless rehashing of the story with others exhausts friends, particularly if the members of the couple are unwilling to make any changes. Doug and I needed to find that sweet spot too. Healing from emotional trauma is a slow process; we need to be patient with it. But it can be achieved with some work.

Forgiveness is a choice to let go of resentments. Forgiveness does not mean forgetting or wishing to reconcile. It does not say you condone the wrongdoer's actions. Forgiveness is making peace with the fact that someone has denied you something you deserve. It is giving up your wish for revenge. It is also treating the wrongdoer with compassion even though they may not deserve it.

Doug and I also had to let go of our grand ambitions about our relationship. We had to accept that when you expect your spouse to be perfect—particularly, if it meant perfectly meeting each other's needs—you will be disappointed.

Everyone loses in divorce. The one who most wants the divorce generally loses the most. I'm suspicious of a congenial divorce. Where's the anger that leads to the decision to divorce? If the anger is not verbalized, it is expressed in more dysfunctional ways. In a divorce, power shifts away from the one who feels guilty to the one who feels betrayed. Some people bind themselves to their estranged spouse through hatred. They feel it gives them a moral advantage, and they fear losing the power advantage. Mediators can help replace rage with reason.

Many men who have betrayed their wives continue to love them. They want to help ease their spouse's pain. But being the betrayer and the comforter to the betrayed person are not compatible roles. When you decide to leave your marriage, attempting to be the support sends contradictory messages.

After Doug's commitment to making our relationship work, I made the same commitment to him. Doug and I began to have more serious discussions, including about my retirement. We talked about where we might spend the rest of our lives together. We sold all our livestock so the farm demanded less of Doug. I agreed to cut back on my work. Being busy with work had almost always felt like an acceptable excuse not to do what I needed to do. Restoring trust takes a long time.

I still had lingering doubts about our relationship. Doug had his heart set on moving to Palm Springs, but Palm Springs had become toxic for me. If things didn't work out for us, I didn't want to be stuck in a place where I did not want to live. But Doug had sacrificed his dream of living in a desert climate to remain in Iowa with me. I thought I owed him that consideration.

When Doug and I forgave each other, it did not mean we condoned the wrongdoer's actions. We say forgive and forget, but we never forget. We needed to remember the traps so we could avoid falling into them again. We had to discover more about each other than we had ever known before.

Some say that forgiveness is a gift you give to someone who doesn't deserve it. I prefer to think of forgiveness as a gift you give to yourself.

I had grown up with the fear I would lose everyone I loved. Early in my relationship with Doug, I expressed my fear that our relationship wouldn't last because I am fifteen years older. Then Doug replied, "If I'm still here in the morning, you'll know I'm still committed."

It's been over a decade since we fought our way through the darkest days of our relationship. But each night when I go to bed, I know that Doug will be there when I wake up the next morning. Our relationship isn't the same one we had when we first made a commitment to each other. We have kept each other a priority; our relationship is more stable and secure but most of all more honest.

I Blew Out My Knee Having Sex

I don't know why sixty hit me so much harder than other birthdays. As my sixtieth birthday approached, I hated it. In fact, I hated it so much I told my husband and my kids to ignore it. I didn't want anyone to sing "Happy Birthday." No party. No cake. I didn't want cards, phone calls, or gifts. I just wanted that day to slip by unacknowledged. I wanted to mourn the loss of middle-age as I joined the young-old cohort while old-old lurked in the shadows.

I usually enjoyed taking my birthday off, and I celebrated each one by doing whatever I wanted to do that day. I had hoped to wake up on my birthday morning to the smell of freshly brewed coffee. Doug had not made coffee but was drinking a latte from Starbucks without having brought me one. He hadn't picked up any of my favorite doughnuts. No card. No greeting. Absolutely no word of my birthday.

Not even a smile as he said, "Don't forget we have an appointment with the attorney this afternoon to go over our wills." Nothing says happy birthday like writing your will.

I was pissed. I held my tongue but wanted to rage, "I know that I said no celebration, but you should have known I didn't mean it!" but my Midwestern taciturn nature kicked in and I held my mouth. My kids apparently got the message too. I didn't hear from them all day either.

Late in the afternoon, Doug called me at work and said, "Todd and Jude want to go out to dinner with us. Are you up to it?"

"Sure," I said, trying to disguise my anticipation. I thought, "This day was a charade. The big fake leading to a surprise at dinner." I was so excited I arrived at the restaurant twenty minutes early. I thought, "I can't go in now! I have to wait until the balloons are blown up, the confetti is strewn across the table, and everyone puts on their party hats." Nothing ruins a surprise party more than having the guest of honor show up early, so I left and went to McDonald's for a cup of coffee.

I laid down two dollars for my coffee, and the young, pink-haired server with ten different colors of fingernail polish pushed back $1.31 saying, "It's only thirty-nine cents for seniors." I wanted to tell her, "I hope you flunk your SATs . . . but then you're probably not even going to take them, are you?"

I got to our table and our friends barely interrupted their conversations long enough to acknowledge my arrival. Worst. Birthday. Ever.

I recently turned seventy eight years old, and my birthday came and went uneventfully. But for the last eighteen years, I've planned my own birthday parties.

A few years after my sixtieth birthday, as I sat at the dining room table in our late 1700s farmhouse, I thumbed through a stack of newly arrived Christmas catalogs. Suddenly, I burst out laughing.

From the living room, Doug called, "What's goin' on?"

"Doug! You've got to look at this!" I couldn't contain myself as I pointed to an ad in the Vermont Country Store catalog that held ads for everything from flannel nightgowns to Walnettos, a childhood favorite candy.

As Doug rushed to the table, I pointed to an ad for the Easy Wipe Extender. The tool had a long handle with a grip on one end and a pincher device on the other end.

I exploded with laughter as I read the description in the catalog, "You fasten a piece of toilet paper to the end of it to extend your reach so you can clean yourself properly, reaching where you can't, ensuring good personal hygiene." In my mind, I pictured a man even much fatter than I am as he sat on a toilet seat, his arms unable to reach around himself far enough to deal with his personal cleanliness.

By then I could hardly breathe enough to ask, "Who would ever . . . ?" Then I abruptly stopped laughing, "Oh, fuck! I need that now!" I had dislocated my right shoulder back in my thirties when I was chased by our mama pig. Arthritis had set in and stolen the range of motion from my right arm. As my doctor said with a smile, "There're just some things we can't do with our nondominant hand." The thought had not entered my mind that someone designed this device to assist all of us who found it difficult to reach those nether regions of our bodies. Nothing spoils a good laugh like discovering you're the one being laughed at.

A few months before I was to have a total shoulder replacement to repair the damage that mama pig Sweet had caused, I traveled through Dallas. Sweating and puffing, I entered the Skylink at the Dallas/Fort Worth airport to transfer to my connecting flight. As I pushed my way into the crowded monorail, I saw one seat remaining, reserved for the elderly and handicapped. Two of us remained standing.

The other person was a rather heavy Black woman I guessed to be about my age. She was loaded down with a large shopping bag and a large roller bag. Given the health risks in the African American community, I imagined she could have diabetes and hypertension. I looked at her, and she looked at me. At the same moment, we eyed the empty seat. I nodded my head for her to take it. She acknowledged my courtesy but silently motioned for me to take it. Unwilling to accept that my age or my race might give me a priority for the seat, I insisted she take it, but she refused. Our dignity intact, we both stood up for the duration of the trip.

My shoulder wasn't the only joint that caused me problems. You may envy me when I tell you I blew out my knee having sex. Don't bother. It was far less dramatic than the incident with the mama pig who was responsible for me having dislocated my shoulder. It wasn't iron-man sex. It was ordinary sex—tranquil, dispassionate, and predictable. In fact, it was so routine that if I hadn't blown out my knee, I wouldn't have written about it.

I don't mean to say that it was bad sex—I don't know that I've ever had really bad sex—but perhaps you've experienced the kind of sex you have with a partner you've been with for many years: Sunday-night-after-the-news sex? You kinda want to do it, but you know you've got a busy day the next day, so you don't want it to take too long. I had a sharp pain in my knee, but my ego felt it had just been thrown from a bucking bronco and landed on the horns of a longhorn steer.

One of the reasons I hated my sixtieth birthday was because my body could no longer resist the pull of gravity. It wasn't just that I'd injured my knee, but the fact that it happened in such an unremarkable way cautioned me that my body was growing fragile. My skin looked like bread mold. I dribbled when I peed. No matter how many times I shook my junk after urinating, the last few drops of piss always ran down the inside of my pant leg. Erections, at best, were unpredictable.

The thought that an old man like me might enjoy sex comes as a surprise to some. To others, it is disgusting. People assume old people have little interest in sex. Or, if we are interested in sex, we are thought of as dirty old men. Some believe we are incapable of sex as if we had an expiration date tattooed on us the day we were born.

I must admit that I'm penis oriented. But I don't think that makes me any different from other men, including heterosexual men. I've seen a lot of penises. For an entire year in the US Navy, I performed flight physicals on healthy young men. I won't say, "If you've seen one penis, you've seen them all," but there are fewer differences in bodies than there are in the way men perceive them. Our penises give us a lot of pleasure, but few things can make men more anxious than when our penises won't work when we want them to.

Adolescents' concerns about erections are much different from concerns of mature men. When I was an adolescent, erections came at the most inopportune times, as I wrote earlier, like when I was reciting in front of class or waiting for my football physicals. The vibrations on the school bus were enough to make me hard, and thinking about the embarrassment of disembarking with a boner didn't resolve the issue. Once I had an erection, it wasn't that easy to get rid of it. The more I thought about it, the worse it got. That is no longer the problem.

I don't remember how I came to believe real men never fail at sex. I assumed men know everything there is to know about sex, even though no one had ever taught me anything about what is normal. I once thought, "Aren't real men ready for sex, anytime, anyplace, with any partner?" My limited understanding of sex was a collage of information I collected in locker rooms, by watching porn, or from reading erotic books. I never heard any discussion about wet dreams. But I never let semen build up to the point I needed to have a spontaneous ejaculation; all of mine were intended. It always seemed the preferred way to remove the pressures about having an erection was to masturbate and move on.

When I graduated from medical school, about all I knew about penises was how to dissect them. I understood the mechanics of sex, but that was it. No one addressed the finer points of lovemaking or how sexuality changes over the course of our lives. No one lectured about penis insecurity and how it constantly torments men. I had to learn all of that on my own. And after practicing psychiatry now for nearly fifty years, I know that most men don't know much more than I did. Some stuff I had to learn the hard way.

Sex makes us feel alive. Some reports suggest that sex also helps us live longer. As we get older, we get better at it. I hate the term sexual performance because it sounds like we're expecting applause or a standing ovation when we finish. Sex is about pleasure, not performance. Aging has the most predictable effects on penises, but age isn't a deal-breaker. When I was about sixty, my sexual function began to change.

It's hard to say when I began to worry about my erections. But somewhere in the middle of my life, erections became less frequent and less reliable. A fleeting thought of sex was not enough. It took something more to get there. And I was never quite certain what that extra something was. Sometimes it was more direct touch, sometimes more lavish fantasies, and sometimes both. A partner can't force an erection any more than you can, and a touch that feels like a demand is counterproductive. Sometimes it is a relief not to be chasing a hard dick all the time.

As I became older, erections were less predictable; any intrusive thought was enough to interfere with an erection. Work, finances, and relationships crept into my thoughts, and an erection would disappear even while making love. It also became more difficult to block out those thoughts. The most critical problem often occurs in the head rather than in the body.

Functioning erections depend entirely on blood flowing into the penis and a restriction of blood flow out of the penis. Think fire hose. But anxiety is like a major leak in that fire hose. Other emotional factors include stress, too little sleep, and emotional exhaustion. At the first sign of losing an erection, anxiety about the loss catapulted me into wondering, "Am I no longer a man? Will I ever be able to have sex again?" And just like in adolescence, the more you think about it, the worse the problem gets. Unlike in adolescence, the outcome of worrying is much different.

Worrying about getting hard almost guarantees that you won't get hard. It's commonly assumed that by the age of forty, about 40 percent of men experience some form of sexual dysfunction. Fifty, 50 percent. Sixty, 60 percent. By the number of advertisements for pirated substitutes for erection enhancers on men-focused websites, I predict that those numbers are higher in the gay community. Perhaps the most significant causes of dysfunction are unrealistic and impossible expectations and lack of understanding about what is normal. Only with experience did I learn what was normal and that if I refocused on the pleasure, I could crowd out those negative thoughts. When I was successful, my erection often returned.

Some of the early fears I had about sexual intercourse was cumming too quickly. The average time it takes men to ejaculate during vigorous intercourse is about five and a half minutes. Early in my life, when anticipation, opportunity, and desire crashed in, delaying ejaculation seemed like an impossibility. Now sometimes I wonder if it will happen at all. Sometimes it doesn't.

Older men don't seem to worry as much about ejaculation as younger men. You can't shoot it over your shoulder as you did in the past. Instead, cum may dribble out the end of your penis. Ejaculation doesn't always happen, and it requires maturity and self-confidence to recognize it isn't necessary for satisfying sex. Enjoyable sex doesn't even have to involve erections or orgasms.

Although my sexual drive and function declined as I aged, they didn't disappear altogether. It's just different. And unlike sex drive and function, my sexual satisfaction diminished little if at all. Men can remain sexually active well into later life, and many men do. Sex stops only if we allow it to stop.

When we're young, a satisfying sex life is all about the number of notches on the bedpost for each partner and each orgasm. As we age, our attitudes shift from measuring sex to experiencing sex. When we get older, if we accept that sex is about making love—sharing an emotional intimacy and a physical one—sexual satisfaction can improve. I think old men make better lovers because we know that slow sex is the best sex. It can be even better than it was when we were younger.

We have many ways to be intimate with someone. Sex should be about giving and receiving pleasure. After I understood that, I began to relax and enjoy slower but more expansive sex. Attitude is the key to penis longevity and sexual satisfaction. The keys to a gratifying sex life are to keep it a priority and to embrace a broader notion of the forms sex can take. We need to reject ageist stereotypes that equate old with undesirable. We need to think slow sex, whole-body sex, playful and pleasurable sex.

Some of the harshest criticisms of old people come from other old people. We are burdened by internalized images of what constitutes an attractive body, but we also have a picture of how we looked when we were younger. We see the differences. We have wrinkles that wrinkle cream can't touch. Our skin begins to look like tissue paper. Our curves start to look like we're a wax figure that came too close to the fire. We don't find others our age attractive because we don't see ourselves as attractive.

Old bodies have more contours, shapes, and curves. Some young men even find them delicious, as I found out on that trip to Oklahoma

City. A bit of a belly can be a comfortable place to put your head. An old body can feel safe and comfortable to hold. Many people, if not most, have some difficulty imagining that old people have sex. I'm seventy-eight years old now, and I can testify to the fact that we do. I have grown more comfortable with my aging body, and it has helped to know that there are those who think a man with a grandpa body is just the ticket.

I've had both my shoulder and knee joints replaced with metal that sets off alarms when I go through the TSA metal detectors. The hooding, as well as cataracts, are gone, so I can see better than I did at forty. My vision is clearer about a lot of things. No longer troubled by the tyranny of testosterone, my lovemaking has evolved into something slower and more emotionally driven.

But could someone please solve the problem of the piss running down the inside of my pant leg?

Don't Call Me Homosexual

The effects of words are social, psychological, and personal. Recently someone asked me, "If *homo* means 'same,' and *hetero* means 'other,' why is it wrong to use the word *homosexual*?" It's a fair question.

Homosexual and *homosexuality* have long been associated with pathology, mental illness, and criminality. These words imply that being gay is sick, diseased, or wrong. When some of us who are gay hear *homosexual,* we hear opposition to our struggle for equal treatment under the law, promotion of "a homosexual agenda," and immoral and corrupt behavior.

One of my most useful courses as an undergraduate was called *Scientific Greek,* and almost every premed student took the course. The professor was a tiny man, always impeccably dressed. He wore a small white mustache that looked like a well-worn toothbrush. His spine was as stiff as his white shirts' starched collars, and he always wore a bow tie.

As he walked into the classroom, he immediately took charge. He presented a list of Greek words that could be used as root words, prefixes, or suffixes. We combined and recombined these terms, Greek to English and English to Greek, to form various medical terms. *Epi* meant "on top," *sub* meant "below," and *derm* meant "skin." Subepidermal, then, meant "below the top layer of the skin." When people say, "It's all Greek to me," they are almost quite literally speaking the truth. When I got to medical school, I didn't have to learn a new language. I already understood what those words meant. I had learned to speak doctor.

This course eased my transition to medical school. All of this professor's students knew that he was invested in our success as physicians. Shortly after I completed undergraduate school, he died. On our first day in gross anatomy lab, we slowly and cautiously unwrapped the swaddled bodies of our formaldehyde-soaked cadavers. One of our small lab groups uncovered the body of our professor. That is how dedicated to us he was.

Karl-Maria Kertbeny created the word *homosexual* because he felt that the commonly used phrases for people with same-sex attractions in the mid-nineteenth century were unfairly pejorative. He wanted to make more neutral terms, so Kertbeny did what our professor had taught us to do. He created the new words *heterosexual* and *homosexual*.

Kertbeny believed that "the constitutional state is only concerned with questions of sexuality insofar as the rights of others are infringed upon." He argued that the state should stay out of the bedroom and not impinge on the sexual freedom of his new category of homosexuals. Ironically, terms used to protect the dignity of LGBTQ people became a term to oppress us.

When you are a stigmatized group such as people of color, gay people, or disabled people, even the minor use of some words can be fraught with small slights and discomforts. Casual, unintentional offenses are forgiven more easily. But sometimes words are weaponized. We all know many words people use as overtly hostile and aggressive weaponry. There is no reason to list them here.

Homosexual probably sounds harmless to most people, including a lot of gay people. It may surprise them to learn that the Gay and Lesbian Alliance Against Defamation (GLAAD) listed *homosexual* as an offensive term as early as 2006. The *GLAAD Media Reference Guide* is intended to be used by journalists reporting for media outlets and media creators who want to tell LGBTQ people's stories fairly and accurately.

Homosexual became an offensive word for several reasons. First, since it contains the word sexual, it focused on sex as the defining characteristic to the exclusion of gay men and women's basic humanity. Second, when I was young, *homo* was a scathing condemnation. Perhaps the most vigorous opposition to the use of the word *homosexual* comes from its association with psychiatric pathology. Until 1973, the *Diagnostic and Statistical Manual of Mental Disorders* of the American Psychiatric Association listed homosexuality as a disorder. When I was in medical school, homosexual meant psychopathic deviancy.

The offense that some LGBTQ+ people take to the term *homosexual* can also be traced to its association with antigay stances heard in Congress, on talk radio, in churches, and around the dinner table. People who still use *homosexual* are usually unaware that the term is a sensitive one, and not all members of the gay community object to it. However, people aware of this former classification feel that the term *homosexual* is overly clinical and implies disease or criminality.

Dictionary.com recently underwent a significant overhaul. It changed more than fifteen thousand entries on its website; many of these changes had to do with the LGBTQ community. The changes are mostly aimed at putting people first and respecting the relationship language has with society's values. It published the following statement:

> Dictionaries are not merely a linguistic exercise or academic enterprise. What are the effects of Black, referring to human beings, being grouped together with black, which can mean, among other things, "wicked"? The effects are social. They are psychological. They are personal. How words are entered into the dictionary—especially words concerning our personal identities—have real effects on real people in the real world.

One of the changes was to capitalize *Black* when referring to people. According to their statement, "capitalizing Black confers the due dignity to the shared identity, culture, and history of Black people." For similar reasons, Dictionary.com urged caution about using the word *homosexual* because of its historical association with pathology, mental illness, and criminality. LGBTQ people also have a shared identity, culture, and history.

So call me gay because I have an "enduring physical, romantic, and emotional attraction" to people of the same gender. Please don't call it my "sexual preference." It's not a preference but an orientation.

Gay is who I am.

"What's the Q in LGBTQ, Grandpa?"

"Grandpa, did you know it takes one sperm to fertilize an egg, but if a different sperm fertilizes the egg, it becomes a whole different person?"

My eleven-year-old grandson is bright and curious, but the question he asked me a couple of years ago surprised me. He and his brother participated in a fifth-grade class in Seattle called FLASH, an acronym for Family Life and Sexual Health.

"Yes, I know," I said with a smile.

My grandson spoke with me openly and without embarrassment or shame. In middle school, he knew more about sex than I did when I graduated from medical school. I certainly could never have had such an open and sophisticated discussion about sexuality with my mother.

On the way to his hockey practice, his older brother, who was twelve or thirteen at the time, said to his mother, "I don't think I'm in puberty yet. I haven't had a wet dream." His comment was as innocent as if he were discussing his hockey practice schedule. My grandsons attended a progressive public middle school, where sex education is a part of the health curriculum. This would horrify some parents.

In my conversation with my younger grandson about his class, he told me that the very first lesson they had studied was about how one in four girls and one in six boys are sexually abused. They learned what they could do if it happened to them.

I told my grandson how some parents object to such teaching because they believe that parents should teach their own children about sex. "But" I added, "parents often don't do it."

My grandson responded, "I can see how it might be uncomfortable for them." He appeared more comfortable than most parents.

Advocates for sex education argue that withholding information about sex from a child would be like placing them in the driver's seat of an automobile without drivers' education. In drivers' ed, adolescents are taught the facts, but they are also taught defensive driving. Defensive sexual education is at least as important. But they never learn to drive until they get behind the wheel.

Parents who oppose sex education in public schools argue that they know their children's needs better than any experts. They say that they should be the ones who teach their children about sex. I wouldn't argue that point. But this fact remains: most parents don't talk with their kids about sex. Unfortunately, many parents who do talk with their children about sex speak about it only in terms of sin and self-control.

Parents teach children about strangers' good and bad touches, but children are not taught about a good and bad touch of their own bodies. Opponents of sex education hold that children are innocent, pure, and nonsexual, and they must be protected. They fear sexually knowledgeable children. They believe children's experience with society will corrupt them. Heterosexuality is sanctioned and normalized. Times have changed, but not for everyone. From Anchorage to Miami, teens across the United States receive wildly inconsistent sex education. Very few sex-education programs are progressive enough to include healthy attitudes about same-sex intimacy.

Since 1982, the federal government has spent more than $2 billion on abstinence-only education. This training teaches that a mutually faithful, monogamous relationship in marriage is the expected standard of human sexual activity. Abstinence-only sex education has had minimal impact on teens' decisions to delay sexual activity.

After our initial discussion about sperm and eggs, my grandson asked me, "What's the *Q* in LGBTQ, Grandpa? Some people say that it means 'queer,' but some kids don't think that's a very nice word."

I hesitated. "Well, when I was your age, *queer* definitely wasn't a nice word. But I've come to like it. It is a word that can mean a whole lot of different things." I explained that the word *queer* has gained some acceptance as a catchall term for a wide variety of sexual and gender expressions. Although it has lost much of its original derogatory origins for young people, *queer* stirs up painful memories for some in my generation.

I also wanted my grandson to know that figuring out one's sexual orientation or gender identity is a process that can occur over a long time. I continued, "The Q can also mean 'questioning' because some people haven't quite figured out their sexuality." He seemed satisfied with that. No doubt he will ask sometime how grandpa could have been straight when he married his grandmother but now says he's gay and is married to a man.

Writers love words. Discovering the precise word that perfectly fits our purposes is like finding a twenty-dollar bill in your jacket pocket that you didn't know you had. But using the incorrect word can unleash a pack of guard dogs that attack at your heels.

The term *bisexual* is not free from controversy. Let me be clear: some people label themselves as bisexual as an enduring identity. Others use it when their sexual orientation is in a state of flux. Many people exist in a sexual purgatory, unsure of what to call themselves. They no longer feel a part of their heterosexual world, but they also don't feel invited into the world of gay men and women. "Questioning" or "curious" may be more appropriate terms, but like it or not, some refer to themselves as bisexual.

The final question my grandson asked was "But what about the *I* in LGBTQI, grandpa? I know it means intersex, but I don't know what that is. I've seen boys' penises and girls' things. It should be pretty obvious that a new baby is either a boy or a girl." The questions were getting more complicated. I stumbled through an explanation of how genitalia don't look all that different during embryonic development and sometimes even at birth.

The *New York Times* queried its readers to discover how readers define themselves. Respondents used a total of 116 words and phrases to describe their sexual and gender identities. Even within the LGBTQ community, people are confused; some consider this acronym too limiting. Others ask, "Why can't we just stop and go back to just the *L* and the *G*?"

When I was much younger, it was far simpler. The Kinsey scale described a spectrum of sexuality from totally straight to exclusively gay. It made sense to me. But it took me some time to figure out where I fell on that continuum. By suggesting people can move to the left or right on the spectrum, Kinsey helped me understand the changes I'd experienced in my own sexual orientation.

Times have changed, and our understanding of sexual orientation and gender identity has evolved. Labels can be useful in allowing ourselves to be more comfortable with who we are. Labels can also be quite damaging when applied to us by others. As we seek to explain ourselves, society, through stereotypes, attempts to define us before we define ourselves.

For those of us who are older, we struggle to understand sexual and gender identity. Shouldn't it really be enough just to say we are all sexual beings who can express that in a wide variety of ways? Calling us all queer might be a lot easier.

Then my grandson showed me a worksheet that was a crossword puzzle entitled "Facts about HIV." Many teens and adults would benefit from taking Family Life and Sexual Health.

My grandson's understanding of sexuality was more sophisticated than that of many adults. Our culture prefers people to be binary: you're either gay or straight. But sexual identity is an abstract concept that one must grow into after having more experience. Sexual behavior is concrete. If someone had asked me during my affair with Roberto if I were gay, I would have responded, "Absolutely not." But if they'd asked if I'd ever had sex with a man, I would have had to answer much differently.

I usually refer to myself as gay because as GLAAD defines the term, I expect it to be an "enduring physical, romantic, and/or emotional attraction to those of the same gender." I'm also comfortable with the term *queer* because it encompasses the myriad of different ways that sexuality is expressed. But don't call me homosexual. I just can't get past the idea that it once meant that I was pathologically deviant.

Aging Allows Us to Say "Fuck Off"

Two things are inevitable as we age: we'll lose people we've loved, and some parts of our body will fall apart. After I spoke to a group of older gay men in Houston, Don raised his hand and said, "I'm eighty-two, and this is the best time in my life." I began to think, "What does he know that I should know?" It changed my life. I began to see that late life is filled with freedoms and opportunities we've never had before. My concerns about age spots, wrinkles, and unpredictable erections began to disappear.

Most of us reach a point in our lives when time becomes urgent. We know we get no do-overs. We begin to ask, "Do I want to spend the rest of my life living the same way I've lived the first part of it?" Sometimes people say men who come out in middle age are going through a midlife crisis. And they are. But this is no red-convertible-sports-car midlife crisis. This is a crisis of identity and values.

When I reached midlife, I began to think, "More days lie behind me than days left in front of me," but I first began to worry about that as a child. My default position was loss. My father died when I was three; Grandpa Koester shot himself when I was six; Grandpa Olson had debilitating Parkinson's disease, so I never really knew him; and an automobile accident paralyzed Lefty when I was nine. Being a man looked to be high risk.

I thought I would die when I was thirteen years old because thirteen is an unlucky number. I registered for the draft when I turned eighteen, and I began to think, "So this is how I am going to die." Midlife was the least happy time in my life, as it is for many people. In a period of six months when I was in my late fifties, I lost my mother, Lefty, and Grandpa Marvin. By the time Grandpa Marvin died, my well of tears had dried up. Love always comes with the risk of losing the ones you love. Some of my friends were dying too. If only I hadn't loved them so much, perhaps I wouldn't hurt so much.

Older people are happier and have better mental health. What I learned from Don in Houston was that we can measure time or we can experience time. Do you ever feel that your life is like being on a six-lane freeway? You pass a sign that says 56 Miles to Next Exit and suddenly you realize you need to pee? Until I got old, time always had that same sense of urgency to me. What time is the next meeting? When is my next appointment?

I was always busy, and in America, busyness is a badge of honor. I was measuring my time. For me, time still carries a sense of urgency, but that urgency is transformed. Time no longer means having endless appointments and moving from one goal to the next. Now the urgency I feel is to experience every moment and not to waste any of the time that remains.

When actor Helen Mirren was asked what advice she would give to her younger self, she said it would be to say "fuck off" more and stop being so "bloody polite." Growing old gave me permission to say fuck off. I refused to do what I thought I should do just to meet someone else's expectations of me. I stopped going to cocktail parties to network with people I didn't really like but who might do something for me. I stopped wearing neckties. I promised I would never sit through a boring meeting or lecture. I discovered that whom I dined with was more important than what is on the menu. I moved things from my bucket list to my unbucket list. I began to enjoy sex in slow time and see it as a time for physical and emotional intimacy.

I deconstructed my old value system and reconstructed one of my own. I learned to appreciate my experiences and the wisdom that has come from both my successes and my failures. I realized that good relationships are always U-shaped, and to hang on to them sometimes requires a lot of work but can take you to a richer place. And I ended relationships with people I found toxic.

I began to get rid of things I once treasured but increasingly felt like just burdensome "stuff." When Doug and I sold our farm and moved to a townhome in Des Moines, we emptied a three-story house, a two-story garage, a barn, and a shed. We made multiple trips to the auction house.

People often asked, "Wasn't it hard?"

We responded, "No, it was liberating."

Whenever a website produces a drop-down list to enter my date of birth, I must scroll down about eight pages to find 1943. In the past, that might have bothered me. Not anymore. I own my age. It took a lot of introspection before I could embrace the word *old*.

When someone says to me, "You look good . . . for seventy-eight," what I hear is the equivalent of "You don't sweat much . . . for a fat person." Why do people qualify it when they say, "You look good"? When they add "for seventy-eight," it sounds as if they are surprised I'm still alive. I just want to respond, "What the hell were you expecting me to look like at seventy-eight? Or are you just surprised that I'm still alive?" If I look good, why qualify it? I want to say, "Fuck off!" If I don't look good, you aren't obligated to say anything.

I know the people who comment on my age want to be kind, and perhaps I shouldn't be so sensitive about it. What I should say is "I don't feel like I expected to feel at seventy-eight." The truth is that both the person who says it and I are reacting to an internalized stereotype of a deteriorating old man. But I do feel slightly offended. Either they're lying about my looking good, or in their head they picture someone at seventy-eight as being ancient and on the decline. What is so wrong with looking seventy-eight? Why does seventy have to be "the new fifty"? Why can't seventy just be the new seventy?

When I came out as gay at age forty, to rid myself of the shame and guilt I felt, I first had to shed the internalized stereotypes of what it means to be gay. Now I must shed those stereotypes of being seventy-eight that I acquired as a child. Now I must come out again as a proud old man.

Age is a number, but it is more than a number. It is multiple representations. I have a chronological age, a physical age, a psychological age, and a sexual age. They vary from one person to the next as well as within each individual. I can be seventy-eight years old, have the body of a ninety-year-old, think like a sixty-year-old, and have the sexual desires of a fifty-year-old. Although Doug is fifteen years younger than me, we don't think of ourselves as different ages because in several of those dimensions, we are the same age.

I know that I am seventy-eight years old, but sometimes physically, I feel like I am in my early sixties. I think more like someone much younger. Somedays I am as horny as a fifteen-year-old adolescent. But the clock doesn't lie. And it keeps ticking.

Society has a distaste for old people, and those of us who are old have swallowed that distaste. We see our future self as inferior to our younger self. That stereotype is easy to absorb and is harder to get rid of. Unfortunately, old people swallowed it too.

Old people are thought to be a drain on economic resources, and young people must pay the freight. People believe it's sad to be old and that old people need care. Many believe that old people are sexless. Sometimes it seems like we have an epidemic of dementia. These are all ageist stereotypes. Medical costs are highest before we die, whether we die at eight or eighty. More economic resources flow from the old to the young than the reverse. (Ask anyone with millennial-age children.) We don't have an epidemic of dementia, but we do have an epidemic of worrying about dementia. And men and women who understand the natural evolution of their sexual function can have satisfying sex well into their late lives.

When I was born in 1943, life expectancy was sixty-four years for men and sixty-eight years for women. When I grew up in Wakefield, Nebraska, not many men lived to be seventy-eight years old. Now, because I'm considered a survivor, I have a life expectancy of eighty-six years. In fact, I have beaten the odds I was given at birth. If I live to be eighty-six, I will have been given a gift of twenty-two years beyond what my life expectancy was when I was born. I want to be able to make the most of them.

I still think about death but not in the same way. I know that it lurks out there somewhere, and I accept that. I don't worry about dying; I do think about how I will die. Doug and I had always promised to be there to hold the first one of us to die as we took our last breaths. The COVID-19 pandemic terrorized me with the fear that one of us might die alone in the intensive care unit of a hospital with no one to hold hands with except a masked and gowned nurse or doctor.

In any relationship, life circumstances can hurtle one into dealing with death or assuming the role of caregiver. I tried—but not always successfully—to think, "Why ruin this moment by worrying about the next ones?" But thoughts about how to leave Doug financially secure when I die boiled in a thought kettle on the back burner of my mind. Love and risk are inseparable, and I wasn't taking any chances. Was my will updated? Check. Life insurance, long-term care insurance, powers of attorney? Check. Check. Check. Advance directives and organ donation? Two more checks. Have I left anything out? Don't leave any stewpot unstirred.

I warned myself, "Don't love too much. You'll always lose what you love. Don't make it hurt too much. He'll leave when he finds someone his own age. Or I will die and leave him alone." If you're always prepared for loss, are you giving everything you have to the relationship you're in? You can't numb feelings selectively. It's an all-or-nothing gamble.

A few years into my relationship with Doug, something unexpected happened. We had met several other age-discrepant couples with fifteen years or more differences in their ages. In three of the age-gap couples in our circle of friends, the younger person developed a terminal illness and died. For the first time in my life, I began to worry, "What if I am the one left behind?" Until then, defaulting to loss had always meant I would be the first to die. Doug has done all the cooking. "Could I learn to cook for myself? He's handled our finances. Where would I even start with that? Could I be alone successfully? Would I be so desperate to find someone new I'd jump into a relationship too soon? Or would I be too old to find another love?" Being the first to die began to look like a preferable option.

Now, thirty-four years into our relationship, we're still alive and together. What a tremendous waste of time it was to worry about all those things over which I had no control.

During my residency in psychiatry at Maine Medical Center, Carolyn, one of the other residents, said, "I've always felt that one day, someone is going to tap me on the shoulder and say, 'Sorry, Carolyn, you really didn't graduate from medical school. We'd like your diploma back.'" This phenomenon is so common it's been named impostor syndrome. It's a pattern where a person feels like a fraud and doubts his or her accomplishments. For much of my life, it didn't matter how many awards or certificates I had, I remained convinced that I had deceived everyone. But I don't feel that way now. My achievements weren't based on luck.

As an old man, I have begun to look at those awards and accomplishments in a different way. I know that I earned them because I worked hard to get them. But I now find that I have a junk drawer full of blue ribbons that meant so much when I was working for them but now have an emptiness about them. The question I ask myself now is "Were they worth the sacrifices I made to achieve them?"

Until my career plateaued, my profession scripted my life. Each step up the career ladder had been dictated to me. One day when I was about fifty, I realized I couldn't climb the ladder much higher. I felt blessed that at least I had put the ladder against the right wall. But I thought, "Now what?" Hugh Grant, as Saint Clair Bayfield in the movie *Florence Foster Jenkins* recognized that his modestly successful acting career held little prospect of being anything more. He said, "I was freed from the tyranny of ambition." I came to that same conclusion.

It has been said, "The two most important days in your life are the day you are born and the day you find out why." Finding my place and my purpose took me more than a day, but not a day goes by now when I doubt I have found them. I am a father, a husband, and a psychiatrist; the rest is just gravy.

As I mentioned earlier, my mother didn't want me to be a psychiatrist because she believed it wasn't being a real doctor. Frankly, a lot of healthcare professionals feel the same way about psychiatrists. But for me, psychiatry suits me. It connects me with others who understand that mental suffering is the worst of human suffering. Psychiatry has given my life a sense of meaning and purpose.

People often ask me, "Why are you, at seventy-eight years old, still working? Do you need the money?" If I needed the money, I wouldn't be working like I do. As I write this, I'm sitting in the Virgin Islands overlooking Hull Beach and listening to the waves crash on the rocks. (Writing also gives me that sense of purpose.) I can work if, when, and where I want to.

Then my cell phone rings and the nurse says, "Dr. Olson, we have a patient in the emergency room who the VIPD brought in. She thinks her mother is possessed by demons, so she attacked her with a meat cleaver." I feel that sense of meaning and purpose. I may get a little anxious, and I'll ask myself, "Do I still have what it takes?" But I know that I'm not an impostor. I know that when I say to the ER staff, "I've got this," it will deflate the crisis. Then the psychiatric team will put our heads together to figure out what needs to be done. Work is only painful when it is devoid of purpose. Work is only work if you'd rather be someplace else.

As the saying goes, "Pain is inevitable; suffering is optional." Pains are the experiences that happen to us: turning sixty, losing our parents, having prostate or breast cancer, dealing with physical changes, and in my case, accepting that I am gay. Suffering is how we choose to deal with our pain. Or not. Or not. Or not. At sixty, I was suffering needlessly. If we neglect our pain, we suffer. Life is a series of distressing events, but we don't have to suffer. We have choices and can make changes. We are responsible.

One night recently, an old friend from medical school and his second wife were coming to Des Moines. I called Lynn to ask her if she wanted to join us since she had known this friend before. Lynn and Doug joined my friends and me for dinner. When the server came to take our drink orders, I said to him, "This is my husband and this is my wife, and these are two of our friends." He looked puzzled for a moment. Then he looked up, smiled, and knowingly nodded his head a few times without speaking.

In *The Long Dark Tea-Time of the Soul*, Douglas Adams wrote, "I may not have gone where I intended to go, but I think I have ended up where I needed to be." My friend and I were out of medical school for

Lynn and Loren eating lunch at the Dolphin Restaurant in Harpswell, Maine, during a return visit to see friends, September 2019. (Courtesy of Loren A. Olson.)

fifty years. None of us at that table had once thought that was where we would be. But on that evening, it felt right to be there. Through the years, I've lost a lot and gained a great deal, and the balance sheet is in my favor.

A couple of years back, I spent the winter obsessing about whether I was too old to get back on a bicycle. I was worried that I wasn't enough of a purist if I purchased an electric bike. After a trial run on an e-bike, reality blew purity away in its draft as I flew down the bike path. As expected, one of my friends, who has been a cyclist for years, scoffed at my choice. But I don't owe him an explanation for why I want an e-boost to take me to places I couldn't go otherwise. *Fuck off!*

A dear friend of mine said, "When you're out on your bike, take some pictures. And I don't mean pictures of you. Pictures of what you see." So I did. Although I had enjoyed the rides through beautiful old-timbered woods and along a lovely creek, I had missed a lot on previous trips. It's incredible how much more you see if you just get off your bike and look. Imagine what we'd all see if we stopped taking countless selfies and we reversed the lenses to take pictures of the world around us. Being in my late seventies is a lot like getting off my bicycle. I didn't need to look for a place in the world. When I began to look at the world around me, I found it everywhere.

Life is much more than a series of painful events, although at one time I might not have believed that. I had to find something in the morning to get up for. I needed to learn to believe that I could handle what my life had to offer me. I needed to learn how to forgive and really mean it. I had to let people know me and know me deeply. I had to learn to say "I love you" without expecting I would hear it repeated back to me. I had to accept that some rules are mistakes and need to either be changed or ignored. I had to shake up my life and rearrange it to become the person I was always meant to be.

Some people suffer because they want their old lives back. Not me. My past is history; I want to let it go. My future is uncertain; it will unfold as it will. I just want to live this moment being mindful of every day.

About the Author

Loren A. Olson MD is the award-winning author of *Finally Out: Letting Go of Living Straight*.

He is a board-certified psychiatrist and a distinguished life fellow of the American Psychiatric Association. He received the Exemplary Psychiatrist Award from the National Alliance on Mental Illness. After more than fifty years as a physician, he continues to practice psychiatry. He believes aging is filled with opportunity.

A highly regarded essayist, Dr. Olson has had his most popular essays read over half a million times. He has been interviewed on national television, national and international radio, and in multiple print and online publications. He is a popular speaker who has spoken internationally and throughout the United States.

Dr. Olson is a father, grandfather, ex-husband, and husband. He lives in Des Moines, Iowa, with Doug Mortimer, his husband and life partner of thirty-four years. His grandchildren see Doug as a bonus grandpa. Dr. Olson believes family is decided by love, not blood.

The greatest rewards Dr. Olson receives for his writing come from hearing from his readers. He invites you to contact him through his website, www.LorenAOlson.com, or any of his following social media:

Facebook https://www.facebook.com/laolson.md

Twitter https://twitter.com/LorenAOlsonMD

LinkedIn https://www.linkedin.com/in/lorenaolsonmd/